WE ARE ONE ANOTHER

The dramatically sited château of Montségur, the sacred shrine of Catharism. During the great siege of 1243–1244 a company of the besieging army ascended one of the precipitous rock faces. The besieged included people who reincarnated in England in the twentieth century and remembered the rigours of the siege.

ARTHUR GUIRDHAM

We are
One Another

A RECORD OF GROUP REINCARNATION

THE C. W. DANIEL COMPANY LTD.
1 CHURCH PATH, SAFFRON WALDEN
ESSEX, ENGLAND

First published in 1974 by
Neville Spearman (Jersey) Limited

This edition published in 1991 by
The C.W. Daniel Company Limited
1 Church Path, Saffron Walden
Essex, CB10 1JP, England

ISBN 0 85207 248 1

Set in 11pt Baskerville, 1½ point leaded
and printed and bound by Ennisfield Print & Design
Wapping, London, England

Introduction

This is a record of group reincarnation. It involves eight people who, alive in the twentieth century, had a previous existence in the thirteenth. In seven out of the eight cases I have been able to trace their thirteenth-century identity. In the eighth case I am aware of the person's Christian name but not of her family connections. None of these figures are historical characters. Their names are not to be found in the text books of any country. They are buried in the voluminous records of the Inquisition.

The group involved lived, in the Middle Ages, in the Languedoc. In the twentieth century they were either born, lived or were educated within a dozen miles of Bristol.

This was not a question of my searching for interesting cases of far memory. I made accidental contact with a person with an amazing spectrum of psychic gifts. She led to a chain of others. In no case did I seek out the other members of this group. In their different ways they made contact with me.

Nothing in this story depends on my subjective reactions to places and people. I am not the kind of person who, on the field of Waterloo, feels inevitably that he must have been Napoleon. I am naturally of a sceptical and cautious nature and am known in my family as Doubting Thomas. I am astonished that the phenomena I have encountered have been revealed to me of all people. I have occupied myself in discovering the significance of names and messages produced in dreams, visions, in states of clairaudience and dictated by discarnate entities. Because of the unusual origin of my data I have to stress all the more carefully that I was for forty years a run-of-the-mill psychiatrist. In the N.H.S. I was the Senior Consultant in my clinical area. I hold a scientific degree as well as being a doctor of medicine. It is all the more necessary to make these points since I claim that

5

this, my own story, is the most remarkable of its kind I have encountered.

The members of this group were all practitioners of the mediæval form of Dualism known as Catharism. Its exponents believed that there were two primary energies of good and evil operating in the universe from the beginning and continuing to the end. They believed also that the world was created by the Devil. These beliefs were an attempt to answer the agonising question, 'If God is all-merciful and, at the same time, all-powerful, why does He permit such horrors to happen in this world?' Though the Cathars preached the word of Christ more than the orthodox, they rejected the idea of redemption by His sacrifice. Purification was achieved by successive incarnations. They believed in complete non-violence. To take life in war or in the course of justice was equally murder. They were vegetarian, except that it was permitted to eat fish. The strict practice of Catharism was only expected of the priests who were known as Parfaits. This was not the name they chose for themselves. They preferred simply to be described as Christians.

A striking characteristic of Catharism was the number of women priests. Three are involved in this story.

A few words are necessary to explain the events to which the characters in this story so frequently return. Their memories are chiefly concentrated on the years 1242–1244. There is a remarkably generalised preoccupation with the massacre of the Inquisitors at Avignonet. This was a gesture of defiance and self-protection launched by the representatives of the Languedoc against the tyranny and cruelty of the French Catholic invaders. The Avignonet affair stimulated the French crown to cut off the dragon's head of heresy. This was the Château of Montségur which had for years been a centre of instruction for Cathar sympathisers and of initiation for the priesthood. The fortress was besieged from 1243 to 1244. It was defended by a small garrison of minor nobles and sergeants-at-arms who fought for the independence of the Languedoc and were sympathetic to Catharism. We are especially concerned with the sergeants-at-arms. The characters in this book tune-in with remarkable precision to the siege, to the evacuation from the castle of the Cathar treasure, probably rare books, and above all, to the last celebration of the Consolamentum before the Cathars perished at the stake after the capitulation. The Consolamentum was the only sacrament recognised by the Cathars. It signified a voluntary renunciation of the flesh and of attachment to the things of this world. Six of the characters in this story attended the final celebration of this rite.

The major events in this story were unfolded between late August 1968 and the early summer of 1972.

I

When I was convalescent from the heart condition which caused
my retirement I sat a good deal in my garden. Once or twice I
saw Miss Mills drive past on her way to work in a nearby town.
I had met her on two previous occasions in other peoples' houses.
She was in no sense well known to me. You could not help liking
her because she was so candid, smiling and spontaneous. She was
quick-moving, vigorous and vivacious. In a neurotic world she
was direct and uncomplicated. In spite of her considerable
momentum she had always time to listen to people. She looked
extremely healthy and had the classical and now disappearing
pink and white complexion the French call *la teinte Anglaise*.
With her smiling face and uninhibited laughter she would serve
as a model of extroversion. She had a gluttonous appetite for
fresh air and I wondered how she stood being immured in an
office.

One day when I was sitting in the garden she came up the
path. She was having trouble with her car and wanted to phone
a garage. My wife asked her to tea. Because my wife thought
her cheerful and forthright company would be good for me, she
invited her to return in a fortnight. Her entry into my life was

banal and unexciting. She began to visit us once weekly. I think she did this from the goodness of her heart. I myself had little to offer. I was dilapidated and without vitality. I thought it was kind of her to call.

Miss Mills did most of the talking. She was markedly gregarious and had no interest in the abstract. She was chiefly concerned with people and phenomena.

One day in late autumn we were left alone together. Suddenly she caught her breath and blushed excessively. 'Do you mind if I ask you something personal?'

'No.' I was still weak and easily exhausted. The pictures on the walls were coming back to life. It was enough to absorb their reborn and intoxicating clarity. But somehow I had no fear that she would tire me with her troubles.

'There are two names which keep repeating in my head.'

'What are they?'

'Raymond and Albigensian. Does it make sense at all?'

'Perfectly good sense. Raymond was the name of the Counts of Toulouse. Albigensian was the name of the heresy which flourished in their territory. You must have picked up the names in history books.'

'I know I did not. But it does make sense and I am not going crackers?'

'I see no signs at all.'

It was a measure of my reduced vitality that I was not excited. For years I had been interested in the Albigensians. A case of far memory for their epoch had provided the high peak of my clinical existence.* Miss Mills knew nothing about the Albigensians. She did not know that they were heretics and that Cathar was an alternative name for them. At that time I had written nothing on the subject. I should have been intrigued by her question but I was too tired to bother.

With the coming of winter Miss Mills' visits were less frequent. She came again with the spring. With her return I had a slight recrudescence of my Ménière's syndrome. I felt swimmy in my

---

* The experiences of Mrs. Smith are recorded in *The Cathars and Reincarnation*. Through them I was able to pinpoint her previous existence and my own in the Languedoc of the thirteenth century.

head and a little off balance. I should have known what it was. By that time I had accepted the cosmic origin of my Menière's symptoms, but I always balanced what I knew with the corrective scepticism of what I thought. I did not know that yet another psyche was beckoning from a former life.

Miss Mills was interesting to talk to because her attention was directed outwards to others and because of her powers of observation. I was diverted by her rapid, graphic and humorous summing up of people. She picked up quickly the atmosphere of places and people. I was not surprised when she raised the question of reincarnation. Most of those I had met who were truly and unsentimentally involved in the subject were vigorous people who led active lives and were more interested by phenomena than theories. I can only accept evidence of reincarnation from people whose belief in it is the by-product of an active life. This may seem illogical but those whose experiences have been most convincing have all been voracious workers. If there was anything of the mystic in them it did not show on the surface but served as a fuel for more than average energy. I am never impressed by evidence of reincarnation from willowy and asthenic people draped in pale mauve and dripping with bangles. As a doctor I prefer to assess not only signs and symptoms but the sources they spring from.

Miss Mills said she had believed in reincarnation since her early teens. She had never read about it or heard it discussed. She had suffered from two recurrent dreams. They began at the age of five when she nearly died of diphtheria. This was not the first time I had observed that recall of previous existences can be initiated by severe illness. It is commonplace that far memory, like other psychic gifts, reveals itself when the personality's hold on life is reduced by disease, exhaustion or danger.

In the first dream she was running away from a castle which, when she later learnt something of architecture, she recognised as mediaeval. The castle was on the summit of a hill. The path by which she descended was rough and stony. It went through woodland to a valley and a stream. There was no menace in the trees and the valley. The horror from which she was running had begun already in the castle. I did not know at that time to which château she was referring. In a year's time the castle and the horror enacted within it were easily identifiable.

The second dream was still more terrifying. She was walking barefoot towards a stake and heaped faggots. There were others with her. On the way someone struck her back with a burning torch.

She had in her childhood a horror of fire. She was seven when a public building in her native city was burnt down. The rest of the family appear to have enjoyed this exhilarating but expensive festival. She herself was uncontrollable and what she called hysterical.

She was also from her earliest childhood terrified of trumpets. This particular dread made a great impression on her but she could not understand it. She ran away and hid herself when organisations like the Boys Brigade blew trumpets in the street outside her house.

She was acutely sensitive to atmosphere. At the age of eight or nine she was appalled at the malevolence of a house she visited. She was so agitated and sickened by it that she had to be taken home. She told me that sometimes in the course of business interviews she encountered people who so radiated evil that she used to vomit immediately. Later she was able on most occasions to hold out until the end of the interview. Healthy, vigorous and outgoing, she does not in the least give the impression of a person prone to psychosomatic symptoms.

At the age of thirteen she went to a theatre and supper party at which her uncle was present. Everybody was happy except herself. She knew beyond doubt that her uncle would be killed. Soon after her premonition was proved true. She admitted that since he was in the R.A.F. this was not altogether surprising.

At first her recurrent nightmares came several times a week. She was too terrified to go to sleep. It was assumed that she was afraid of the dark and she was given a nightlight. This concession continued for years until the nightmares became less frequent. At the time she met me they were still occurring several times a year. They stopped just before or just after she first came to tea. She was following in the footsteps of other patients with far memory whose dreams had stopped after I met them.

Miss Mills could not tolerate any form of organised religion.

She had never been to church since she was a schoolgirl when attendance was obligatory. She was surprisingly cynical about medicine and had little use for doctors. She believed in leaving things to nature but in no fanatical sense. She had no dietetic fads and had indeed an impressive appetite. She believed in exercise, fresh air and 'getting a move on'. The latter was her shibboleth. She repeated it with the same constancy as the faithful recite the Litany but with more conviction and in ringing tones.

Because of her views on doctors and her robust appearance I was all the more surprised when one day she asked me to look at her hip. She had a pain just internal to it. I was reluctant to do this because I was not a general practitioner and in any case I had almost retired. I indicated that it was a matter for her doctor and it was only when she said that it was probably a trifle and that she would leave it that I said I would look at it. I knew that otherwise she would not see the doctor. The pain had lasted for two months. She described it as muscular. She said that it was 'also in the joint'. She wondered if she had strained something. I was convinced that she was suffering from a colon disturbance. The colon is a sensitive organ in the psychic and I was quite prepared for her to be afflicted by one of the traditional maladies. What I did not anticipate was the result of my examination. The pain stopped that day and did not return. It was inevitable that I should wonder if this was comparable to the cessation of her nightmares and those of psychic patients I had met. Was this another example of a symptom being stopped by an act of recognition between two psyches who had known each other in a previous existence? This was no more than a presumption and a vague intuition.

In any case the pain stopped permanently. I was pleased for her sake and unaware that my diagnosis was wildly inaccurate. The origin of her pain was far more dramatic than a sensitive colon. It was two more years before I learnt the truth.

But the examination revealed something more dramatic and mysterious than her pain and its causation. When I looked at her left hip I saw, slightly above it, a belt of strange protuberances arising from the skin. I have never in my life seen anything comparable. Some of these structures were an inch long. Some were bladder shaped and at first sight resembled polypuses but they were without stalks and attached to the skin by a relatively broad base. In shape and appearance they looked like large blisters produced by burns. The difference was that there was no fluid in their interior and they were semi-solid.

The distribution of these semi-solidified vesicles was significant. They extended from above her hip across her back to the midline. 'I suppose this is part of your dream. This is where the burning torch hit you.' I spoke lightly and not at all insistently.

'Yes,' she said simply.

Any clinician seeing these swellings would at first sight consider them to be burns. Similar isolated cystlike protuberances may well exist but I have not seen them. I know no condition which could produce such swellings disposed in a band in the position I have described. Anyone with a flair for pathology could say that they were burns which had suffered some peculiar process in that the fluid inside them had either been reabsorbed or discharged by the rupture of the vesicle. It had, in fact, become congealed. I suppose that the passage of seven centuries can act as a prolonged embalming process. It may be that, where people with psychic potentialities die violent deaths, the reincarnating psyche carries with it the imprint and vague outlines of an ancient wound. It brands the new individual with the marks of an old torture. It is intended that these scars remain as evidence.

I had read that birthmarks are sometimes scars from the wounds of previous lives. I regarded this as an interesting supposition. I was impressed by the story, in the *Christ at Chartres* by Denis Saurat, of the French official who bore in his hands the marks of old tortures. I was prepared to believe these things possible. I did not expect that I myself would be presented with such evidence. I was not only impressed by the nature and position of this strange eruption and by the way it bore out the truth of Miss Mills' recurrent dream; the circumstances in which it was revealed were also significant. Was it the disclosure of this lesion which induced the disappearance of her pain? Was my sight of this disfigurement a graphic resumption of psychic contact? Certainly her pain disappeared almost immediately.

It appeared that I was again in the middle of one of those circuits of communication which I have described elsewhere as open periods. During the latter I was especially involved in chains of telepathy, clairvoyance and healing. It is as if different individuals in these chains ignite in others the capacity for psychic communication. During such periods any strong intuitive impressions are usually valid and subsequently confirmed. I began to think of Miss Mills as a Cathar.

She dwelt little on this disfiguring lesion. She said that she and I must have met in a previous reincarnation. From some people this kind of talk is at best wildly presumptive, often a little fatuous and sometimes nauseating. Miss Mills was talking impersonally and in relation to presented phenomena. She accepted that recognition by far memory of another person as a friend or colleague in previous centuries must be very rare. She indicated clearly that she was unable to remember such a connection. She said that it must nevertheless exist because of the effect it had produced in stopping her dreams and her pain. This dogmatically clinical opinion was confirmed later by evidence from a discarnate source. She believed that, where people who have known each other in previous incarnations meet again, they must have been in constant contact in the years between. She said that such contact could not be conscious in the accepted sense of the term.

About this time I had a curious experience. Suddenly I felt off balance, swimmy in the head and with noises in my ear. I had no doubt that this was an echo of my Menière's syndrome. Some hours later Miss Mills came to tea. She had cast her shadow before. When she arrived I was still a little troubled by my symptoms.

She told me that in 1954 she visited France towards the end of July. She had originally planned to go only as far as the Loire. Suddenly she felt an irresistible impulse to see Carcassonne. She could not explain this compulsion. Nobody had advised her to visit this town and she knew nothing of its history. She arrived in August and was immensely moved by it and especially by the country to the south of the city. She spoke with emotion of the scent of the broom on the hills to the south. She had not realised that she was traversing a region drenched in the history of Catharism. She described this two-day visit to Carcassonne and its environs as an unforgettable experience. She could not imagine why this should have been so.

During her short visit my swimminess and feeling of being off-balance disappeared. It came to my mind that these labyrinthine symptoms began in August 1954. They had coincided with Mrs. Smith's first look into the past when she mounted the stairs at St. Jean Pied de Port. I could not fail to notice that, in the same month of the same year, Miss Mills had been drawn to an area which to me was both beautiful and fatal. It seemed that psychic communication was operating at maximum intensity in the late summer of 1954 and that it continued to operate on the afternoon of Miss Mills' visit to me. When she came that afternoon she dispersed the symptoms of the Menière's syndrome which had coincided with Mrs. Smith's and her own visit to France in 1954.

What happened at this visit convinced me that the brief reappearance of my symptoms was a sign that I had moved again out of time and was in contact with reality. I knew from previous experience that with me Menière's syndrome was a signal that the past was knocking at the door. I kept on wondering if Miss Mills had been a Cathar. In spite of the increasing evidence I rejected the possibility. I regarded my previous experience of the thirteenth century as a supreme revelation. I could not believe it would be repeated.

In the late summer I went on a Sunday morning to the Botanical Gardens. I went early to avoid the crowds which visited them on Sundays. I was surprised to find Miss Mills examining the dahlias with her usual vivid and effortless interest. In spite of her vivacity she seemed very tired. I had always thought of her as an inexhaustible battery of energy. We sat down together and looked at the long border. I asked her how she felt.

'It's these horrible noises in my ears, and my head is swimmy.'

Here, I thought, was another with Menière's symptoms. 'How long have you had it?'

'Off and on for years but never as bad as these last few days.'

Looking at her pink and white complexion I was surprised that she had ever suffered from anything. 'What troubles you most?'

'The noises in the head. Tell me, does it mean that one is being prepared for something?'

'I don't know what you mean,' I lied.

'Does this horrible singing in my ears mean that I am becoming especially receptive?'

'Receptive to what?'

'I am suddenly besieged by masses of people coming to see me with their troubles. It is night after night and I can't escape them. They say I do them good. They even say they do not know what they would do without me. I hate talking like this but it's all so tiring. I have an idea that hearing these noises and being helpful to people is one and the same process. It's something to do with being more receptive. I cannot explain it.'

'You may get the noises and swimminess because you are already tired by people.'

'I think it's the other way around.'

I did not say any more because I had no wish to influence her way of thinking. I knew she was right. The suffering recognise instinctively when certain psychics are in a state of heightened receptivity. They know that to consult such people at these times is to receive increased consolation from them. I knew also that in some cases of migraine and Menière's disease the symptoms are a sign that the ground is being prepared.

Because I had little to do that evening I decided to write up my diary. My first requirement was the date. I looked at the calendar and found that it was August 24th. This was the plexus in time from which issued my first attack of Menière's and Mrs. Smith's first experience of *déja vu* phenomenon. Now it was the date of Miss Mills' first admission to consciousness that another form of experience was being perceived by her psyche. It was also significant that some days previously I had had a re-echo of my Menière's disease and that this had disappeared when she spoke of Carcassonne. I felt there was more to come.

From now onwards Miss Mills spoke frankly to me of her thoughts and intuitions. She had read little or nothing of psychic matters and her convictions were based on experience. Her explanations were all her own and she had not previously discussed her experiences with anybody. One day I began to explain to her what I meant by open periods. I used this term to describe those days or weeks when one seems to be enmeshed in a web of telepathy, precognition and inexplicable manifestations of healing. She astonished me by saying that in such synchronisations I was acting as a transmitter. She divided those with psychic capacity into emitters, receivers and transmitters. What she said corresponded with my own ideas on the subject except that I had given little thought to the problem of emitters. The sub-division of psychics into these three categories is interesting. The individual receives the truth through the particular mechanism with which he is especially endowed. In time to come Miss Mills was to reveal beyond doubt that truth disclosed by revelation more than equalled that achieved by the philosopher or scientist. This statement applies not only to truth in the transcendental and religious sense of the term but also to the facts of history.

I could hardly credit that this bustling extrovert could think and feel in these mysterious terms. Perhaps this was my error. She was so open and uninhibited that she was able always to establish contact with people, places and atmospheres. Perhaps her extroversion extended to the cosmos. For this reason she was able to produce intuitions usually associated with introversion.

Because her dreams stopped when she met me, and because the same phenomenon had occurred with other patients with far memory, I considered it possible that we had met in another life. Where brief, impersonal meetings in psychic people produce the sudden cessation of long standing symptoms it is often evidence of resumed psychic contact, or a void being healed. In such meetings as this a state of Oneness is restored. The symptoms cease because in this state of restored unity the persons concerned are moving out of time. It is only in a timeless medium that healing of this nature can occur.

I may have stopped Miss Mills' dreams but I could not prevent the psychic barrage now levelled at her. Her own feeling that she had become especially receptive was justified. It was soon obvious that someone or something was trying to get in touch with her.

2

The bombardment first came in the form of voices. At first Miss Mills thought these voices were speaking in dreams. She said later she had heard them in a half waking, half sleeping state impossible to describe. This was a new and dramatic departure in the history of my contact with Dualism. It had been knocking for years on the door of the unconscious. The knocking, beginning with earlier patients, was reaching a crescendo. The pressure on the door was so tempestuous that it swung wide open. I realised now that dramatic and almost physical methods were being used to draw my attention to Catharism and the thirteenth century. Miss Mills' case was unique in that I saw clearly, from day to day, the various mechanisms used to draw our attention to events and attitudes manifested seven centuries ago but vital to us in the world of today.

The voice spoke several times at night, and every night for a week. It told her that I must write, talk and do everything in my power to increase people's knowledge of Catharism. When this phenomenon first began Miss Mills wondered if the voice was that of a deceased friend who had died exactly a year earlier but afterwards she became less certain. She was convinced at this stage that she was being addressed by a single entity. Later she felt that more than one entity was involved. These questions were to be clearly answered some months later.

At odd times in the last two years I had felt it possible that somebody from the thirteenth century was trying to make contact with me. I should make it clear that, at this stage, this was a deduction rather than a perception. If I was correct in this assumption it was merely a matter of being right by accident.

The voice insisted that Miss Mills must confide in me. It said that one of her troubles was that she could not accept that I was 'directed'. The voice assured her that I was and also it appeared that I was to be trusted. This smacks of the sentimentality one associates with inadequate mediums. In actual fact this attitude was logical and completely justified. The voice was, at times, to refer back to esoteric instruction begun seven centuries earlier. It was reasonable that it should be stressed that I was capable of receiving a confidential communication.

Thirdly, the voice gave advice. Its maxims were not moralising nor pretentious. Jung said that when the archetypes spoke they tended to be pompous. The instruction given to Miss Mills was basically mystical but simply expressed and concerned with the nature of time. At the beginning the exhortations were simple enough, a kind of beginners' manual for other worlds.

At this time there was another significant incident. I was visiting a hospital for geriatric patients. I was to all intents and purposes retired and it was a pleasure to fulfil my comfortable duties without pressure. Before doing my round I chatted idly to the matron over a cup of coffee. Perhaps because she was accustomed to seeing me in a hurry she talked more freely than usual. She was not a person with whom I had ever discussed anything other than patients and hospital administration. On this particular day she began to talk about the state of the world. Speaking of the troubles in Northern Ireland she said there must be something radically wrong with Christianity. I said that I believed that Christianity had become so distorted that it was unrecognisable compared to its primitive beginnings. On this occasion I mentioned the word Catharism. I say this with intention because I am not accustomed to discussing this subject with people not specifically interested in it. I described it as the resurgence of primitive Christianity. We then went upstairs to see the patient.

The latter was a lady of ninety-nine years with a hawklike and imperious visage and far-seeing eyes and with the profile of Dante. She had been seventeen years in the hospital. I have never encountered anyone who preserved into extreme age such insight into life and people and such an unflagging interest in the world about her. On this particular day she looked more than ever like an Old Testament prophet. I was astounded when she began to speak of the Pyrenees. She said the early sects who had lived there had searched always for the truth. She mentioned the Albigensians. She said that what they had said must again be disseminated and that the matter was urgent. She spoke with fervour. I was astonished because the old lady continued the theme I had mentioned downstairs. It was another example of the process of ignition which, at certain periods in my life, runs in all directions like a low fire. Precognition, clairvoyance—do these names matter so much as the general truth and sanctity of communication? And suppose she read something of what was in my mind when I entered the room. Does one discredit or minimise the process by calling it telepathy? What is important is not that such a process should have occurred between us but that it should have occurred at this time. The old lady was exhorting me, in the same way and on the same lines, as the voice which had spoken to Miss Mills. It was also remarkable that, after seventeen years, I should find another person with Cathar interests on my own doorstep, in the hospital where I had started practice thirty-five years previously.

But what is perhaps most significant of all is revealed by the circumstances under which this lady was admitted to hospital seventeen years previously. She had implored me on that occasion to get her away from the power of evil. She said that the house in which she was living was drenched in its atmosphere. She expressed what could have been considered to be vague delusions. In speaking of delusions I am referring to her reaction to the evil in the atmosphere. At this time I had not accepted the basic truths of Catharism that there are two primary principles of good and evil in the universe, that these were present at its beginning and will remain till the end of the world we know. I did not know at that time that her relatives had also registered the evil in the atmosphere. In thirty-six hours this patient was without symptoms and remained so for years, demonstrating a degree of clarity, insight and, at times, inspiration such as I had never seen previously in one of her age. She stayed in the hospital not because of her symptoms but because of her own imperative wish to do so. She regarded it as having a good atmosphere. In her acute perception of forces of good and evil she was exemplifying the basic principles of Catharism.

In these early messages to Miss Mills the approach to the question of time was mystical and designed to convey that chronological time was an illusion. Later the voice was to say, "You cannot enter time except by escaping from it but you cannot escape from time by entering into it." I read this as meaning that it is only when we quit our time-dominated personalities that we can escape through the psyche to the time-less and spaceless world of the Spirit.

At this time Miss Mills asked me if I believed in the existence of a group soul. I wondered whether she was trying to explain to herself how, in her limited area of country, there were several people who had met again after centuries. I had never thought much about this aspect of the matter. I had some vague idea that a soul, still tied to the wheel of life could, in returning to earth, continue to exercise a magnetic compulsion on those who had, in a previous existence, felt affection for the personality it had inhabited. But Miss Mills was less concerned with the mechanics than with the purpose of group reincarnation. It was obvious that, like me, she had not thought deeply on the subject. She admitted later that she had been told by her nocturnal instructor that, where a group of people were reincarnated together, it was inevitably for a good purpose. I did not find the prospect attractive. To me, at that time, all ideas of purpose were a little wearying. I had set myself too many goals in this life and the idea of being chained to the same destiny and with the added handicap of gregariousness was a little deflating.

Nevertheless there were others who took her view. Paul Beard, the Head of the College of Psychic Studies, told me, from the evidence he had acquired from mediums, that in the last ten years people were reincarnating in groups to achieve some common, constructive aims. He believed that many Cathars were being reincarnated. It seemed that, though there were not many people in England interested in Catharism, I was destined to meet them all.

3

At the beginning of 1971 things became exciting. For Miss Mills they were not only exciting but frightening. She had a telephone by her bed. She had always kept beside it a writing pad and pencil to take down messages. One morning she saw there was a message scribbled on the pad. She knew she had made no note that morning and wondered if this was something forgotten and left over from the day before. She picked up the paper and read a cryptic remark about the nature of time, and another comment on a line underneath urging her to accept direction. She was, in fact, seeing in writing what she had previously heard from the voice. She felt tense and disquieted. She had absolutely no recollection of making a note. She is businesslike, meticulous and with a remarkably good memory. Nor is she the kind of person to write down on paper ideas which she finds interesting. She has no literary ambitions, no philosophical interests and her nature is the reverse of metaphysical. She could neither account for the writing on the paper nor could she bluff herself that sooner or later she would discover some reasonable explanation. She waited trembling for further information. She did not have long to wait.

On a few occasions she saw no writing when she awakened but found it under the bed later in the morning. The paper must have fallen from her hand when she wrote in whatever state of amended consciousness she existed in during those moments. I saw the handwriting. It was undoubtedly hers but wider-spaced and sprawling. It was splayed out like any handwriting done very quickly and with a sense of pressure. The messages on the writing pad repeated what she had heard previously from the voice. She had to trust me. There were further and more complicated reflections as to the nature of time. The following statements were typical. 'To live from moment to moment is to live intensely. To realise eternity in time is to love with intensity. Time is but a keyhole and mankind holds the key. Liberation is the ability of the soul to live beyond the time unit.'

Other messages were esoteric. 'Memory is a cloud that drifts back and forth.' There were aphorisms as to the nature of truth.

'Truth is built up from vibrations. You cannot find it by thinking about it. You have to experience it.'

At this time she was tired and agitated. She asked how long was it going on, what did it all mean and did I think she could stand it?

The situation was all the more painful when she noticed that the messages were intensifying round the anniversary of her father's death. She said that she detected a change in the handwriting. She said it resembled her father's a little. The handwriting I saw at this time was smaller and more constricted and in this it resembled her father's writing. I was shown an example of the latter. I did not think the change of style was very significant but I have no knowledge of graphology. To me the handwriting was indubitably Miss Mills'.

I cannot dogmatise as to the mechanism involved in this nocturnal writing. This is a matter for the specialists. I assumed it was a variety of trance writing and that Miss Mills was acting as a medium. She had no recollection of passing from sleep to the state in which she wrote the messages. In view of what happened later it is doubtful whether the phenomena described were attributable to mediumship.

After this first run of written messages the voice intensified. It spoke to her day and night. She tried again to define it for me. Speaking of the source of the nocturnal messages she said, 'You could call it a voice, perhaps an inner voice. It was not a voice in the sense of what we hear in ordinary conversation when we are awake.' Certainly it was something more distinct and audible than a demanding thought or a strong intuition. Its main theme was still philosophical and concerned with the nature of time.

The voice by day sometimes resembled what she heard at night. On other occasions it 'just came to me in the course of work. Sometimes it comes very suddenly when I am busy. I don't know how you can tell.' Here the auditory perception was complicated by intuitive and visionary factors. It is interesting enough to reflect on the mechanism responsible for her communications. What is more important is to know if they make sense.

For the first time she relayed messages which were unmistakably Cathar. She telephoned me and asked if there was a

Cathar sacrament,* and if it was always bestowed by a bishop. I said there was such a sacrament but that a bishop could not always have been in attendance. As there were never at any time more than five in the Languedoc it seemed to me impossible that the common practice was for a bishop to officiate. She went on to say that priests called deacons could also be present.

She asked me with considerable confusion and hesitation if I had heard the words filius major and minor. I had. These were names given to the bishop's next in command. When a bishop died he was succeeded by the filius major. The latter's role was taken over by the filius minor. She had learnt these titles from the voices. She could never have heard of or seen these words before. They are not part of the stock curriculum at an English Boarding School for Girls. In any country they must be known only to a handful of people instructed in the structure and function of the Cathar Church. In this country these terms would be known by still fewer by, indeed, a number so small as to be negligible.

This was her first excursion into Catharism except for the question she had posed earlier in our acquaintance about the connection between the word Raymond and Albigensian. I had answered this quickly and with confidence to the effect that the Christian name applied to the Counts of Toulouse who were great protectors of the heresy. When she was literally invaded by Catharism in 1971 I still believed that I had answered her first question correctly. As we shall see later Raymond had nothing to do with the Counts of Toulouse. Similarly I believed I was correct in denying that bishops were invariably present at the Consolamentum. Nevertheless I had learnt with Mrs. Smith to know that extrasensory perception can be more accurate from the scientific point of view than historical research. She had known a quarter of a century before the savants that Cathar priests in certain areas and at certain times wore dark blue robes rather than the prevailing black. When Miss Mills had rung off I picked up in a desultory fashion and without much hope the first book on Catharism which came to hand. This was Nelli's translation of *The Ritual of Lyons*. The latter is one of the truly

* She was referring to the Consolamentum, the only sacrament recognised by the Cathars.

authentic remnants of Cathar Liturgy. There I discovered that the Consolamentum was bestowed by what in the text was called L'Ancien, literally, the old one. According to Nelli and Deodat Roché the latter was a bishop or a deacon. Once again I was in error. This woman, who had no conscious knowledge of Catharism, was able to give the details of its hierarchy.

It is interesting that I found what I wanted in the first book I picked up and that I opened it at the required page. As this was the first time I had done it I could only regard it as a coincidence. But afterwards, in verifying Miss Mills' statements and in answering her questions, I constantly went to the right book at the right page and often at the right line or paragraph. Previously I could never have believed that I would be able to perform one of the classical criteria of occultism and go to the particular book indicated at the specific page. I did this constantly in confirming Miss Mills' statements. This indicated a radical change in me. I had always accepted that I could never find anything I was looking for. I believed sincerely that will was an impediment in these matters. But was I using will in going to the book which gave me the answer? Was I exercising choice at all? Was it not possible that, whoever guided Miss Mills, was exerting an influence so powerful that, though directed primarily at Miss Mills, I was equally and accurately guided by it?

In February 1971 the messages from her guide were accentuated. One phrase she kept hearing was 'make me a good Christian'. She asked me if this phrase had any particular significance. I replied that it was so vague and commonplace that one could not credit it with any importance whatever. In actual fact I knew that she had alighted on something. I was unforthcoming because I thought it was better to encourage her critical faculties. I asked against what background she had encountered these words. She said that they 'came as a kind of prayer'. I knew she had given only a part of the full sentence which runs 'make me a good Christian and bring me to a good end'. I was absolutely certain that this sentence occurs at one of the most sacred moments of the Cathar Consolamentum. The latter was not only crucial in the life of a Cathar, but as we shall see later it was the spiritual peak of Miss Mills' existence in the thirteenth century. I told her the full and accurate quotation of which her words were only the beginning. I said that this was without doubt part of the Consolamentum. She was clearly disappointed. It was obvious that she thought otherwise.

That she was well on the track of Catharism was revealed by her next words. 'What do apparellamentum and amelioramentum mean?' I told her that these were the names of two specifically Cathar ceremonies. The former was a kind of monthly confession of sins. I regretted that for the moment I could not tell her exactly what the amelioramentum involved. Again she was disappointed. I assumed this was because of my failure to describe the amelioramentum.

Over a period of eight months she reverted to the quotation of 'make me a good Christian'. It was clear that she could not accept that it was part of the Consolamentum. I do not know why I took so long to discover my own error. I supose it was the usual question of a curtain descending and of my standing in the way of my own enlightenment. 'Make me a good Christian and bring me to a good end', had nothing to do with the Consolamentum. It was part of the amelioramentum. The latter was not a religious service but the simple ritual of bowing three times before a Parfait and uttering the sentence I have mentioned. My errors in verifying Miss Mills' statements, and the accuracy with which she instructed me, should be borne in mind by the reader who is asking himself how much she obtained from me by telepathy.

It was now clear that one was confronted with someone with memories of Catharism in the thirteenth century. I could not accept easily that I was dealing with another case of reincarnation. I did not believe in my own luck. I did not know at this time that, because of the existence of human catalysts, one case can lead to another. Nevertheless, I had to accept that in one way or another Miss Mills had memories of the Cathar epic. What she produced of her past came out of the past. Her knowledge of French was minimal and prevented her from reading any books in that language. By this time she had read *The Cathars and Reincarnation*, which came out nearly two years after I met her and which contains no references to filii minori and the like. She was not historically minded. She was only concerned that her revelations and intuitions should be proved to be fact. Though she showed signs of strain and exhaustion during her nocturnal bombardment, she did not slide into a neurosis nor did she undergo agonies of doubt as to her sanity. Her line was more, 'What is it all about? The stuff about time is Greek to me. Why do they pick on me?'

Any idea of Miss Mills being a psychiatric casualty is absurd. Certainly she heard a voice in the absence of a physical presence. So also did St. Paul, Mohammed and Joan of Arc. A hallucination is described as a false perception. This is a poor definition because the experience is real to the person hearing the voice or seeing the vision. The definition of hallucination needs to be altered. We are entitled to ask if such voices as Miss Mills' have some constructive purpose which can be verified and fulfilled. Nobody will deny that the voices heard by St. Paul on the road to Damascus and by St. Joan at Domrèmy were creative and produced tangible results. There can be nothing more constructive than the knowledge gained for us by Miss Mills in the course of her experiences. It proves clearly that truth by revelation adds also to the facts of history.

The acid test is that pathological hallucinations occur against the background of manifest psychiatric disorders. The patient is diagnosed by his disturbances of behaviour rather than by the simple fact that he has what we call hallucinations. In diagnosis the number and nature of the latter are of great importance. Miss Mills had no signs whatever of psychiatric disorder. In making these assessments the background and temperament of the individual is crucial. Hallucinations and delusions occur mostly in those of schizoid temperament. The latter involves shallow emotion and the withdrawal of interest from the environment. Miss Mills' disposition is completely different. In the paranoid varieties of schizophrenia the victim, before the onset of disease, is guarded, hostile and suspicious of others. Miss Mills is as open as the day and with the capacity to infect others with her own vivacity. Whatever the origin of her voices and, later, of her visions, it was completely unrelated to psychiatric disorder. When she was receiving her revelations of maximum intensity I suffered from the continuous hunger induced by a rapidly emptying stomach. This happens constantly when someone on the same wavelength as myself is under great pressure or suffering acutely.

4

The guide who spoke and dictated to Miss Mills veered sharply away from the philosophy and liturgy of Catharism. These variations of direction were to occur more than once. I wondered at times if more than one guide was involved. This guess was later to be justified.

About the middle of February 1971 there was a glut of Italian references. Names like Vicenza, Sorano, Brescia, Desanzano and Treviso all appeared on her writing pad. 'What is all this stuff about Italy? Is it important?' she asked. Then she added, 'Am I getting this from you?' She had the same obsessional honesty as Mrs. Smith and the same tendency to search for the most rational explanations. I could only tell her that Catharism had been very strong in Northern Italy and that it had been practised openly in Lombardy long after it had been persecuted and gone underground in the Languedoc. I noted that, except for Sorano, all the names she had quoted were from Northern Italy. I could not find Sorano but I assumed it to be Italian.

The next Italian reference was far more striking. She had found the name Jean de Lugio on her writing pad. Underneath was written 'He was the filius major of the Bishop of Bellesmana'. This was astonishing. Jean de Lugio wrote the basic classic on Cathar theology, *Le livre de Deux Principes* (*The Book of the Two Principles*). I had no idea that he was a filius major or of the name of the bishop he served. I set out reluctantly to search through my library. Once again I found, without effort, in the first book I came to, that Jean de Lugio was a filius major. The book, as it were, opened itself for me.

I was pondering Miss Mills' words, 'Am I getting this from you' when something happened which took us beyond the sphere of possible telepathy. The latter had never really been a valid proposition because my knowledge of Catharism in Italy was negligible. The path of her revelations lurched suddenly towards the Balkans. On February 16th she wrote down what was a complete mystery to me.

On that morning Miss Mills found the words Trogarium and

Sorano on her writing pad. Sorano had occurred before and I had previously assumed that it was in Italy. I felt sure that the word Trogarium was not Italian. I could not explain these names. What was written on a second piece of paper was still more mysterious. The word Nikolski meant nothing. All I could offer was that it was Slavonic.

Then something curious happened which gave a partial answer to these questions. The woman who has translated three of my books into French appeared in England on a professional visit with a set of proofs. I had forgotten that when I last saw her in France she had spoken at great length and very earnestly about her five months' residence in the Balkans. She had been almost obsessionally preoccupied in showing me the ornaments she had collected there. In Bulgaria she had visited with passionate interest the tombs of the Bogomils who were the Balkan precursors of the Cathars. On her brief visit to me in England she returned at once to the theme of Dualism in the Balkans.

It appeared that what had interested her most in Bulgaria was an ancient Rosicrucian cross. The Rosicrucian cult was one of the examples of Dualism gone underground after the persecution of the Cathars. She was worried that its Bulgarian owner did not appear to appreciate its significance and value. The lower arm appeared to have been sawn through obliquely so that the base with its three significant curves was missing. She had brought with her a book on the Rosicrucians and demonstrated, on one of its illustrations, the point at which the cross had been mutilated.

I was astonished by what she told me but made no comment until I had been to my study and examined my diary for 1964. There I found a drawing I had made of a cross I had seen in a vision on waking from sleep. It was identical with that seen by Madame Brelet even to the oblique line where the cross had been mutilated. The only difference was that, in my vision, as time went on I saw three brilliantly illumined concentric circles with curved edges. These were placed one inside each other at the intersection of the arms of the cross. At the time I noted this experience I did not realise that I was seeing a Rosicrucian symbol. I regarded the cross as of Manichean design. It was only later that I realised that what I had seen was a Rosicrucian cross with a glowing rose.

In all the years following this vision I had never wondered why the lower arm of the cross should be broken. Is this to be taken as a form of symbolism expressing the persecution of Dualism and also its persistence? There is surely more to it than that. Why the very specific phenomenon of the oblique saw-cut in the lower arm? I drew my design years before I met Madame Brelet or even knew of her existence. Surely this sharing of an exact experience by a woman awake in Bulgaria and by a man waking from sleep in Somerset, separated from each other by years in time and by hundreds of miles, could indicate some personal connection in another epoch. At least it signifies a capacity on the part of two people to escape from chonological time, and in the same direction. But surely this cannot be the whole story. Madame Brelet appeared in the middle of Miss Mills' Balkan revelations. Had she cast her shadow before and induced the latter to remember such items as Trogarium and the Nikolski gospel? At the time of her visit I had not discovered the significance of these names.

It may well have been that Madame Brelet, who herself had psychic gifts, had stimulated in Miss Mills the recall of memories associated with the Balkans. The latter was to reveal later her capacity for psychic communication with someone she had never met, who lived in another country and who had the identical psychic experience as herself but ten years later.

Some days after I asked for Sir Steven Runciman's *Mediaeval Manichee* from the local library. I had raced through parts of it some years previously when I was writing *The Cathars and Reincarnation*. I had no intention of hunting for anything Slavonic. Had I wished to do so I would have consulted Obolenski's book on the Bogomils. The Nikolski mystery was solved first. I discovered that this was the name given to the Slavonic Gospel of the Bosnian heretics. The latter term includes the Bogomils and Paulicians who were fore-runners of the Cathars. In the Nikolski Gospel the Lord's Prayer includes the additional words beginning 'For thine is the Kingdom'. In this it resembles the Cathar and Anglican forms and differs from the Roman version.

At the same time, the mystery of Trogarium and Sorano was solved. Sir Steven states that the former was the centre of the heretic church on the Dalmatian and Istrian coasts. Its doctrines were Dualist. The church, with others in the vicinity, had strong missionary traditions, working in Italy and even in France. He adds that the Albigeois are said to have derived their doctrine from the church of Trogarium. The latter is now known as Trogir.

This book also clarified the question of Sorano, Vicenza and Desanzano. In the thirteenth century there were two varieties of Catharism in Italy. One was centred on Desanzano. The bishops of this branch of Catharism lived in Sorano and Vicenza.

Why this sudden switch to the Balkans? Why should Miss Mills' invisible guide give her accurate details in scraps concerned not only with the Cathars but their Bogomil precursors in what is now known as Bosnia and Herzegovina? Clearly she was insistent that Miss Mills should know as much as possible of the origins of Catharism. I had known before that the roots of the faith were in the Balkans. I had not known of the special missionary function of the church on the Dalmatian coast and that it sent agents to the Languedoc. At this time there was a rush of seemingly fortuitous circumstances pointing to the Balkans. A lady I had never met sent magazines containing pictures of Bogomil tombs in Yugoslavia. Had she not done so, would I have visited the Yugoslav exhibition in Paris a few weeks later and been fascinated by these tombs? It seemed a natural apotheosis that the Yugoslav savants in Paris should have showed an intense interest in my book *The Cathars and Reincarnation*.

Was Miss Mills' guide stimulating her to recall some specific connection with the Balkans? Was this an attempt to present the credentials of Dualism from its very beginnings? Were the references to Dalmatia the vestigial recollections of something Miss Mills herself had heard in the Languedoc in the thirteenth century or was this evidence of an earlier incarnation?

I could answer none of these questions. All I could do was to marvel that in the middle of Miss Mills' Balkan excursion Madame Brelet should come to England for three days and provide startling evidence of some connection with the near East. She and Miss Mills had never met and the latter had never been farther East than Florence.

5

After her shift towards the Balkans Miss Mills veered sharply to the Languedoc. One day she found by her bed a paper inscribed with something more positive than reflections on the nature of time.

What was written on the paper was

'Raymond de Perella.
Sun—No.
Treasure—No.
Books—Yes.'

She wanted to know if this meant anything to me. It could not fail to do so. It clearly and unmistakably referred to the siege of Montségur. This was organised by the French in an attempt to cut off for ever the dragon's head of heresy. The great siege came towards the end of the ghastly wars launched against the Albigeois at the instigation of Pope Innocent the Third. Montségur is the château where the forces defending the Cathars made their last stand. This was, in effect, the death blow to the resurgence of primitive Christianity in modern Europe.

I knew that Raymond de Perella was the owner of the château of Montségur. It did not occur to me that this was the Raymond referred to by Miss Mills as far back as the autumn of 1968 and whom I had negligently identified as the Count of Toulouse.

'Sun—No.' can have only one meaning. It has been argued that the site and construction of Montségur were determined by cosmic and astronomical considerations and that in previous times it had been the centre of sun worship. For the Manicheans, who were forerunners of the Cathars, the rising and setting of the sun and the dates of the spring and autumn equinoxes were of special significance. These questions have been discussed by such savants as Fernand Niel. On the other hand we have the firm 'No' of Miss Mills' nocturnal informant. I do not think that here we are being asked to choose between the specialists and those who transmit truth by revelation. What the voice is saying is that Montségur was not a centre of sun worship in the days of

Raymond de Perella. Miss Mills herself had no knowledge of this subject.

'Treasure—No, Books—Yes' is easy to explain. Much ink has been spilled over the treasure of Montségur. It is an historical fact that four Parfaits were lowered from the walls of the castle carrying unspecified treasure. This occurred either just before or after the burning of two hundred Parfaits in the meadow below the château. Earlier in the siege other envoys left secretly carrying the treasure to the caves of the Upper Ariège.

What was the nature of this treasure? The first obvious suggestion is that it comprised the sacred writings of the Cathars. The more romantically inclined have gone so far as to suggest that it was the Holy Grail. The latter hypothesis is simply not tenable. Had this cup still been in existence in the thirteenth century it would have been of no interest to the Cathars. They were not concerned with possessions and incapable of undue attachment to inanimate objects. A reasonable supposition is that the treasure was simply money. The Cathars needed funds as much as any other organisation. But Miss Mills, quite uninstructed in Cathar thought except for the fragments of philosophy she had received from her guide, was positive that the treasure consisted of books.

This was the beginning of Miss Mills' instruction in the history rather than the philosophy of Catharism. It was as though her guide, having found her a puzzled and not very apt recipient of metaphysical instruction, had deliberately reverted to history. Or was it that the discarnate entity wished merely to establish his or her credentials? Was it intended that Miss Mills should collect the data and that it should be verified by me? However fanciful it may seem I am convinced that this was the intention.

By now my fatigue was less and I had recaptured my interest in Dualism. I had never before been confronted with a day-to-day contact with another century, in the process of which I was supplied, two or three times weekly, and sometimes more often, with information from the mouth of someone who had lived seven hundred years previously. I was not to know that more than one invisible teacher was concerned with Miss Mills' education. I did not realise that after she had served a painful and harassing apprenticeship her instructors would cease to be

34

invisible and present themselves to her. Most important of all I could not realise that Miss Mills, utterly uninstructed in the subject, would make solid and fascinating contributions to our knowledge of the history and nature of Catharism.

At this time Miss Mills was intensely interested in Raymond de Perella. She bombarded me with questions about him. Did he have a family? I said that I felt sure that he had one daughter and that she and his wife had been burnt as heretics at Montségur. This was not enough for Miss Mills. 'Did he have another daughter? I feel convinced that he had other daughters.'

'Why?'

'I cannot tell you. It just comes to me.' She spoke unexcitably but firmly. In spite of her control I felt the rising tension inside her. It was as if she were distracted by names she had almost recalled but the memory of which had again receded.

She wished also to know if Raymond de Perella had estates other than Montségur. I had no idea at that time. In 1972 I visited Pereille and saw the few stones left of the château from which he took his name.

At this time the word Mirepoix was repeating itself insistently in her brain. I told her that this was understandable because this town was the nearest place of importance to Montségur. I omitted to tell her that Pierre-Roger de Mirepoix was the captain of the garrison at Montségur. It never occurred to me that Mirepoix meant to her a person more than a place. When she first raised this question I did not know that Pierre-Roger de Mirepoix was the son-in-law of Raymond de Perella. If I had ever read it I had forgotten it. Certainly she was little enlightened by me as to the members of the family in which she was so interested.

I was away for a few days at the end of February. When I saw her again she was as open and friendly as ever but there was in her cheerfulness a note of strain and determination. I especially noted her eyes. Normally they are clear and light blue and one has the impression that they see naturally and without effort the finest detail. The whites of her eyes were dulled and their light extinguished. 'Do the fourteenth and sixteenth mean anything?'

'The fourteenth and sixteenth of what?'

'Of March. They are dreadful dates, I tell you, dreadful. And the second was awful, but anyway it's over. Yes, I think it was the second.' She ruffled through her diary. When she came to the page I could not help reading, 'Why am I so depressed?'. It surprised me that she had even recorded her state of mind. She raised her head and looked at me solemnly and with unwavering intensity. I had the idea that she wondered if I was concealing things from her. 'Did anything awful happen on these dates? Will anything happen on the fourteenth and sixteenth?'

I mumbled something about anxiety states. I had in mind to tell her that tension always projects itself to the future and gives us the feeling of impending horror. For shame's sake I had to desist. She was in far less an anxiety state than I was. I would not say that she was pushed to the limits of endurance but this was because she was an especially tough specimen. I knew in my heart that she was remembering something, but all the time I was afflicted by a professional conscience which told me that when in doubt one should be sceptical and that on no account should one encourage illusory thinking in others.

I was really remarkably obtuse. This could well have been another example of the protective curtain which descends within you when you are not ready to be enlightened. Nevertheless there is something to be said in my defence. I was handicapped and confused because she had given three dates instead of one. Had she spoken only of the sixteenth the light would certainly have dawned.

On the night of March 3rd there was another instalment. It was clear that the mouthpiece of eternity had been working overtime. The following words were written on a single sheet of paper.

> Sorba
> Sicillia
> Sibilia
> Jean de Cambiaire evêque.

I was interested to note the circumflex accent on the word evêque. I was sure that Miss Mills' French did not extend to such niceties.

I had only a single clue but it was valuable in that it pointed definitely towards the Perella family. I knew that one of the female members was called Corba. I could not remember whether she was the wife or daughter of the owner of Montségur. I wondered if Miss Mills had written Sorba for Corba. When she discussed this paper with me I suggested that one should be allowed a few spelling mistakes in recording messages from another dimension. She was unimpressed by this argument. She was unable to allow for varieties of language and spelling across seven centuries. In these matters she was rather pernickety. On the conscious level she was over-meticulous and had a tendency to reject whole patterns if the detail was not as she thought it should be. My suggestion that Sicillia and Sibilia were two attempts at Cecilia was rejected out of hand.

Three days later she discovered the single word Lantar written on a piece of paper.

I verified that Corba was the wife and not the daughter of Raymond de Perella. His three daughters were Phillipa, Arapaïs and Esclarmonde. Miss Mills' Lantar referred to Marquesia de Lantar. She was the mother-in-law of Raymond de Perella. Raymond was thrice bereaved at Montségur. His wife, his mother-in-law, and his daughter Esclarmonde were all burnt as heretics.

With what knowledge I had of the tragedy of Montségur I could see that Miss Mills' guide was steering her in that direction. She herself was bewildered and weary of the whole business. When I commented on what she told me I did so briefly and to reassure her. It was one thing that she should believe that there was something in it, because in taking this attitude she avoided considering herself pathological. It was quite another to share with her what I knew of Catharism and thus to encourage attempts to remember. I do not think my attitude made much difference. She was tense at that time and not enjoying the experience. She protested constantly that she could see no purpose behind it. It was obvious that she sensed a purpose but could not accept that she was its instrument.

I discovered further evidence that her memories were tied up with Montségur and the Perella family. Cecilia, or to give her her full name, Cecilia de Montserver, was married to Arnaud-Roger de Mirepoix. The latter was the brother of Pierre-Roger, commander of the garrison, who was married to Raymond de

Perella's daughter Phillipa. It was an exciting discovery to me that Miss Mills' memories should be so centred on the mountain refuge that had haunted me for more than thirty years and that her guide should know the names of the family who owned the château. My pleasurable excitement did not communicate itself to Miss Mills. She clearly doubted that Sicillia, taken down in a state of amended consciousness at the dictation of a discarnate entity, could spell Cecilia in modern times. At this time I found her didactic attitude a little exasperating.

My excitement was, in fact, wrongly directed. For me the key word should have been Montserver. This name was vital for Miss Mills both in her present life and her previous incarnation. It was also crucial for me. It is not every day that one is led to someone who knew you in 1242 and can tell you what you were like and what you were doing. I did not know what the Montserver family had meant, and was still to mean, to Miss Mills and myself.

Jean de Cambiaire was more of a problem but was ultimately discovered. He was a Cathar parfait who, along with three others, was seized in 1235 by the order of Raymond the Seventh of Toulouse and burnt as a heretic, a gesture to propitiate the Pope and the French. The Count sent two preliminary emissaries who satisfied themselves with making the prescribed Cathar genuflections before the Parfaits, after which they retired whence they came.

I was intrigued by the appearance of the name Cambiaire. To me it was obscure and unimportant. I assumed that if Miss Mills were on the point of producing a flood of recollections all manner of minor characters would be involved and that these would add to the validity of the total experience but would have no special interest in their own right. I was not to know at this stage that this man was a finger pointing to the main characters in an entirely new story.

Jean de Cambiaire was described by Miss Mills as a bishop but appears in the records as a deacon. The latter was one of the higher grades of the simple Cathar hierarchy.

One morning Miss Mills woke with an acute pain in both wrists and shoulders. She wished to talk to someone but did not want to bother me too much. When I asked her how bad the pains were she described them as very severe but her manner was detached and undemanding and I assumed that this was because I was not her doctor. She was usually prompt, business-like, posing questions or problems in a simple form and preferring concise answers. It was obvious that she had something more to ask. It came out eventually. When she put the question she sounded diffident and hesitant and it was obvious that she was despising herself a little. 'When people were burnt at the stake did they have their arms tied behind their backs?'

'Why do you ask?'

'Oh, nothing, that was what it felt like.'

'Let's see,' I said, 'What date is it today?' I had not forgotten that she had predicted horror on two days in March. I looked at the calendar and found it was the sixteenth. It came to me without any effort at all that this was the day the Cathars were burnt at Montségur. This was no feat of memory on my part. It was a date I remembered with ease like those of Waterloo and Trafalgar. I had failed to respond to it at first because she had mentioned it alongside the 2nd and the 14th of the same month. I had no idea what the latter could signify. 'I've no idea how people were tied to the stake. I've no doubt one could find out easily enough but I'll leave it till I go to France in the summer.'

I saw Monsieur Duvernoy in September. He is the meticulous historian of Catharism who checked my book *The Cathars and Reincarnation* for possible errors. He said that the wrists were secured behind the back with chains.

I now considered it was time for me to elucidate whether the 2nd or the 14th had any particular significance. I was prepared to believe that in a psychic person with a possible Cathar in-carnation, a horror like Montségur would still reverberate after seven centuries, not only in the subconscious but the near conscious. I was ready to credit that this remembered agony could extend itself over the month of March. I had no confidence whatever that I would find that any particular event had hap-pened on the other dates mentioned. I was prepared for a long search but found what I wanted immediately. I was to exhibit for months this capacity to go immediately to the book I needed at the right page and line. It was hard for me to understand that I found so inevitably what I was seeking. I did not understand that, in a way, I was not seeking anything. Was it not rather that my will was in abeyance and that I was being guided to the books?

The significance of Miss Mills' echoes of past agonies was truly startling. The surrender of Montségur was determined by conditions unique for the Middle Ages. It involved a fourteen-day truce which is inexplicable on military or political grounds. It is said that this extraordinary delay was to enable the Cathars to celebrate the Manichean Spring feast known as Bema. This is conjecture but what is certain is that a truce of this nature involved the presence of Cathar sympathisers in the investing army. March 2nd was the day the truce was arranged. Its terms demanded that the garrison marched out as free men on the 14th, leaving the Cathars to be dealt with by the Catholic authorities.

What did all this amount to? In her previous life Miss Mills had been burnt at the stake. I could not doubt her after I had seen on her back the mark of the burning torch. At the back of my mind I had wondered whether she had suffered at Montségur. It was hardly remarkable that this thought should not occur to me at times. In her dreams she had run from a château on a hill by a rough path to a valley with woods and a stream. Montségur and its environs answers accurately to that description. And for more than thirty years I had been haunted by this mountain. I had been drawn to it and had, at the same time, recoiled from it because of some sinister and inexplicable significance it had for me. The pains on the morning of the sixteenth were striking enough in all conscience. The depression on the 2nd and the 14th were equally explicable. If she had been a Cathar at Montségur she, as one of the four hundred people in the fortress, would know immediately that, by the terms of the truce drawn up on March 2nd she was under sentence of death. As for the 14th, it is not hard to imagine her feelings when the garrison marched out and left the sheep helpless to the wolves.

Later in the year I was to receive still more striking evidence of her capacity to reverberate in the present to other tragic dates. on August 15th she rang to say that she could not get Carcassonne out of her mind. While she went about her work its name kept repeating itself and was accompanied by a feeling of misery and tension. Had something happened in Carcassonne that day? I felt that she was near the target because I knew that the city fell to de Montfort's crusaders in August. I did not know the exact date. I felt it was too much to expect that she had done it again. Carcassonne fell to de Montfort on the fifteenth of August.

What was still more extraordinary were the questions she posed in November of that year. Did anything happen at Termes, was it something to do with the water supply and was there an outbreak of disease? The word Termes had obtruded itself on her consciousness. She did not know where she got the idea about water. 'It just came to me while I was working. I can't say positively it was a voice. It just kept bothering me. It could well be nonsense.'

Termes I knew well enough. It is one of the Cathar castles which put up a vigorous resistance to the Crusaders. I had seen its ruins on a green hill scented with aromatic shrubs. Its seigneur, Olivier de Termes, defended his patrimony with great vigour. After a period of drought the water supply was exhausted. The besieged were ready to parley when there was a terrific thunderstorm, as a result of which the cisterns overflowed and obviously became contaminated. The garrison drank copiously, there was an outbreak of some serious malady, possibly typhoid or dysentery, and the castle was surrendered. My researches, or rather my sudden dip into the right book, informed me that the date of the capitulation was November 23rd 1209. Equally easy investigations disclosed that this was also the date on which Miss Mills telephoned.

Little enough is known in Britain of the Albigensian wars. Those who know a little have heard of the sack of Béziers and the fall of Carcassonne. How many in this country have ever heard of Termes, let alone of the flooding of its cisterns more than seven and a half centuries ago? Miss Mills does not confine herself to this. She remembers that the garrison were treated for their intestinal condition with an infusion of mint. She knows a good deal about infusions from her apprenticeship as healer to be described later. Mint still grows in profusion at Termes on the hill below the castle. Miss Mills is one of those historical sounding boards which become resonant on certain dates.

From early in March 1971 she was obsessively preoccupied

with the question of hostages. Time and again she returned to this theme. Were certain persons offered as securities to the besieging forces? I could not help her at all. I said it was unlikely and also that, after this lapse of time, this was something which almost certainly could not be verified. Then it occurred to me that I had been stupid. It is established beyond doubt that Pierre-Roger de Mirepoix, the captain of the garrison, stayed on himself after the defenders had marched out. This is well known because he arranged for the treasure to be evacuated either just before or after the burning of the Parfaits but definitely *after* the evacuation of the garrison. It seemed to me that, in staying on after the soldiers had departed, Pierre-Roger was acting as a hostage. I was a little proud of this effort and passed it on to Miss Mills. She was very polite and obviously unsatisfied.

Later in the year I found the answers to her question. Raymond Perella's son Jordan was in the hands of the enemy as a hostage. So was his cousin Arnaud-Roger de Mirepoix.

In the month of March she was inundated with Cathar recollections. Her remembrance of the tragedy of Montségur had sparked off other memories. These consisted simply of lists of names. None of the latter involved what could be called historical characters. Some were positively obscure. That they can be identified at all is due to the depositions made before the Inquisitors, to the latter's mole-like persistence and to the industry of their scribes.

On March 14th there were three lines of names. One line was written as follows, 'Arapaïs. Guiraud.' This explained itself two nights later with the single inscription Guiraud de Rabat. Arpaïs and he were wife and husband. What is more important is that she was one of the daughters of Raymond de Perella. What is still more fascinating is that the two names came through on the night of the 14th. This was the very night on which Arpaïs and Guiraud must have said good-bye to each other. He was one of the garrison freed by the conditions of the truce. She was detained by the Inquisitors and made a deposition on March 18th. This deposition is of great importance to us. It describes her agonising parting from her mother Corba and her sister Esclarmonde who were to be burnt as heretics. Arpaïs saw Esclarmonde and her mother for the last time on March 14th. If

Miss Mills was burnt at Montségur this was two days before her death. No wonder March 14th was a terrible day for her. It seemed that her perception of the echo of tragic dates occurred not only when she was awake but in the state of consciousness in which she made her notes at night. Perhaps her guide or guides were especially active on these tragic anniversaries.

On April 7th Miss Mills produced her most comprehensive list of names. Lantar, Corba, Fornera, Raymond, Phillipa and Arpaïs. This is clearly and beyond all doubt the Perella family. We have already identified Corba as Raymond's wife, Marquesia de Lantar as his mother-in-law, and Phillipa and Arpaïs as his daughters. Who was Fornera? I discovered that she was the mother of Pierre-Roger de Mirepoix, who married Raymond's daughter Phillipa. (The degree to which these heretical families intermarried was notorious.) It should be noted that Miss Mills wrote the Occitan version Fornera rather than the frenchified Fournière.

Can we now say who Miss Mills was in her previous incarnation? I think we can do this without doubt. The evidence from her dreams, their cessation and from the marks on her body, point to her having died at the stake. Her reaction on the three days in March suggests that she perished at Montségur. This should be established without doubt when we are dealing with her detailed recollection of the siege which preceeded the burning of the Parfaits. We have noted her detailed knowledge of the Perella family and the persistence in her memory of their Mirepoix relations.

But there were two other members of the Perella family whose names were not written by Miss Mills in her copious annotations. The name of the third sister, Esclarmonde, never appears, neither does that of the brother Jordan. Miss Mills was particularly persistent in wanting to know the number of Raymond's daughters. She knew without being informed by me that there was another other than Arpaïs and Phillipa. By a process of exclusion it was clear to me that Miss Mills was Esclarmonde. Neither Phillipa nor Arpaïs perished at the stake. Neither were complete heretics, that is to say they had not received the Consolamentum. Esclarmonde had done so years previously. She had never married and had devoted herself to a life of piety. As a practising Parfaite she was doomed. The reason why Miss Mills had never written Esclarmonde was that there was no particular point in recording her own name.

She remembered that she had a brother even though she could not recall his name. Perhaps the necessary chord of memory did not vibrate because Jordan was away from Montségur at the time of the final tragedy.

Next followed a remarkable testimony, from this incarnation, as to the accuracy of my suppositions. I saw Miss Mills on June 5th. She had returned some days previously from a holiday in Ireland. On this day I made up my mind to mention her previous identity. I have always been reluctant to strike positive attitudes with sensitives of her type. I have a dread of influencing them in any way. In addition, I am reluctant to impart too much information on any subject in which they are interested, in case I direct their thoughts and feelings in any particular direction. I believe, indeed, that my experience with Miss Mills may have been ordained to enable me to adopt a more positive attitude in these matters. I remain essentially the passive recorder.

I said I felt she must be Esclarmonde because of the constant references to the names of Mirepoix, Perella and Montségur. She received this quietly with an apologetic smile. I had the impression that she was less concerned with her previous identity than with other matters. 'I don't know what you will make of this,' she said. 'It was a dream I had on holiday. I dreamt I was sitting on this couch, yes, in this very corner. You were sitting in your chair as you are now. You were telling me exactly what you are now. I can't swear to the actual words but it wouldn't surprise me if they were the same. Anyway you were saying that I must be Esclarmonde—is that how you say it?—because I talked so often about the Perella family, the Mirepoix and Montségur. It struck me as odd at the time.' She was very tense that day. I think, from sheer exhaustion, she was understating the case. 'Anyway', she continued, 'it seemed so odd that I made a note in my diary.' For some time now she had kept a diary, irregularly and without rigidity, noting down her principal visions, dreams and intuitions as a supplement to the evidence dictated to her. I think she did this because I had at one time said that, had I not kept a diary, I would not have seen clearly the connections in the psychic synchronisations in which I became entangled. She was no more a slave to her journal than I had been. She only used it to note what was of first importance.

At the end of the interview I asked to see her diary. I trusted her completely but the scientist in me demanded that I see the evidence. My excuse was that I wished to verify if I had recorded the nocturnal messages in the right order. She usually handed them to me in batches and I made a note of the night on which they occurred. I saw clearly recorded in her diary the dream in all its details. The date was May 29th.

So far as I was concerned that was conclusive, but on August 13th there was further evidence. Her written communications for that night began with the following statement. 'Mars 16me 1244 trois generations de femmes.' The reference to three generations in association with that particular date can only refer to the Perella family at Montségur. Marquesia de Lantar, her daughter Corba and her grand-daughter Esclarmonde de Perella, all perished on that day and in that place.

But if this bleak unpunctuated statement had a weird fascination after seven hundred and twenty-seven years, what followed later was more astonishing and detailed and more intensely personal. Towards the end of 1971 and at the beginning of 1972 she was pouring out all kinds of details of her training in healing and meditation in the thirteenth century. She said that in learning to meditate she had not adopted any of the special positions recommended for others. She suffered from a pain in her left hip and walked with a limp. Her left leg was shorter than the other. For these reasons she was allowed to sit on a stool when meditating. She said, 'I am certain that I had something the matter with my left hip. Could it have been a tubercular hip joint? I had a cough, too, but the hip was more important. Anyway there was something the matter with it because that is why the pain stopped when you touched it last year.'

'Why are you so sure?'

'Because you stopped the dreams too.'

'I accept the dreams because it has happened with other people. But this, you say, is a pain from a disease you had in another incarnation. Can you explain that in the same way as the dreams stopping?'

45

'I don't know why but I'm sure you stopped it.'

I said no more. I thought of the marks on her back. If she could bear permanently on her body the scars sustained in a previous incarnation, a pain of a few weeks' duration but without demonstrable signs was surely easier to account for. The pain in her left side had only appeared after she met me. As well as being a memory of the past it was a pathological announcement of our previous contact. It stopped almost immediately after I had touched the affected area. It seemed I was wrong in attributing her previous pain to colon disturbance. The truth was something more exact and personal than any generalisation that the colon is a sensitive organ in the psyche.

There is still more to come. I learnt later that Esclarmonde was described in the records as 'infirme'. This implies that she was unmistakably an invalid. It is not likely that a vague disturbance like an irritable colon would attract attention in the thirteenth century. It should also be remembered that when, a year earlier, I had offered my explanation to Miss Mills, even at that time she had insisted, against my medical experience, that the pain she felt was in the joint itself.

6

In the names recorded by Miss Mills in March 1971 I have only mentioned those which testify to her identity, her membership of the Perella family and her association with Montségur. Another group of names was of more specific significance. They were absolutely unknown to me. In verifying previous Cathar references I had encountered the names of many obscure persons wholly forgotten except by a few savants who had disinterred them from the files of the Inquisition for specialist works of small circulation. This new batch was still more obscure.

It began on March 9th with Isarn de Montserver. It was clear that the name had made a big impact on Miss Mills. She seemed to assume that I must be familiar with it. I was satisfied, and with reason, that I had never encountered it previously. On March 19th we had the inscription

Montserver
Braida
Cisilia (*sic*)

The word Montserver occurred again on March 31st. This time it was accompanied by Queille. I did not know whether the latter was the name of a place or a person.

This means that the name Montserver was written three times in March. In studying the written evidence provided by Miss Mills I went on the assumption that the names which repeated themselves most often would be the most important for my theme. This supposition was generally correct.

In March the name Braïda occurs twice. It appears first in association with that of Montserver and Cisilia. I went later to my works of reference. I found that Braïda de Montserver was a woman who became a Parfaite after recovering from an illness. She was burnt as a heretic round about 1242. She had a son, Isarn de Montserver. He became ill, received the Consolamentum and died at Queille in 1235. She had a daughter Cecilia who, as we have seen, married Arnaud-Roger de Mirepoix. As the word spelt Cisilia appeared on the same night as Montserver and Braïda we can surely assume that it refers to Cecilia de Montserver.

Miss Mills' spelling of Cecilia and her leaving off the two dots above the i in the name Braïda are errors which add to the validity of the experience.

We are therefore following the tracks of a new family. I had no idea when I first encountered the name Montserver that it would be crucial to my story. I anticipated that it was another obscure name which would enable us to ponder the degree to which we can tune in to detail from seven centuries ago. It was something to marvel at, be thankful for and forget. I did not realise that it would lead to a new world of experience and a new attitude to life.

Among the names written in March were Laureta, Ransane and G. de Lahila. They were repeated on different occasions during the following summer. G. de Lahila was later identified as Guillaume de Lisle. Miss Mills gave different versions of his name. Lahila is the original Occitan. He was a knight strongly sympathetic to the Cathars, who was mortally wounded at Montségur. It was only fitting that these three names should appear together. Laureta was the mother of Guillaume de Lisle. Why should Ransane be recorded with them? The explanation became clearer when I learnt from a deposition of the Inquisition that all three were seen together at a meeting of heretics.

Another name which appeared in March was that of Raymond Sanche. As we shall see later he plays a shadowy but significant rôle in our story.

A curious phenomenon occurred after the first appearance in the records of Isarn de Montserver. Miss Mills became pre-occupied with the number 609. Time and again she asked if it had any significance. I could not see how a number of this nature could be related to the Cathar tragedy. I made several wild guesses. Was it the number of the Cathar Parfaits at that time in the Languedoc? After a time I wondered whether it was the number of some Inquisitorial folio but as I did not live in Toulouse or Paris this was of little use to me. I thought of writing to the appropriate authorities but deferred because I was busy at the time and because I felt that if one waited long enough something would turn up. Consulting authorities too early can be like influencing witnesses. In this particular matter I had to wait five months for enlightenment. It came on August 31st, 1971. The night previously Miss Mills had written in large letters, on a single piece of paper, '609 Montserver.' This diverted one's mind positively in the direction of numbered documents. This was all the more so because there followed eight small pages written in a somewhat smaller hand. The message was as follows. 'Dans les propres maisons de les hérétiques le temoin avula (sic) Braïda sa belle fille et Cesilia fille de Ladite Braïda ainsi que laieul de la femme de Raimon Sanche et P. Andoys. Elle dit egalement quelle a vu dans la maison de Na Laureta a Mirepoix tous sauf que Guillaume de Mirepoix qui n'aiment pas les hérétiques adorent la les dit heretiques il y a environ 16 ans.'

I stuck at one point in the translation. I could not work out the meaning of the word 'avula'. This was a simple phonetic elision of 'a vu là,' that is to say, had seen there! The full translation is as follows : 'This witness has seen in their own houses Braïda, her daughter-in-law and Cecilia, daughter of the said Braïda, also the grandfather of the wife of Raimon de Sancho and P. Andoys. She also said she had seen (these heretics?) in Na Laureta's house at Mirepoix. All except Guillaume de Mirepoix who disliked the heretics, made the ritual genuflexion before the said heretics. This was about sixteen years ago'.

We have already encountered Cecilia de Montserver in the names appearing in the middle of March. It is clear that she was Braïda's daughter and that the Montserver family is important in our story. Braïda had been mentioned twice previously in March. She was clearly a key figure. It was equally evident that the latest message was an extract from an Inquisitorial deposition. The form and the stilted wording were obvious. It was only natural that I should assume that this was an extract from an as yet unidentified document labelled 609. My supposition was correct but I had some way to go before I discovered its origin.

In assessing Miss Mills' performance in writing this extract we must take account of the following factors. She produced this record before she, or I, knew that such a document existed. That I recognised it as couched in the style of the Inquisitors was no proof of its authenticity. She wrote it in French. She is unable to write French in the modern idiom. She is quite incapable of reproducing the style of the Inquisitorial records. Only a small proportion of the latter have been published in French. I knew that Monsieur Duvernoy had made his own translations but that a number of these had not been printed. Certainly so far as I knew at that time such a reference to Braïda and her circle had never been printed. Miss Mills has, in her small flat, little space for books and her library is limited. The one book she possesses on Catharism is my *The Cathars and Reincarnation.* It contains no reference to the Montserver family. The Inquisitorial records are in Paris and Toulouse. Until I told her she was not even aware of their existence.

I felt sure that, with the aid of Monsieur Duvernoy, I would find the source of this reference to Braïda de Montserver and her family when I visited the Midi in late summer. Against the background of what had happened the reference Montserver 609 was pretty significant. But the route to enlightenment was indirect.

Just before I went on holiday in September Miss Mills rang me to say that she must have been entirely wrong about 609 being the number of a folio. She had just been looking through *The Cathars and Reincarnation*. She pointed out that in a statement about Pierre de Mazerolles I had quoted a reference. This was Folio 609 in the Archives at Toulouse. At first I was astonished. My own book was the last one I would have examined for the reference, and indeed I had not done so. Then I remembered the circumstances perfectly. In September 1969 I had visited Monsieur Duvernoy in Toulouse. I had wished to know what happened to Pierre de Mazerolles, one of the main characters in *The Cathars and Reincarnation*, after the murder of the Inquisitors at Avignonet in 1242. Monsieur Duvernoy had translated for me from Latin into French the references to de Mazerolles. I remembered distinctly how, when I collected this translation, he said to me, as though surprised by my insouciance, 'But don't you want the number of the reference?' He wrote it down for me at the end of the interview.

That seemed to me to be the end of the matter. Folio 609 related to Pierre de Mazerolles and his circle and I had been looking in the wrong direction. The mistake I made at that juncture was that I never realised that folio 609 was a large affair and contained the depositions of several people. I was prepared to leave it at that. Nevertheless, I felt strangely sorry for Miss Mills. I will not say that she showed disappointment but it was clear that 609 was a big issue to her, possibly because she assumed it had contained some references to the Montserver family. There was a great deal in the messages she received which she could not understand. For the most part she was content to shrug these off with statements that they meant nothing to her. At her most exhausted she longed for them to stop. But her attitude to the Montserver family was quite different. One day when she asked me what I knew of Braïda de Montserver I was surprised to see her eyes filled with tears. It was inevitable that I wondered if the two had been connected in a previous incarnation. I could never have imagined how close they were to be to each other in this present world. I felt inclined to write a long string of questions about Folio 609 to Monsieur Duvernoy in

Toulouse. Again I decided to wait. Miss Mills was providing so much material that I wondered if she would supply her own answer. I contented myself with a letter to Monsieur Duvernoy mentioning my interest in the Montserver family and asking if he could inform me about them when I visited the Languedoc in September.

When I saw Monsieur Duvernoy in September 1971 he translated from Latin into French several passages of Folio 609, from the archives at Toulouse, which contained references to the Montserver family and which I had never encountered previously. Queille, the home of the Montservers, appeared four times in the document. Pelegrina, wife of Isarn de Montserver, is also mentioned. Later Monsieur Duvernoy sent on to me the full translation of this deposition. I was able to see that Miss Mills was preoccupied with the figure 609 because it was concerned with the destinies of the Montserver family.

In 1972, and again through the offices of Monsieur Duvernoy, I was able to trace the origin of Miss Mills' message about Braïda, Cecilia and Raymond Sanche's relative which I have mentioned previously in this chapter. It consisted of sentences, varying a little from the original, but clearly deriving from the deposition of Pelegrina, the wife of Isarn de Montserver.

It was clear that the 609 written on Miss Mills' writing pad and reverberating in her mind was a clue offered by Braïda to establish her own credentials. Monsieur Duvernoy weighed in with further assistance when he sent me also, though I had not asked for it, the deposition of Arnaud-Roger de Mirepoix contained in the Doat collection in Paris. On April 20th, 1244, five weeks after the burning of the Parfaits at Montségur, Arnaud-Roger made the following statement. 'I saw at Limoux, in the château of Isarn de Fanjeaux, my mother-in-law Braïda now burnt (as heretic) who had taken ill there. Then Raymond, the Bishop of the heretics arrived with another Parfait and received the said Braïda (i.e. into the Cathar faith) in the following manner.' He then goes on to describe the ceremony of the Consolamentum and gives a list of the people present.

Arnaud-Roger describes also how Braïda's son received the Consolamentum. 'When Isarn de Montserver, my brother-in-law, was in Guillaume Baudoin's house at Queille and suffering from the illness of which he died, he asked me to bring the Bon-shommes (Parfaits) to him at all costs because he wished to give himself to them. I then brought to the sick man Guillaume Tournée and his companions who were Parfaits, and as I led him to the house where the invalid was lying a messenger arrived and told me that the Bailiff of the Count of Toulouse had seized four Parfaits from the Château of Montségur and that I should go there straight away. I set off at once to Montségur and left the Parfaits in the house.'

Arnaud-Roger does not mention the names of the Parfaits seized by Raymond the Seventh in a discreditable attempt to keep the Catholic French in play. But we know one already through Miss Mills. When the names of the Perella family first came through on March 3rd they were accompanied by that of Jean de Cambiaire, described by Miss Mills as a bishop but so far as we know no more than a deacon. Cambiaire was seized while Isarn de Montserver was on his death bed. The name of the latter appeared on Miss Mills' writing pad for the first time six days after the first mention of Cambiaire. Miss Mills was remembering back to the years before the final tragedy of Montségur in 1244. At this time the Perella family were installed at Montségur and had been from the beginning of the century. Miss Mills could well have recalled Jean de Cambiaire because he was associated with a member of a family whose intervention in her life was to become crucial. At the least this extraordinary and obscure recollection shows how much the name Montserver reverberates in the memory of a woman in Somerset in 1971.

Folio 609 is of specific importance to us because it contains so many references to the Montserver family, but it gives also other information equally vital for our purposes. The mistake I made all along was to believe that 609 was a small folio containing only one or two short depositions. This folio contains several references to Guilhabert de Castres who is an important figure in my story. I had never conceived it possible that any of the main characters of Catharism would intrude in my history. I have always reacted against those whose previous incarnations involve the well known and distinguished. Guilhabert de Castres does not appear in the history books but he is constantly referred to in works on the Cathars. That he should be involved in my story was beyond my aspirations. But, come to that, did I ever imagine that the Parfaits would visit Somerset?

The reader will have noticed that in these revelations the small gentry play a prominent role. The explanation is simple. In most of the European heresies those who went to the stake were chiefly members of the unprivileged classes. Perhaps the prototypes of the superior artisan were the main victims. Weavers, for example, were especially prone to heresy. Catharism is unique in that so many of the victims were among the minor nobility. In some heretical movements the aristocracy backed the heretics, as was to some extent the case with Luther. Catharism is the only heresy known to me where the nobility, and particularly its female members, were so ready to die for their beliefs.

7

We have said enough already to show that the Perella and Mirepoix families were closely related to each other. Raymond de Perella was, after all, the father-in-law of Pierre-Roger de Mirepoix, the commander of the soldiers who garrisoned his château. Both these families were allied to the Montservers. Cecilia de Montserver was the wife of Arnaud-Roger de Mirepoix. There were other marriages between members of these two important families. The heretical nobility of the Languedoc were markedly intermarried.

Now none of the three above-mentioned families played any part in the history told in *The Cathars and Reincarnation*. In the latter book I was concerned with two families, those of Fanjeaux and Mazerolles. These two were also intermarried. As Roger-Isarn in the thirteenth century I had a sister Hélis. She married Arnaud de Mazerolles. Is there any evidence that the group of families figuring in the stories of Mrs. Smith and Miss Mills were known to each other? Even without detailed evidence this must have been so. All the five families mentioned were active supporters and protectors of Catharism. All had provided Parfaits or Parfaites for the cause. They must have been well known to each other because they were members of the nobility with a fervent common interest in which they acted together, and living in a restricted area the size of Somerset. But we have much stronger evidence than this.

Raymond Sanche reappeared twice in the list of names. His role would appear to have been of some importance.

Long before Miss Mills wrote his name I had noted in my diary an extract from Deodat Roché's book, *L'Eglise Romaine et Les Albigeois*. The incident described was not exciting but it made a considerable impression on me. It was recorded that Raymond Sanche, with Isarn de Montserver and Pierre de Mazerolles, had acted as escort to conduct the Bishop Guilhabert de Castres from Montségur. They had stopped en route at the château of Durfort. The latter was part of the estate of the family to which I belonged in the thirteenth century. I had imagined that it was for this reason that I had made the note and also because Pierre de Mazerolles, the source of my nightmares described in *The Cathars and Reincarnation*, had been mentioned. I had no idea that whatever was echoing in me was important not entirely because of these names I knew well, but because Guilhabert de Castres was present. I doubt if the fact that I made the note was near-conscious far memory on my part. I think it is more likely that the discarnate entity from the thirteenth century was drawing my attention, through Miss Mills, to the rôle played by Guilhabert de Castres.

What struck me after I read the names of Guilhabert's escort was that here we had a positive bridge between the families I had encountered in my other contact with the thirteenth century and with those I met through Miss Mills. This was further emphasised when I was able to study at leisure the French translation of Arnaud-Roger de Mirepoix's deposition. It stated that when Braïda de Montserver received the Consolamentum, Isarn de Fanjeaux and Isarn de Montserver were present. The former's wife, Ransane, came in and went out during the ceremony. As she alone failed to 'adore', that is to say to bow three times to the heretics, it can be taken that she was not a practising Cathar.

After she received the Consolamentum Braïda spent her convalescence in the house of Isarn de Fanjeaux, brother of my thirteenth century precursor. That she should have done so is indisputable evidence of the links between her family and that of Fanjeaux. When she had recovered she set out for the 'house of the heretics'. The latter term means a kind of convent for women Cathars. To which did she go? It is almost certain that later in the thirteenth century Miss Mills went to the same institution.

It is quite clear that the guide was directing Miss Mills', or rather my, attention to Folio 609. What was the aim of this particular gesture? Two factors stand out clearly. Attention is being directed to the Montserver family in general and to Braïda de Montserver in particular. It is not for nothing that we are treated to a description of the latter's illness and convalescence and to the details of how she disposed of her possessions when she became a Parfaite.

There is further evidence of the inevitable connection between Mrs. Smith's families and those of Miss Mills. The deposition referring to Queille, the family home of the Montservers, and to Isarn de Montserver's wife Pellegrina, was made by Ermissende de Mazerolles. Folio 609 contains also the records of the interrogation of Pierre de Mazerolles. The latter, in being the night visitor intruding himself in Mrs. Smith's and my own nightmares, can from some points of view be regarded as the spark which ignited the whole chain of recollection. It is undoubted from the records that Hélis de Mazerolles and Isarn de Fanjeaux, the sister and brothers of Roger, my precursor in the thirteenth century, visited Montségur regularly, the former as an earnest Parfait and the latter as the emissary of the Count of Toulouse. There can be no doubt whatever that they were well known to the owners of the château and to the commander of his garrison. The main characters of Mrs. Smith's and Miss Mills' stories were known to each other and lived at the same time. It will be seen later that Miss Mills' characters spill over copiously into Mrs. Smith's territory and for a particular reason. Is it possible that these two women's thirteenth-century prototypes were known to each other? This is more than probable. It becomes even more likely if we take into account Miss Mills' extraordinary reaction the morning I received a letter from Mrs. Smith. She had never met the latter and was unaware of her name and address. She informed me that I had received a letter that morning. At this time I was hearing from Mrs. Smith at the rate of once a year.

Can we at this stage clarify the purpose of Miss Mills' guide in getting in touch with her? Did she wish to enlighten Miss Mills as to her previous incarnation or was she concerned with offering her own credentials? Certainly the clues given were enough to identify Miss Mills in her thirteenth-century rôle without too much difficulty. But this could never have been done had she not referred her messages to me. It needed someone with a modest knowledge and a greater interest in Catharism to decipher these messages. What is my rôle in the grand strategy of this occult campaign? We must leave discussion of this until we have all the evidence. Certainly Miss Mills' spirit guide was identifying herself for a special purpose.

8

Early in April 1971 Miss Mills' revelations took a curious turn. The shower of undeniably Cathar names and references ceased. They were not to be renewed again until the end of July. I was slow in interpreting this sudden change of direction. I had had two similar examples before. I was slow to see that this could mean that there was more than one guide. Miss Mills herself made this suggestion earlier than I did. This was not difficult to understand. She was in closer contact with them and became familiar with their particular interests and preoccupations.

The flood of writing in May, June and July was clearly divisible into five groups. These were Biblical quotations, drawings and crosses, quotations in Latin, French and English from sources which were obviously liturgical, names of classical authors and philosophical reflections. The messenger did not follow any particular order. One group did not succeed the other. If I deal separately with the different categories it is in order to simplify the story.

During this period the visions, voices and intuitions continued. The guide, or guides, dictated at greater length and with particular intensity. Miss Mills was tired and troubled. There was never any deep-seated, fulminating revolt against her instructors but she was more tense than before. She wondered again why she had been chosen as a vehicle, above all because she could not understand clearly what she was transmitting. It was not till she achieved a more 'personal' contact with the other world that she heaved a sigh of relief and settled down to her allotted rôle. Talking directly to people, or beings, was something she could do and understand.

May began with a flood of Biblical references. These were to continue regularly for three months and spasmodically for some months afterwards. There is no point in discussing these references in detail. Many were prescriptions for spiritual development and could be followed with profit by anybody. Naturally what I searched for were implications particularly applicable to Catharism in general, or Miss Mills and myself in particular. I did this by searching for fundamental common denominators. These were being revealed by those passages which repeated themselves most often. It was curious that among the first quotations to which her attention was directed was a reference to trumpets in Corinthians I. This particular quotation was repeated later. In itself it did not appear to have any particular significance. Psychic communication of this nature can often descend to uninspiring detail. Or was it related to her life-long horror of such instruments? I wondered if the invading host at Montségur had been addicted to the blowing of trumpets. Had the burning of the Parfaits been preceded by an appropriate fanfare? I decided after several scrutinies of the lists of quotations that if this particular verse was significant its meaning was incomprehensible to me. I did not discover till the year afterwards that the most ghastly and crucial episode in the siege of Montségur was preceded by the blowing of trumpets.

The most cardinal point is easily made. Quotations from St. Paul were overwhelmingly predominant. The references were almost all to the epistles. Those to the Acts were almost non-existent. Quotations from St. John's gospel were a very poor second. The Pauline preponderance was unmistakable. Corinthians I was the favourite epistle.

To anyone with some knowledge of Catharism it might be surprising that so many quotations were from St. Paul. The liturgy of Catharism was based on the first chapter of the gospel according to St. John. The Parfaits carried with them a copy of this gospel. Why our guide's prediliction for St. Paul?

The answer is simple. Among all the Apostles Paul is the supreme interpreter of Christianity from the occult point of view. His speciality is its Spiritist aspect. When he talks about a body corporeal and a body spiritual he is discussing briefly what has been expanded by modern spiritualists, theosophists and followers of Steiner. His outlook ties up directly with modern conceptions of etheric and astral bodies and the like. Orthodox Christians may jib at the idea that early Christianity was characterised by psychic communication and spiritist phenomena. What was to be revealed later to Miss Mills indicated clearly that primitive Christianity was of this nature.

There are more specific reasons why Miss Mills' Cathar guide should refer her to St. Paul. Catharism itself was essentially a spiritist religion. Lucifer or the Devil made the world of form. God ruled over the world of the invisible. The good God made the good spirits. But Catharism is not alone in being a religion concerned with spiritist phenomena and psychic communication. We have before our eyes the example of modern Spiritualism in its different aspects. Did Miss Mills' guide or guides lead her through these references to anything more specifically concerned with Catharism? Is there any citation which illustrates the particular nature and specialised theology of the latter creed?

Corinthians I, chapter 15, verse 45, is repeated no less than five times in the weeks given over to these scriptural references. 'And so it was written, the first Adam was made a living soul, the last Adam was made a quickening spirit.' Now this is specifically Cathar. It is no good passing it off as part and parcel of the Christian inheritance. It is one of those passages people accept without reflection because of their spiritual content but which are nevertheless not part of Christian orthodoxy. This particular verse implies that a living soul is in man from the

58

beginning. This is contrary to orthodoxy, particularly of the Catholic variety. The latter regards the soul as something which grows with consciousness and which sleeps after death till the Day of Judgement. The Cathar idea is quite different. Man is born with his full psychic complement. This is an essential feature of the doctrine of reincarnation. After death the psyche does not pass into any such state of cosmic somnolence as is represented by the concept of limbo. It embarks on a process of reincarnation. 'The last Adam was made a quickening Spirit' refers to our ultimate development in being emancipated from matter. This, to the Cathars, was the *raison d'être* of our existence. They recognised that there was every gradation between matter conceived of as inert spirit and, at the other extreme, matter so spiritualised that Christ could appear on earth and reveal the true nature of his spiritualised body to the disciples at the Transfiguration.

This verse is the bedrock of Cathar teaching. That it appears in the scriptures does not mean it is part and parcel of contemporary Christianity. Every form of this religion has depended on the same written sources. The vital difference between orthodoxy and so-called heresy can only be in the interpretation.

The issue is further clarified if we read what comes before and after verse 45. Some of this is the basis of ordinary Christianity but its scope is wider than this and contains matter which predates Christianity. 'All flesh is not the same flesh, but there is one kind of flesh of man, another flesh of beasts, another of fishes and another of birds.' Paul is dealing with the different degrees to which matter is impregnated with spirit. This is basic Cathar doctrine. If we like we can call this an esoteric interpretation of Christianity, but if one does so, the latter is very close to Catharism. In making this statement Paul was influenced by prechristian sources and the cultural background against which he was reared. What he says is another version of Schiller's statement that God sleeps in the stone, wakes in the plant, dreams in the animal and lives in the man. This ties up not only with Cathar doctrine but with modern ideas of physical, etheric and astral bodies and their different distribution in the animal kingdom.

It is no good describing this as orthodox Christianity. The

latter could affect to agree that the aim of life is to enable the spirit to escape from matter. But does orthodox Christianity, be it Catholic, Anglican or Presbyterian, believe in the existence of a spirit body? Essentially, Catholics do not believe even in the Spirit as intrinsic to the nature of man. To them the Spirit is something granted by grace from on high and preferably by the intercession of the priesthood. 'For this corruptible must put on incorruption' means, in Dualist terms, that we are essentially imprisoned in matter at birth and must free our spiritual body from the fleshly envelope. The former then becomes one of the good spirits in the form originally created by the good God.

In some of the other references the subject matter is concerned with the evidence for life after death, that is with the recognition by witnesses of the continued existence of spiritual bodies. Again, it is no good taking it for granted that this is orthodox Christianity. The latter uses Christ's appearance to the disciples after His crucifixion as evidence of His resurrection but fails to draw the conclusion that after this world man, as a whole, passes to other planes of awareness where, under certain circumstances, he is still visible and his voice audible. Orthodox Christianity still adheres, far more than the sophisticated recognise, to the idea of a long sleep and a Day of Judgement, or, among the more enlightened, to a sudden partial dissolution in a world of spirit, of being wrapped up and obliterated in Abraham's bosom. The Pauline interpretation is applicable to the phenomena of Miss Mills and the presence which speaks to her at night. How, after all, did Braïda get here? This is presumably why the latter is supplying the references.

There is other evidence that we are on the right lines in regarding the Pauline quotations as referring to Catharism. The latter owed a great deal to the faith of Bogomil which had flourished previously in Bulgaria. Bogomilism in its turn was grafted on the beliefs of a considerable sect called the Paulicians. The latter had a long innings in the Balkans where they are first noted in the sixth century and where they existed until the tenth century, especially in Bulgaria. The Paulicians were unmistakable Dualists who received this name because of the emphasis they laid on the Pauline writings. We begin to see an increasing significance in Mme. Brelet's interest in Bulgaria and in the flood of Balkan references with which Miss Mills was inundated in the first months of 1971.

However, the most dramatic evidence of the importance of the Pauline writings on Catharism in general, and in particular on the education of Miss Mills, came later in the year. In September I was on holiday in Montségur. My hostess was renowned for her knowledge of philosophy and, in particular, for that related to Dualism. One day she was telling me that ten years previously she had had a vision of St. Paul. I listened intently and made no comment. She continued to tell me, with obvious diffidence, that St. Paul did not restrict himself to a visual appearance. He had dictated to her a whole string of scriptural references.

'Yes,' I said, 'and the great majority was from the first book of Corinthians.'

She looked very startled. 'How could you know?'

'How could I fail to?' I then explained how Miss Mills had also been instructed to read St. Paul.

How do I explain this episode? I cannot dismiss it as coincidence. It is so much a natural component of the whole pattern of this story. Can it be telepathy? We must beware of this word. It is becoming as dangerous an umbrella phrase as was 'suggestible' in earlier days when extra-sensory perception was not accepted except by a tiny minority. Can this be explained as telepathy when there is a gap of ten years between Miss Mills' experience and that of my hostess at Montségur?*

Miss Mills' references were often abbreviated. Thess, for instance, sufficed for Thessalonians. Later in the summer, as the dictation was intensified, her writing deteriorated but was always decipherable. The numbers of the chapters and verses tended to flow into each other without intermission. But never once in the deluge of quotations, which amounted to one hundred and twenty-eight, did she offer something which was not verifiable. She never gave the number of non-existent chapter or verse.

* While I have always analysed these synchronisations in relation to chronological time, and felt that it is necessary to do so, one has to admit that there is something illogical in the procedure. After all, time is an illusion and all psychic experience, even the simplest varieties of extrasensory perception, is inevitably tinged with the implications of timelessness.

On one occasion I thought she had erred. Written on a piece of paper she found the words, Job, Wis of Sol and Ecclesias (sic), with the appropriate chapters and verses. The somewhat inelegant Wis of Sol was identifiable as Wisdom of Solomon. It seemed to me that she was off-beam from two points of view. Her third reference appeared to be to Ecclesiastes. The chapter quoted was thirty-eight. There was no such chapter. It was only on scrutinising the paper a second time that I saw it was written as above. It clearly referred to Ecclesiasticus which contains fifty-one chapters. But to me the reference to Ecclesiasticus contained a second source of error. The Old Testament was anathema to the Cathars. This was inevitably so because they held that the Jehovah of the Old Testament was the devil. It was, however, permissible to read the prophetic books. The reference to Job was therefore in order. Ecclesiasticus could not be described as coming under this heading. Then I realised that in certain Cathar communities the books of the Apocrypha were also allowed. Wisdom of Solomon I knew to be Apocryphal. I was not so certain about Ecclesiasticus and was relieved to find that it came into this category.

But the reference to Ecclesiasticus was still striking for another reason. It came late in the history of the Biblical quotations. It was not written till the first week of November 1971. It was for this reason that I thought she was wide of the mark in giving the Old Testament references. Had she, as it were, written herself out in the course of her midsummer bombardment? By the time the reference to Ecclesiasticus appeared the guide had switched over to another subject, that of healing. The latter had been introduced in May but in a symbolic form which I did not recognise. It intensified in November and was to achieve its incredible apotheosis in February 1972 when there was no doubt whatsoever that she was the favoured recipient of a revelation. What was contained in Ecclesiasticus, chapter 38? It referred graphically to the virtues and functions of the physician. This is very important because to heal the sick was one of the two basic injunctions required of the early Christians. Once again this function was allowed almost to disappear during the greater part of Church history. Nevertheless it was actively revived by the

Cathars. Many of the Parfaits were doctors and all were to some degree educated in medicine.

It could well be that this message was more personally directed and that Miss Mills was being exhorted once again to confide in me. It was quite unmistakable that at the time she received this message she was reluctant to do so. This happened from time to time. A certain degree of ambivalence is inevitable in people like Miss Mills, but one could not call her a moody person. I noticed that she never hesitated to disclose the historical facts of Catharism or the references to the Scriptures. She was at times reluctant to disclose the philosophical messages. She described them as somehow more personal. When she acted like this I never pressed her. It will be seen later that the explanation of her reluctance was not difficult. It was in part inevitable in view of her past allegiances. On the other hand the fact that she took this sensitive attitude about her philosophical communications necessitated a reminder from Braïda that I was to be trusted.

There was another specific and personal reference in Ecclesiasticus. This was the quotation which says, 'The Lord hath created medicines out of the earth.' Less than a week after this Miss Mills was inundated with recollections of the preparation of medicines and of dressings for the treatment of wounds. This quotation from Ecclesiasticus ushered in appropriately an amazing period of months devoted to the subject of healing.

The question of healing had been introduced earlier in the context of the quotations. On August 16th Mark, chapter 16, verses 18 and 17, was recommended. 'And these signs shall follow them that believe. In my name they shall cast out devils; they shall speak with new tongues. They shall take up serpents; and if they drink any deadly thing it shall not hurt them; they shall lay hands on the sick and they shall recover.'

At this time Miss Mills took up no serpents and, as far as she knew, cast out no devils. But two strange phenomena were occurring. The first was dramatically related to the statement in Mark. She had always been the sort of person to whom other people took their troubles. This tendency was at this time, and from the rationalist point of view, inexplicably intensified. Night after night, when her work was done, she was besieged by the physically sick and mentally anguished who derived more comfort from her than they received elsewhere. But now she manifested a specific and unmistakable sign that she had developed the gift of healing. Sometimes she stretched out a hand to comfort her visitors and touched them on the forehead, hands or shoulders in an involuntary and comforting gesture. She noticed that her hands began to burn and that she felt in her fingers an intense, pricking sensation associated with the gift of healing.

Those who visited her commented on the burning they felt in their flesh and that there seemed to be a great force which emanated from her. This was the palpable manifestation of what Mark had said, 'They shall lay their hands on the sick and they shall recover.' What was to be dramatically revealed later was the emphasis on the hands. Was it striking and unusual that an active, competent good mixer such as Miss Mills should be developing the gift of healing? I suppose it would have been for anybody watching from the sidelines. It would have been equally mysterious to those who felt the burning in their skin and the great healing force which emanated from her. To me it was less surprising. She had been a Parfaite in the thirteenth century. In coping with the troubles of others she was merely taking on where she had left off in a former incarnation. I did not realise how completely she was returning to her previous role. I had no idea of the immense significance of her physical impulse to reach towards people with her hands. Mark had said also, 'They shall speak with new tongues.' At this time Miss Mills was, independently of time, using French, Latin and, later, Occitan.

It was interesting that in taking down the reference Miss Mills wrote the verses from Mark in the wrong order. On another occasion she repeated the same performance with a Cathar prayer. It is interesting that Mrs. Smith recalled one of Roger's favourite poems with the verses in a different order from that printed in Professor Saintsbury's book of French lyrics.

There were other references which were significantly Cathar but which I do not quote because they could apply to any even mildly esoteric approach to Christianity. The several references to the Holy Spirit came into this category. There were other isolated citations which had a specific and striking significance.

'Greet the brethren with a holy kiss.' The kiss of peace was later described by Miss Mills. It occurred at the conclusion of the Consolamentum. In this the Cathars were repeating the rituals of primitive Christianity.

9

The Biblical quotations noted by Miss Mills had various implications but before they had run their course they turned definitely in the direction of healing. Most of the references were dictated from May to the middle of August. Those dealing more specifically with healing, such as the big quotation from Ecclesiasticus, were delayed till November. By the late summer I was beginning to wonder whether more than one guide had taken responsibility for Miss Mills' instruction. A similar conclusion could be drawn from a study of her drawings. Once again I wondered whether the explanation could be the same and that these seeming changes of direction were because different teachers were entrusted with different systems of instruction.

On May 8th, when she was being submerged by her first tide of references, chiefly Corinthians I, she found at her bedside the cryptic message, Tau Cross.

I did not even know that these words were related to each other. I had no idea of the significance of the word Tau. This will give the savant some idea of my knowledge of these matters. I was busy at the time and had no intention of conducting an immediate search for the meaning of this word. I walked across the room to a book lying on the sofa. It was called *The Philosophy of Compassion*, by Esmé Wynne Tyson. The book had been obtained from the county library while I was away on holiday. I did not even know it was on order and had not opened it. It seems that months previously my wife had put it down, without my knowledge, on the list of books required from the library. There was no reason in the world why I should have anticipated finding anything to help me in this book. Nevertheless I looked at the index. There I saw Taw. The relevant extract was, 'Justin believed that the Crucifixion was pre-ordained and that the blood of the Passover was sprinkled on the Israelites' doorposts in the form of a cross, as Taw, the last letter in the Hebrew alphabet, foretelling the sacrifice on Calvary.'

The fact that Miss Mills had written TAU rather than TAW did not worry me unduly. I assumed that she had recorded the French version. This was confirmed by Larousse. I learnt later that Tau is the common English usage. Miss Mills had recorded it with her usual accuracy. Larousse also pointed out that it was the nineteenth letter of the Greek alphabet. As the derivation of the Tau cross was obviously ancient I could not see that we were dealing with an exclusively Cathar symbol. This was borne out by the fact that it was accompanied on the same day by seven designs on a second piece of paper. These were as follows:

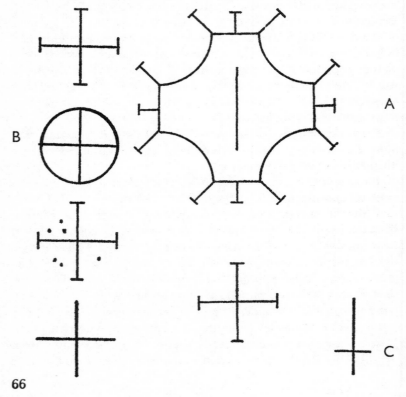

I am not competent to discuss the meaning of these crosses. My only comment is that, except for the one marked C, which is the cross of St. Peter, they have all equal arms and are therefore of Greek rather than Roman origin. B, with the cross surrounded by a circle, is Celtic. Like the Greek, it is non-Roman in origin. In Roman crosses the inferior arm of the cross is longer than the others as is depicted here.

Miss Mills saw to it that Cross A was a problem. During all the period of her revelations she had two or three insistent preoccupations, and this was one of them. All I could offer was that it resembled the emblem of the Languedoc except that at the end of each arm there were three miniature crosses rather than semicircular protuberances. I thought this suggestion was good enough. I never quite succeeded in getting Miss Mills to see that, after more than seven centuries, the evidence as to the significance of a symbol was hard to come by and often imprecise.

She asked me if the cross had anything to do with Fanjeaux. I could not find that it had been at any time the seal or emblem of this town. It was drawn on another occasion with what looked like the word DUFTONIS written above it. I could not be sure of the letter F. Later still, in the autumn, it appeared with the word FANJEA written below it. The latter was an obvious abbreviation.

Towards the end of the year I picked up an article on healing, in *Man, Myth and Magic*. I skipped through it quickly. The more I had experienced the realities of healing, the less I was inclined to read about it. It seemed that the Tau cross was one of the symbols of healing. I still did not see in what way this cross was particularly related to Catharism. I knew well enough that the latter accepted the obligation imposed on primitive Christianity to heal the sick. I did not, I could not, have realised to what extent healing was a deeply studied art and science in the Languedoc of the thirteenth century. I had to wait until the guide appeared before Miss Mills in the robes she wore in the thirteenth century. She was wearing also the cross which had become something of an obsession to her pupil. What it denoted is part of Braïda de Montserver's story.

IO

On June 28th, 1971 Miss Mills had the following to show for her night's rest. 'Grant us to know what thou knowest and to love what thou dost love, for we are not of this world and this world is not of us.'

This certainly rang a bell. It was familiar and it puzzled me that I could not identify it exactly. I assumed that it was part of the Consolamentum. I found the answer in turning rapidly the pages of Nelli's translation of the *Rituel de Lyons*. A Cathar prayer by Jean Maurin is appended at the end of the translation from Occitan into French of the ritual of the Consolamentum. I was bewildered not only by the fact that she had written the words in English but by the perfection of the translation. I give Professor Nelli's French text of Jean Maurin's prayer. "Puisque nous ne sommes pas du monde et que le monde n'est pas de nous, donne nous a connaître ce que tu connais et a aimer ce que tu aimes.'

I do not know why, in the French version, the statement that we are not of this world is in inverted commas. Equally I do not know why Miss Mills inverted the order of the sentences. There was a second instalment the same night.

> We entrust this holy prayer to your keeping
> Receive it from God and us and from the whole Church
> May you have strength to say it all the days of your life

I guessed again that this might come from the Consolamentum. I could not claim to recall the words of the latter rather lengthy sacrament. My guess was correct. What is fascinating is that once again we have a perfect rendering of the original French. Miss Mills' knowledge of the latter language would quite unfit her to produce such an elegant translation.

On July 5th she switched over to Latin, of which she has no knowledge whatever. I inevitably suspected that what she had produced was an extract from the Consolamentum because it was clear that her attention was being directed to the Cathar

68

liturgy. The words she quoted were uttered just before the bishop or deacon conferred the Consolamentum by touching the head of the aspirant with a copy of the gospels. 'Pater sancte, suscipe servium tuum in tua justitia, et mitte graticam tuam et spiritum sanctum tuum super eum.' There is in this extract a grammatical nicety of great importance to us. The Latin varies according as to whether the bishop or deacon is addressing a man or a woman.

The output on July 27th was striking. 'Then they arose up on a sky of glass and for everyone that rose aloft another fell and was lost and God came down from Heaven with the twelve apostles and took ghostly shape in Holy Mary.' I was almost sure that this was a further extract from Jean Maurin's prayer. I verified that this was so. Once again I was astonished at the elegance of the translation from the archaic French of the original.

In reading the original French I was puzzled by the last sentence, 'il s'adombra en Sainte-Marie.' I could not understand what God had done in the Holy Mary. Still less could I understand why Miss Mills had translated this with such confidence as 'took ghostly shape.' She herself was unable to explain her performance but said that she regarded this verb as meaning that God became spiritualised in the Virgin Mary. I consulted three dictionaries without success. One evening two months later I was nagged by the idea that I had not yet found a translation for this elusive verb. I went to the bookcase and quite inexplicably took out Duvernoy's *L'Inquisition à Pamiers.* Certainly I was not hoping for translations of s'adombra in a work edited by this painstaking and meticulous author. I opened it at a passage in which the Curé of Montaillou is speaking to Beatrice de Planisolles. I did not expect any transcendental philosophy from this gentleman. He had been too adroit at adapting theology to his own purposes and was a menace to the local women. I was astonished to read immediately on opening this book that this ingenius mountebank, who thought gymnastically in order to justify his own licentiousness, had explained to the women he had seduced how God 's'adombra' in the Virgin Mary. Two months later I saw Monsieur Duvernoy in Toulouse. I asked him how he would translate s'adombra. He said that estomper was an approximate meaning, that is to say that God took shape in the Virgin Mary.

This phrase is expressing the Cathar idea that Mary herself was not incarnate in the flesh but herself clothed in a spirit body. To some Cathars neither Mary nor Christ were incarnate. What is astonishing is that Miss Mills was not only able to perform this extraordinarily exact piece of translation from old French—'took ghostly shape' is after all more precise than 'God took shape'—but that, in spite of her non-metaphysical equipment, she should have grasped the philosophical significance of the statement.

What we derive from this is more evidence that Miss Mills can break the language barrier in the state of awareness in which she receives her messages. This can occur precognitively. We saw previously that, in one of the references to Braïda de Montserver, she could translate into French from mediaeval Latin a text she had never seen. In the course of one's life it has become crystal clear that all extrasensory perception occurs out of time. This is easy to see and even to prove in the commoner psychic gifts such as clairvoyance and precognition. I have had less opportunity to see this independence of time manifested in the rarer attribute of the gift of tongues. It is only in the case of Miss Mills that I have seen demonstrated beyond doubt that this latter gift is manifested outside the limits of chronology.

II

Is there anything else we can deduce from this direction of attention to the Cathar liturgy? The Cathar prayer is interesting because it expressed so poetically and precisely the basic principles of Catharism. Can we learn anything from Miss Mills' preoccupation with the Consolamentum? Isn't this inevitable in any reincarnated Cathar? This sacrament was, after all, the only one recognised by the cult but its importance to the believer exceeded that of any individual sacrament in the Catholic community. But apart from the written messages, Miss Mills was at this time dreaming and seeing visions at night which pointed to the Consolamentum. It also kept coming to her by day. There was one occasion when she saw a table covered with a plain white cloth. A bowl of water and a small book were standing on the table. The book would almost certainly have been the Gospel according to St. John. She is describing exactly the arrangement made for the simple but transcendental ceremony of the Consolamentum.

She was also insistent that the Consolamentum was not the final initiation I had thought. She said that for some at least it was only the first step to the deeper initiation. Without the latter the Parfaits would not have been able to step willingly on to the faggots when they were burnt at the stake. Catholic sources constantly refer to the willingness with which the Parfaits went to their deaths. They have hinted, with ludicrous inaccuracy, that this was a manifestation of a suicidal impulse. She insisted that without further initiation the Parfaits would not have been able to heal the sick. She was particularly concerned with healing. I felt that she made a case. I had always regarded it as beyond the bounds of possibility that the Holy Spirit could enter into a man at a single ceremony and that, hereafter, he could be endowed with the gift of healing and the capacity to withdraw into his spiritual body to such a degree as to be impermeable to physical agony. This might happen once or twice in the world's history but it seemed to me fantastic to assume that it was a regular occurrence. To heal the sick and to escape the agonies of burning were surely the end results of a long process of preparation. I agreed with Miss Mills that what she said was reasonable but required more evidence than her visions and dreams and compelling intuitions. Also, on this question of the Consolamentum, she demonstrated a brief but definite reluctance to discuss details. I did not have to wait much longer to build hypotheses from the information she had already given me. By the middle of August new characters were appearing on the scene. Through these she was able to tell me details of this further training and of the aims and details of the forms of meditation practised. I wonder whether anyone else has ever added in her manner to a knowledge of a lost and persecuted religion.

Her interest in the Consolamentum was not entirely devoted to its religious significance and general nature. She was looking back in agony to a particular evening when the Consolamentum was celebrated. In a later chapter we can pinpoint this date with accuracy. I said that the Latin prayer which begins 'Pater sancte, suscipe servium tuum' contains a grammatical subtlety. The Latin varies a little according as to whether the bishop or deacon is addressing a man or a woman. At first I was disappointed that Miss Mills had quoted the form used when the recipient was a man. But this was as it should be. She was not looking back to the night when she herself, as Esclarmonde de Perella, had received the Consolamentum. This had happened years before that night when the Sacrament was celebrated for the last time at Montségur and when she watched while others received it. We must wait to discover who were present with her at this last ceremony.

By this time I had obtained from Miss Mills' revelations a much deeper insight into the nature of Catharism. I had not yet reached the stage where I was to receive accurate, dictated therapeutic instructions as to the methods used in healing. The fact that the latter proved so sensible, efficacious and valuable inclines me all the more to treat with respect the other varieties of information we received from the guides.

What I had learnt so far was that Catharism was deeply rooted in primitive Christianity. This was implied in the scriptural references. It is often said that Catharism had deep roots in the Manichean faith. This is a justifiable statement in that all forms of Dualism had much in common but, because of what I learnt through Miss Mills from the high exponents of Catharism in the thirteenth century, there can be no doubt that the practitioners of this faith went back directly to their Christian forebears. How otherwise can we explain the flood of scriptural references? The latter paint for us also a clear picture of the nature of the Christianity of the first two centuries after Christ. It was very obviously a religion of emanation and of psychic communication. The spread of the faith was a psychic contagion rather than by theology. It is obvious that Catharism was of the same nature. Matthew leaves the seat of custom immediately to follow Christ. Men-at-arms at Montségur, offered their freedom, prefer to die with the Cathars. Sober historians have pointed out that the way back to Catharism is through the occult. The whole basis of Catharism is that the invisible world of spirits was made by God and the world of form by the devil. But most of all I know that Catharism was concerned with the world of spirits because the latter had chosen years previously to make more or less direct contact with me. They had tried to announce themselves previously in different ways and through different people. Now their methods were becoming more direct. I was able later to talk with confidence about Catharism because of information received direct from its thirteenth-century exponents.

Because this is my story we need not discuss in detail the clear likeness between the ritual of Catharism and that of primitive Christianity. The service of the Consolamentum resembles that of the simple sacrament of primitive Christianity. But is there anything else we can add from what to me are indubitably revealed sources? (A time was to come when Miss Mills could learn by direct conversation the details of life in the thirteenth century). The answer is definitely Yes.

In the middle of the summer session of handwriting, for a period of two or three days, Miss Mills produced several sheets of paper inscribed with the names of non-scriptural authors. These were divisible into two main categories. The first group extended from Pythagoras to Plato and included Chrysippas, Archimedes, Euripides and Democritus. The second was neo-platonic. The third extended from the birth of Christ to the age of the Plotinus and Porphyry. It included Iamblichus. The name of Plotinus was repeated several times.

All the names in these two categories occur against the background of a Greek or Greco-Roman culture.

The third category consisted of two mystery religions. Miss Mills wrote the names of Mithras and the Eleusinian mysteries.

What is the significance of these non-biblical quotations? Why Plato and Pythagoras? Because in the broad sense of the word these two philosophers were Dualist. Plato shares with the Cathars the belief in the entry of the fully developed soul into matter. He clearly regards this as a disaster. It is strange how so many with a smattering of Greek culture regard the latter as based on a serene, semi-pagan optimism lost to the world with the advent of Christianity. This is nonsense. Equally Platonism was not pessimistic. The idea that enlightenment consists in the free man's constructive and unfanatical emancipation of the spirit from matter is far less depressing than the belief that we are dependent on grace transmitted to us from a distant deity through the intermediary of a capricious and tyrannical priesthood. Platonism and Catharism were neither optimistic nor pessimistic. As well as being mystical they were realistic and based on the truth of experience. Also, neither of these philosophies was puritanical. It is surely significant that Platonism, neo-Platonism and Catharism flourished against the background of the most refined and sophisticated civilisations of their age.

Pythagoras, the universal man, was also a Dualist. The way in which he related his catholic interests to his religious attitude is characteristic. He reveals to us clearly how a Dualist attitude is inevitably imposed by contemplation of the phenomena of nature. The latter is typical of Catharism. It can be seen to this day in the Languedoc where those interested in the Cathar heritage are saturated with the nature and folklore of their region.

There is another reason why Miss Mills should be referred to Plato and his precursors. Christianity has two main roots, the Hellenic and the Judaic. In orthodox Christianity the two are balanced, though some would say that the Jewish influence was paramount. Such phenomena as Sabbatarianism point in this direction. But there is no doubt whatever that Catharism leans back affectionately to its Greek roots and precipitately away from its Jewish origins. The latter attitude is shown by its very wholesale rejection of the Old Testament. One can say with certainty that the predominance of the Greek over the Judaic influence is one of the cardinal features distinguishing Catharism from orthodox Christianity.

Plotinus, Porphyry, Iamblichus and Chrysippas are easy to answer. Three were Neoplatonists who interpreted the teachings of Plato in the centuries following the birth of Christ. The chief among these was Plotinus, who lived in the third century A.D. and is mentioned several times in Miss Mills' recollections. He taught that the creation occurred in successive zones as the forms of emanation passed farther and farther from the original and divine source. His teaching is very close to Cathar Cosmology.

The name of Porphyry in Miss Mills' messages is significant. He was a pupil of Plotinus and records, in his life of the master, that, 'His writings are the records of these researches and revelations given him by the Gods.' So are those of Miss Mills. Her guides, as returned Parfaits, were invisible and visible spirits who had lived previously under the direction of the Holy Spirit.

The gnostic fathers had a good deal in common with the neoplatonists. Generally speaking they believed that salvation lay in self-purification through different incarnations, and that the cleansing process was essentially an emancipation from matter. They regarded the latter as being evil in the sense that it was uninfused with spirit. This led inevitably in many gnostic sects to a belief in the active principles of good and evil, in fact to frank Dualism. Now there is no doubt that Catharism had many roots in gnosticism. Deodat Roché, one of the chief modern exponents of Catharism, is greatly preoccupied with the derivation of the latter faith in the philosophy of Origen.

These classical and neoclassical references show that Catharism had affinities with earlier forms of Dualism, whether or not these latter were Christian. The non-Christian roots of Catharism are revealed in Miss Mills' third category of non-scriptural references. The key words were 'Mithras' and 'Eleusinian mysteries.' The former is easy to account for. The cult of Mithras is almost universally accepted to be Dualist. It was indeed one of the first religions to be concerned with the opposition between the Light and the Dark, between the forces of good and evil. The Eleusinian mysteries involved an esoteric cult of nature. I do not know to what degree Dualism was incorporated in its practices. One can only repeat that all forms of Dualism are concerned with the reaction of nature and its innate forces. That is why they are so fundamentally sensible as well as mystical. Can we infer from this that primitive Christianity was one of the aspects of Dualism? I have no doubt that this is true.

Another question arises. Has Catharism, and therefore primitive Christianity, any philosophical likeness to Buddhism? Certainly there is a strong resemblance in external observance. Buddhism, like Catharism, advocates complete non-violence and

chastity and abstention from flesh foods. It also believes in reincarnation and that enlightenment consists in emancipation
from matter. It would therefore be fascinating were Miss Mills
able to supply us with something of the basic metaphysics of
Catharism and early Christianity. This is all the more necessary
because Christianity differs from Buddhism, in that its original
scriptures contain so little of purely philosophical nature. There
are exhortations to consider the lilies of the field, but this is
poetical insight rather than philosophy. Again there is no clear-
cut psychological system in the Gospels and Acts comparable to
that of Buddhism in which, from the word go, life is described as
suffering. This suffering is attributed to desire, and desire in its
turn held responsible for our being tied to the wheel of recurrent
lives. It would therefore be more than instructive were Miss
Mills able to provide us with specific philosophic reflections as to
the meaning and conduct of existence, and more enlightening
still if these showed any affinity with those of Buddhism.

From some points of view Miss Mills' messages as to the nature
of time had a distinctly oriental flavour. I do not think that this
is any evidence that Catharism provides a specific bridge between
western and oriental philosophy. I think it is merely that any
Western philosophy which can claim to be transcendental contains elements resembling those in the older systems symbolised
by such writings as the *Upanishads*.

12

Towards the middle of August there was a positive flood of
references. These were mostly of very obscure names. This out-
pouring of names may be explained by Miss Mills' penchant
for anniversaries. Her agonised recollection in March of the
crucial dates in the Montségur tragedy has already been noted.
Carcassonne fell on August 15th, 1209. It was just before this
date that she was positively inundated with references.

It is impossible to give a day-to-day record of her experiences without hopelessly confusing the reader. My best course of action is to take in turn the main trends of her narrative and follow them more or less to their conclusion. Even then a considerable amount of overlapping is inevitable. When she was frantically writing the names of obscure persons whose significance was incomprehensible to her, she was also having dreams and visions of a man preaching, of meetings in woods and in large rooms, and of receiving instruction in meditation. At this stage it seemed that two guides were operating. One gave her in writing the detailed history of Catharism, while another was concerned with its principles and practices.

It was interesting that there were no written messages while I was away on holiday but that the dreams and visions continued. The same pattern had been followed during her absence in Ireland. Did this mean that I functioned better as a catalyst when I was somewhere in the vicinity? This could hardly be so, seeing that the dreams and visions continued. The written messages at this time were concerned with straight history. Perhaps my main function was to pinpoint dates and events and it was for this reason that the historical evidence ceased in my absence. I am not greatly concerned with these possibilities. What is of outstanding importance is that in my absence on holiday I became, if not superfluous, more easily dispensed with. Something more than a substitute took over in my absence. When I went away I was replaced by a more satisfying confidant.

In a way I regretted that Miss Mills should have belonged to the Perella family who owned Montségur. I do not care for reincarnation stories involving the eminent. That my personal pilgrimage should end at Montségur was fitting enough. The mountain had haunted, frightened and consoled me for thirty years. Nevertheless on the whole I would have preferred the decent obscurity of *The Cathars and Reincarnation*. Roger-Isarn was, so I thought, a modest figure in relation to other members of his family and Puerilia was an unidentified peasant girl. But if I needed a change from the big families it was certainly on the way.

On the night of August 16th a single name was written on a piece of paper. I had not the remotest idea of its meaning. Still

less did I realise that it was a spark which was to lead rapidly
to the final conflagration. The name was Brunasendis. All I could
think of was that it was a Latin noun in the genetive case. I
could not begin to guess its meaning. I deferred looking through
my books because the quest seemed so hopeless. But one day
the usual thing happened. I cannot remember what I was looking for at that time. The names Brune and Arsendis literally
leaped to my eyes. Brunasendis was a composite phonetic
rendering of two separate names. The two people concerned
were women. They were the wives of sergeants-at-arms and were
burnt at Montségur.

The next night the words "salt, pepper and wax" were written on three separate lines on the same sheet of paper. Miss
Mills was diffident about producing them. 'I don't know what
you'll think,' she said. 'It isn't just that they mean nothing to
me. They seem so senseless.' In actual fact this was something I
understood immediately. The Parfaits doomed to die distributed
spices, condiments, cereals and other oddments to the garrison
before the latter marched out to freedom. We can therefore
give an accurate date for what Miss Mills was recording on the
night of August 14th/15th, 1972, in Somerset. The distribution
to which she referred occurred early on March 14th, or late on
March 13th, 1242. The guide dictating these messages knew that
among my limited distinctions as a schoolboy was a devotion to
history, but in those far off days I never anticipated that I would
be asked to study it in such detail.

On August 15th the names

Arnold
Dom
Pons
Narbona

appeared on four separate lines. Again these names meant nothing
to me and once again their meaning was literally thrust at me
from the first book I consulted. Arnold was the English for
Arnaud. Dom was an abbreviation of Domerq. Pons Narbona
was as she wrote it. These two men were sergeants-at-arms. They
were burnt with their wives at Montségur. The names of their
wives were Brune and Arsendis. When I had first identified the
latter I had not discovered the names of their husbands.

I was particularly fascinated and moved by this discovery. As I have said, I had always been touched by the story of the sergeants-at-arms at Montségur. That a handful, free to leave with the garrison, had preferred to die with the Cathars, is possibly the most eloquent tribute ever paid to the goodness of the Bonshommes. It is something like the story of the penitent thief that these mediaeval toughs should have preferred death with the Parfaits to freedom to continue killing for hire. One does not expect to find the hired soldiers of the Middle Ages attracted to the doctrine of non-resistance. When I first read about Montségur I seized on this story and never forgot it. In *The Cathars and Reincarnation* I excluded my personal reactions. If emotional responses to a memory can be counted as evidence in these matters, my reaction to the sergeants is worth considering.

On August 21st two more names came through. Tournabois and Calavel were later identified as Raymond-Guillaume de Tournabois, and Brasillac de Calavello. As she moved towards her finishing sprint in August, Miss Mills often wrote the sur-names of the men, and the Christian names of the women. Was this fatigue? Was she failing to keep pace with the dictation? I was astonished to find that these men were also sergeants-at-arms and that they had also been burnt at Montségur. Brasillac had no significance for Miss Mills or me. We were to find later that it meant a whole world to another caught in the circle of communication.

When Miss Mills wrote salt, pepper and wax on her piece of paper she was thinking back under the direction of her guides to March 14th, or probably the evening of the 13th. But surely she was steering towards a still more crucial and significant date? The marching out of the garrison on March 14th was appalling enough. Was it as tragic as the last celebration of the Conso-lamentum at Montségur? The reader may remember that, months previously when she recalled the Latin of the Conso-lamentum, she wrote down the version which applied to the reception of a man. What, in fact, she was remembering was the last celebration of this sacred rite ever to be witnessed at Montségur. She was tuned-in particularly to the reception of a man. Was it one of the sergeants-at-arms?

79

There was only one word written on the night of August 22nd. This was Fay. I knew that this applied to a woman and that she had made a deposition. I had no idea of the latter's contents. I did not know that Fays de Planha was the wife of another sergeant-at-arms. The latter appeared now to be redressing the balance which had previously favoured the more privileged classes. I discovered that at a crucial stage in the siege, when the besiegers had seized the barbican and were close to the fortress itself, Fays was among the women and men who asked for the Convenanza. This was a request to ensure that, if the individual was gravely ill or mortally wounded, a Parfait would come as soon as possible to administer the Consolamentum to him. Fays was steering us to the same date as Miss Mills, that is, to the day on which this sacrament was administered for the last time on Montségur. After she had made her request Fays went back with the other women and men to fight against the besiegers.

The importance of Fays in our story is emphasised by the fact that two nights later her name was recorded again. The record on a single piece of paper read, 'Plaigne, Montségur 65.' The lady's full name was Fays de Plaigne. (Planha in Occitan.) The numerals were a complete mystery.

At this time I found another reason why, months earlier, Guillaume del'Isle had recurred three or four times in the record. On one of these occasions his name has been bracketed on a single sheet of paper with that of Marquesia de Lantar. He was grievously wounded in the ferocious fighting of the last days of Montségur. He received the Consolamentum. Marquesia de Lantar was also present. The sergeants-at-arms must have received the Consolamentum on the same occasion. This is obviously the particular ceremony Miss Mills is recalling. When she wrote down the Latin extract from the Consolamentum she was registering the exact moment when one of the soldiers was receiving the Sacrament.

At this time I obtained her diary once again to see if I had appended the right dates to the pieces of paper and to other messages which she had given me. By this time I was past being astonished. I knew that she was reliving her life in the last days and hours of Montségur. Nevertheless it was fascinating and a little eerie to discover that from August 17th to 18th she had made three entries describing in detail the Consolamentum. She wrote these descriptions before she noted the names of the first sergeants-at-arms. Her recollection began with a dream on August 17th of a simple table with a white cloth on which were standing a book and a bowl of water. The dream ended with the priest washing his hands but the memory continued during the next two days in visions and by a voice which uttered prayers which she cannot recall clearly. She insists that the Lord's Prayer, as used by the Cathars, was different from ours. It is known that the word suprastantial was used instead of daily bread. She says that there were other differences. Her preoccupation with the Lord's Prayer may be explained by the fact that it was only intensively used by the Cathars after they had received the Consolamentum. Its constant usage was a kind of gift. Once again she may know more than the savants. What she saw in her visions concerned chiefly the end of the ceremony. A man kissed another and the latter a third and the ritual continued in this manner. The women did the same but there was no interchange of kissing between the sexes. This is an accurate description of the kiss of peace which followed the Consolamentum.

In these dreams in August, in the temperate and capricious summer of Somerset, Miss Mills was looking back, with unerring accuracy, to the evening preceding a harsh spring morning in another country in another age. The date was March 15th, 1244.

13

The sergeants-at-arms are important from another aspect. We see them receiving the Consolamentum and giving themselves up to the Spirit. Miss Mills recalls also when they were still very much in this world. Her guide indicates clearly the act of violence with which they were associated.

It began for me on March 8th, 1971. This was Miss Mills'

time of great depression when she was recalling the last days of Montségur. Perhaps in sleep the vibrations of her horror were communicated to me but there was nothing terrible in my dream of the eighth of March. The dream was in colour. At that time colour dreams were of special significance for me. I was traversing a harmonious green country of hills and hollows. There were steep roads going up the hills. At first I thought of the Dordogne. I came to a village at the foot of a hill. I went into a house and asked for the doctor. It was not because I was ill. I wanted him for some other reason. I wondered, was I looking for myself? They knew all about him but they did not know when he would return. The people were kind and considerate but the whole thing was a mystery to them. They could tell me nothing.

Then it came to me in the dream that this country was not the Dordogne but the country round Puivert. This place is in the Pyrenees. Puivert is a village with a château on a low green hill above a gentle valley. It has none of the harsh majesty of Queribus, which looks with unremitting vigilance at the broken teeth of the rocks below it and the pockets of vineyards descending to the plain. Nor has it the remote and emanatory magic of Montségur, which sends out light from its bleached, scarred watchtower across the valley and the years. Puivert is a gentle château with a musicians' gallery. It is set in country that is green and smiling.

The dream was clear and peaceful. But, though Puivert was as peaceful in the dream as it is today, does it cast a shadow on our history? I discovered that Alpaïs, the chatelaine of Puivert, was an admitted Cathar. She died there in 1208 having received the Consolamentum. It was fascinating to find that she was the sister of Raymond de Perella, and therefore Esclarmonde's Aunt. As she had died in her bed three decades before Montségur I assumed she had been dragged into the story as further evidence of the Perella connection. Miss Mills was soon to prove that Puivert had a more specific significance.

Another thread was picked up again in the feverish psychic activity in August. On the 16th the names Imbert, Otho and Alzeu were scrawled in huge letters on three separate sheets of paper. Imbert meant something to me. It was obvious by now that Miss Mills' flood of recollection was concentrated on the siege of Montségur and the events which led to it. It was clear, too, that we were again dealing with the sergeants-at-arms. Imbert was a sergeant-at-arms who had made a deposition before the Inquisition in which he described the behaviour of those who murdered the Inquisitors at Avignonet. I did not realise at this time that the guide was acting as she had done on more than one previous occasion. She was directing the memories of Miss Mills into a narrower channel than the siege of Montségur. This was all the more clear when I discovered the identity of Alzeu and Otho.

I undertook the search for those two names without enthusiasm and in a desultory fashion. The shower of references was confusing and at the time of their reception it was difficult to trace the pattern which became clearly evident at a later date. Once again I was literally given the verification. I opened a book at the exact page containing the name of Alzeu de Massabrac. He and Otho were the sons of Alzaïs, daughter of Guillaume de Mirepoix. We have already seen in one of Miss Mills' excursions into French, that Guillaume was present in a certain house of heretics at the same time as Braïda de Montserver and her family. Alzeu and Otho were involved in the massacre of the Inquisitors at Avignonet.

It seemed to me now that the latter event was becoming one of the major themes of the narrative. This was all the more fascinating because from some points of view it was the biggest issue in Mrs. Smith's story. Her nightmare of Pierre de Mazerolles returning from Avignonet was the incident which enabled me to know at what date I, and my girl-friend Puerilia, had lived the supreme crisis of our lives. It was almost uncanny to discover that Miss Mills, in her turn, was harking back to the same incident. It was hardly credible to discover that Arnaud Domerq and Pons Narbona, the husbands respectively of Brune and Arsendis and burnt with their wives at Montségur, had also been concerned in this affair.

The matter was clinched by the two references to Fay de Planha, whom we have already mentioned in relation to the final Consolamentum. Her deposition includes an extraordinarily detailed description of the arrangements made for the massacre of the Inquisitors at Avignonet. The latter event is inextricably connected with the onslaught on Montségur. Without it the siege may never have occurred. Fays gives the names of many of those who rode from Montségur on May 28th, 1242, to take part in the attack on the Inquisitors. Her deposition contains the names of the men-at-arms we have noted and of knights such as the brothers Massabrac. Our old acquaintance Guillaume de l'Isle was also concerned in this episode. But what is of greater significance is that she mentions Pierre de Mazerolles. On the eve of the massacre, Pierre Roger de Mirepoix, with one body of men, met Pierre de Mazerolles leading another troop in a wood at Gaja-la-Selve. This association between the characters of Mrs. Smith's story and that of Miss Mills is important not only from the historical point of view but because it confirms the validity of the psychic experience of both women.

There was further evidence as to the importance of the Avignonet affair in our story. Autumn was well advanced before I discovered the significance of my Puivert dream. The latter was not simply something thrown in to make weight, for the chatelaine was Raymond de Perella's sister. Her son Gaillard de Congost was involved in the plot. The embers of this affair burnt up a little in November. The names 'Sicard-Puivert' came through on a piece of paper. I am not sure whether or not Sicard was another member of the chatelaine's family or merely derived from Puivert. What was interesting was that he was described as either a sergeant-at-arms or a squire, and, *mirabile dictu*, he was also concerned in the Avignonet affair.

14

It is almost too much to have been taken back to the massacre of the Inquisitors at Avignonet. It is also poignant and eerie to have been diverted to a specific day when a world ended seven hundred and twenty-seven years ago. Beyond doubt Miss Mills had tuned in to the last Consolamentum at Montségur. These things were enough for me. I would never have credited that I would also have been given information about the disposal of the Cathar treasure.

The known facts are that four Parfaits, who had previously stayed hidden, left the château on the morning after, or the evening before, the Parfaits were burnt at the stake. The nature of the treasure they carried is unspecified. Another clandestine expedition with a similar aim took place just before or just after Christmas 1243. It is said also that another attempt had been made previously, possibly as early as May 1243. It is believed that the treasure was hidden in caves in the Ariège valley. Those are the simple facts. A considerable amount of ink has been spilt in their embroidery. At this time I was not sure whether two or more attempts had been made to dispose of the treasure. I knew of other conjectures which had been made in relation to the nature of the treasure and its disposal. I knew that the names of some of the men concerned in the clandestine excursions were still unknown to us. I myself did not know these names.

Way back in the beginning of her protracted séance Miss Mills, ignorant of the function of Montségur as a place of instruction, had written the word treasure. Now, in this feverish month of August, her guide returned to the subject. On the 15th the names Amiel and Hugo were written together on a single piece of paper. I discovered that these were the names of two of the four men who took the treasure from the château when the Parfaits were burnt. It was very significant that she recorded these names on the same night as she had written salt, pepper and wax on another piece of paper. Evidently all this was happening at the time of the final break up at Montségur. In 1244 arrangements for the disposal of the treasure and the distribution of salt, condiments and other objects were taking place at the same time. The salt and pepper could well have been given out on March 15th. The authorities say that the treasure was also evacuated that night or the following morning. It is almost uncanny that Miss Mills' recollections of the distribution of the condiments and of assignments for the treasure should occur on successive nights in 1971.

The next night, August 16th, she found, on one sheet of paper, the names Clamens, Corson and Marti. It was some days before

I had time to understand their significance. The name Marti was familiar. I knew that the bishop of this name had been present at the end of Montségur. I could not be sure this was the same man because I considered Marti a common name. Corson was difficult to understand. It sounded so Anglo-Saxon. Nevertheless I succeeded in tracing these names just after nine o'clock one evening. What was more remarkable than my modest efforts was the fact that Miss Mills had telephoned me between five and six the same evening to say that she saw four people going from the château. They were accompanied by a guide.

I discovered that Clamens was a Parfait and a deacon. At the beginning of the siege on May 13th, 1243, he went with three other Parfaits to Caussoh. Corson is how an Anglo-Saxon would take down the name were it dictated. The other members of the party included R de Caussa and his son. Corsa is the phonetic spelling of this latter name. I was satisfied now that the fourth name applied to the Bishop, Bertrand Marti, who was at Montségur during the siege and was burnt at the stake. I had no idea how important he was to become in the story.

This accounts for the four Parfaits described in the records. What of Miss Mills' statement that she thought there was a guide with them? It is said in a deposition made before the Inquisition that the four Parfaits were accompanied by two sergeants-at-arms. Was one of these two the guide referred to by Miss Mills? I was not deeply interested in the subject of the treasure. I incline to Duvernoy's sensible view that it could well have been money. The Cathar Church needed funds as much as any other organisation. When Miss Mills informed me on August 25th that she had had two words written on a sheet of paper and that these words kept repeating in her head, my reactions were mechanical. One word was "bonnet" and the other "Mass". So far as I was concerned the former was probably some form of headgear worn by the Parfaits. As to Mass, I could only assume that she was referring to the Catholic ritual but I could not see in what connection. I was turning the pages of Niel's book on Montségur when the words Pierre Bonnet caught my eye. Once again it was a question of my lighting immediately on something important for me. There is no index of names in Niel's book. I learnt that Pierre Bonnet, a Cathar deacon from Toulouse, accompanied by a heretic called Matthew, left Montségur with gold, silver and a large amount of money. They took the treasure to a spoulga, or fortified cave, in the Sabarthes. The spoulga belonged to Pons Arnaud de Castelverdun. This is revealed in the testimony of Imbert de Salas. This latter had already come through on Miss Mills' recording apparatus.

Miss Mills told me about these two words before I saw the sheet of paper. I saw from the latter that Mas was spelt with one S and had nothing to do with the Catholic ritual. I knew that Mas was a meridional word meaning farm or estate. As such it was, and is still, used as a person's name. Miss Mills was referring to Pierre de Mas, a Parfait who, during the siege, invited nine sergeants-at-arms to eat with him in his cabane.* The Parfaits were concerned in maintaining morale. Among the nine present were two, Imbert de Salas and Brasillac de Calavello, whose names had been written previously by Miss Mills.

The date of Pierre Bonnet's expedition was either round about Christmas 1243 or perhaps somewhat earlier.

Some days previously Miss Mills had written Montségur 65. She now returned to the charge with greater insistence. She felt sure it was some kind of reference number. I found later that it was the number of the note in Chapter 3 of the second part of Niel's book on Montségur. Miss Mills does not possess and has never had this book in her possession. Braïda was asking me to divert my attention still further to the disposal of the treasure of Montségur. It is clear that she was saying definitely that it had been placed in the cave belonging to Pons Arnaud de Castelverdun. So far as I am concerned this settles once and for all the question of where the treasure was deposited. Was Braïda herself involved in this matter? In the middle of the writings referring to the treasure, the words Montserver and Queille were repeated. Both were written together on a single page. Later Miss Mills had dreams and visions of a castle and a sizeable town surrounded by wooden houses. She felt that this place had been a temporary repository for the treasure.

Two days later we were still on the trail of the treasure. A single sheet of paper was occupied by Isarn de Fanjea Dalion.

* A kind of hut.

The first name is obviously Isarn de Fanjeaux with the name of the town incomplete. Isarn was an emissary of the Count of Toulouse. He visited Montségur frequently and even kept in touch with it during the siege.

In considering the word Dalion I wondered if we were harking back to Avignonet and if Dalion were some kind of attempt to reproduce the word d'Alfaro. The latter was the bailiff of Toulouse in whose house the massacre took place. This was a feeble, exhausted misinterpretation of the efficiency of Miss Mills and her guide. The word we are looking for is le Alion. Miss Mills' rendering is accurate except for the apostrophe. These niceties must be allowed for in taking dictation from discarnate entities in a state of altered consciousness.

Bernard d'Alion is an obscure character who only enters the narrative by the side door. Nevertheless he fits in with the pattern and is associated with a secret expedition from Montségur in May 1243. He gave hospitality, through his bailiff, to Raymond de Caussa, previously mentioned by Miss Mills, another heretic and two sergeants-at-arms. Bernard is described as an ardent supporter of Catharism. This little party was bound for the Château of Usson in the Donnezan. The latter is an area of the Ariège which is traditionally regarded as the region where the treasure was hidden. Bernard himself lived near Castel-verdun. The latter name should be noted carefully. If this were a treasure hunt the searchers would be regarded as getting warm. A few days later the evidence was more positive. It was presented in the most extraordinary form.

The message on the night of September 2nd was brief, dramatic and unique. Miss Mills chuckled when she rang up about it. By this time she was convinced that there was a purpose in these experiences but obviously regarded this message as near-farcical and wondered if the fault was in her. She said she had taken to drawing and that what she had produced was 'either a half moon or an abnormally bent banana'. The single name Bellessen was written beside the drawing. She asked me if there could be any possible meaning in the message.

It is at such times as this that one realises how the whole operation was beautifully dovetailed and fitted a pattern. I *did* recall the name Bellissen. It rang a bell in my brain and was associated with the phrase 'sons of the moon', and, in some dim way, with the Comté of Foix.

When I saw the paper it was clear that the drawing was indubitably a half moon. I was particularly intrigued by this message. The word Bellissen accompanied by the symbolic drawing was an utterly new method of communication. It was all the more impressive in being difficult to classify. I discovered, again by going straight, for no concrete reason, to the right book and the right page, that the chief family at Lordat, like those at Rabat and Castelverdun, derived from the female branch of the Bellissen family. I could not discover why the latter were known as sons of the moon. What is of more immediate significance is that once again we are being referred to the Cathar treasure. Bernard D'Alion who, as we have seen, could well have been concerned in the disposal of the treasure, lived at Castelverdun. So far as Rabat is concerned, we have connections there already. Arapaïs, daughter of Raymond de Perella, married Guillaume de Rabat. As for the reference to the family at Lordat, the connection with the treasure is still more specific. It is curious that we have evidence about this place from contemporary sources. Years ago an expedition was digging near the castle ruins there. The project was abandoned in some disorder. One member became deranged and others had psychiatric disturbances.

My friend Paul Beard made some interesting comments about Lordat. One of his chief responsibilities is to pick out the sheep from the goats among those claiming to be mediums. No doubt this sharpens his perceptions. He said that there is an abrupt variation of the atmosphere in the neighbourhood of the ruins at Lordat. At one point it is good and, at another, thoroughly bad. I wonder whether the good atmosphere comes from its Cathar affiliations, and the bad from some who, across the centuries, have dug for gold? Or is it just that, wherever psychic goodness has operated at its maximum intensity, it attracts to itself the presence of evil? If this were so one would perhaps feel the menace of evil at Montségur. After all, the Crusaders and chanting, triumphant priests could well have contaminated the atmosphere. Yet Montségur remains inviolable in its persisting serenity. These matters are beyond our full understanding.

It would seem that the treasure, or some of it, arrived in the lower reaches of the Ariège valley. Has Miss Mills anything to add to our knowledge? Of some things she is certain. The last expedition from Montségur was by no means the most important. The other evasions from the castle were not merely to arrange hiding places for the treasure. A proportion was carried each time. The expedition of Amiel and Hugo on March 15th or 16th, 1244, completed an operation which had begun ten months previously. It is possible that not all the treasure reached its intended destination at the first attempt. Some may have been hidden en route.

What was the treasure? Beyond doubt books. Miss Mills agrees that there were also bags of money but in other bags she saw clearly in her visions the outline of books. The bags were leather with a peculiarly shaped neck. They were tied at the neck with some kind of cord. When Mrs. Smith, as Puerilia, set out to find Fabrissa, she also carried a leather bag closed at the neck with a cord.

I think many investigators may be misled as to the nature of the Montségur treasure. Were the sacred books not necessarily secret, esoteric writings but rare books which had been very difficult to obtain, which were greatly valued, and which were concerned with subjects related to Dualism? Miss Mills mentioned such writers as Iamblichus. Democritus and Porphyry. There cannot have been many copies of the writings of these authors extant in thirteenth-century Europe. What were available would be more likely to find their way to the Languedoc because its standard of culture was higher than anywhere in Europe. There is another reason why, at this time, rare works of Greek and neoplatonic authors should have been especially available to the collector. The fourth Crusade had been launched against Byzantium, in the early years of the thirteenth century, by the same Pope who instigated the campaign against the Cathars. In the near East, as in the Languedoc, the Crusaders ran true to form. After the horrors of the Fourth Crusade there was a steady exit of scholars, works of art and manuscripts from Byzantium. The idea that this civilising flood only began with the fall of Constantinople in 1453 is quite erroneous. The Cathars could well have acquired many valuable manuscripts after the Crusade of 1204.

15

As the written messages tapered off in August another phenomenon occurred. Miss Mills was seeing persistently recognisable faces in dreams and visions. She had seen people and faces before but had been unable to remember them as separate individuals. She saw many people in dark blue robes. This was the colour worn by the Parfaits at this particular period. One figure was repeated in several dreams and visions and was clearly recognisable. This was a short, thickset man with a chubby face and grey hair. She estimated him at well over seventy. He was older than his youthful expression caused him to look. He was the first of five faces which were to become familiar to her.

After the first few days of September the written messages ceased. Miss Mills was glad of a respite from an exhausting experience often accompanied by positive anguish. She did not know that the written messages were to be replaced by a more direct method of communication.

One night, towards the middle of the month, she was awakened by the barking of her spaniel who sleeps in the room with her. This animal is a splendid watch dog who reacts immediately to the lightest sound or footfall. Miss Mills opened her eyes and saw an old lady standing at the foot of the bed. She had dark eyes, classical features and a straight and well-formed nose. Her face was criss-crossed by a thousand fine wrinkles but was nevertheless charming because of her open and friendly smile. She wore a small Juliet cap on the top of her head. Her grey hair escaped sideways from the edge of the cap. She was under middle height. She wore a dark blue robe. The blue of her robe was not as dark as the colour we call navy blue. Miss Mills described it as French navy, as something approximating to a dark royal blue.

Miss Mills was not in the least afraid. The outlines of the old lady were misty and that first night she could not see clearly the simple ornaments the latter wore, except that there was some kind of chain round her waist. At her first visit the old lady said nothing. The insistent inner voice continued. Now its messages were of the simplest and to the effect that God is love and that we should love one another. It seemed that no other messages were necessary. The presence which had previously expressed itself in dictated messages and as a voice was now here in visible form. She had proved her identity. There was no longer any need for her to establish her credentials in the form of details of Cathar history. She was now completely accepted by Miss Mills. It was almost as if they could relax together.

After the old lady's first appearances Miss Mills wondered if she was a figure in a dream, but on two succeeding nights the dog barked immediately when she appeared. Does a dog bark at a figure in a dream? At her fourth visit and afterwards he made no sound whatever though he was always restless. He obviously got used to her visits. The most striking effect of these visits was simple. Miss Mills was so much better for them. She was at peace and happy. She had been through an exhausting and frightening experience. The old lady was a great comfort to her. They were happy in each other's presence and Miss Mills looked forward to her visits. She spoke of her as she spoke of people she especially liked in real life. She spoke without reverence or respect but with positive affection. It was clear that she gained more from the old lady than from any living person. She said she brought great peace. It was obvious to me when I returned from France that Miss Mills was much happier and in the process of being transformed by the experience.

After several visits the outline of the lady in blue became clearer. Miss Mills could see what she wore. She had a chain round her waist. It was made of silver, or of some metal resembling it. It was composed of circular links. The latter were either plain or decorated with a little cross and the two types alternated with each other.

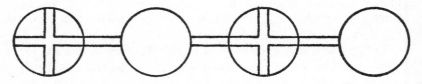

Was this chain one of the decorations worn by the Parfaits or Parfaites? Mrs. Smith was concerned with what the Parfaits wore round their waists. She had rejected the idea that it was merely a girdle, and was preoccupied with a buckle with a strange design. It seemed as though, at this time, the whole aim of the operation was to acquaint Miss Mills with the simple everyday principles and practice of Catharism. This was done by an intensification of dreams at night and visions by day. The fact that the old lady appeared at night did not lessen the visionary experiences. It did replace or reduce the writing. It was interesting that the old lady did not herself appear in the dreams and visions. The latter, illustrating life in a Cathar community, were centred round the chubby faced man. I did not realise that the old lady was introducing him judiciously to Miss Mills and, through her, to me.

Throughout the early autumn Miss Mills continued her dreams and visions of people in dark blue robes, and of meetings in a castle and frequently in forests. It is a matter of history that the Cathars met often in the woods. The chubby faced man with the pleasant smile was almost invariably present. Sometimes he wore black, probably when going on journeys, but dark blue was the prevalent colour for the Parfaits. This was the reverberating theme of Mrs. Smith's revelations. I was happy to find confirmatory evidence from Miss Mills. I had previously accepted the explanation that dark blue was worn as a disguise in certain areas in the times of persecution. At this time Miss Mills' memories were centred round Montségur before the siege began. No one living in or around the castle was anything other than a Cathar or a Cathar sympathiser. One wonders whether dark blue was in any sense a disguise.

As to the question of girdles and chains Miss Mills is positive that ordinary male Parfaits wore girdles. The latter were knotted on the left side with a loop left dangling over the left hip. The female Parfaites wore a silver or silver-like chain such as that worn by the old lady. The chain was tied and looped in the same way as the girdle. There were two varieties of metal used in these chains. The design was the same in each case. I do not know what this difference in the two qualities of metal signified.

The two bishops who will later decorate our pages wore leather belts fastened with a buckle. The design of the latter was as follows.

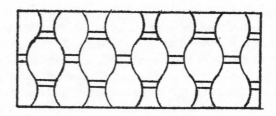

It appears that this belt and buckle were not confined to the bishop but were worn also by others of high standing in the simple Cathar hierarchy. They may well have been worn by deacons and by the aspirants to bishoprics known as filii majori and minori. Mrs. Smith was almost obsessed by the buckle I wore and the design with which it was inscribed. The sign ⊐⊏ which she remembered is constantly repeated in Miss Mills' drawing. This implies that Roger held a rank higher than that of an ordinary Parfait. I had not been aware of this before.

From all the details we have been given the lady in blue can be none other than Braïda de Montserver. The narrative thread running through Miss Mills' recollections pointed clearly to the Montserver family in general and to Braïda in particular. We have received accurately, and in verifiable detail, the names of the other members of her family. She was the only member who practised as a Parfaite. We learn from the deposition of Arnaud-Roger de Mirepoix how she embraced the faith and disposed of her worldly goods somewhere round the age of thirty. That she was certainly Braïda is borne out by evidence we shall receive later from another source.

16

Late in October something astonishing happened. Braïda began to speak. She spoke with a pleasant light voice in what Miss Mills described as a hard accent. She noticed that the consonants were sharply accentuated. Miss Mills did not know what the language was but she said calmly and unhysterically, without insistence but with conviction, that she knew what Braïda was discussing. She was utterly serene in making her claim. She had come a long way from the brisk extrovert with her breezy and satirical descriptions of her more trying colleagues. 'It's just no good my trying to define it. I know we speak through our thoughts and the language is secondary. What I say may sound silly but I know it's a fact. And I got a few foreign words.'

This did not trouble me at all. I had now begun to see the especial significance of one of the references to Paul written down by Miss Mills. In this particular verse he refers separately to the gift, and the interpretation, of tongues. Here was a living example of the latter. When people hear the speech of discarnate entities talking in foreign tongues they are tuning in not to words but to a system of vibrations which the listener translates according to his own language and culture. This is the gift of the interpretation of tongues as distinct from the sudden capacity to speak unknown languages. Miss Mills, in her writings, had already demonstrated this gift. How otherwise could she have written in French the translation of a Latin deposition she had never seen?

At first Braïda described or discussed little. She said that she brought peace, and that Miss Mills would achieve it with patience. This lasted for two or three weeks. Then Braïda appeared to be more clearly visible. Her outlines were more defined and she was seen against a background of light rather than shadow. When she spoke she began to move her hands and arms more than previously. She would sometimes nod her head as if to emphasise a point she was making. Miss Mills saw that the chain she wore round her waist carried a medallion. This was decorated with a symbol which, one night in December,

Miss Mills saw clearly to be that which had obsessed her throughout the summer. It was the Maltese type cross with the small Tau crosses at its periphery. There was one slight difference. Its centre was occupied by a Celtic cross.

Miss Mills was interested but not unduly excited by her identification of this symbol. I suppose it was commonplace compared with the fact that she had been speaking so many nights with a discarnate entity. To me the fact that Braïda wore the cross was a turning point. I did not yet know its significance but that Miss Mills had seen it months before, and that it was worn by an entity from another world, was a watershed in my life. I had always thought that truth by revelation was essentially a mystical and indefinable experience. I now saw that it could be concerned also with historical detail and that in some cases it could be the only reliable evidence offered. After seven centuries we are more likely to learn the meaning of this symbol from Braïda than from any modern savant. She has the advantages of having lived in the Languedoc seven hundred years ago and of being still with us.

Miss Mills now repeated the course of instruction she had received in the thirteenth century. There was nothing philosophical or mystical about it. It was eminently practical and, what is more, medical. In dreams, visions and in conversations with Braïda she learnt how to make infusions and potions of plants and berries. She was shown infusions of grasses which were used as sedatives. A similar preparation of rosemary was widely used for coughs. I began to understand more clearly my own passionate love of rosemary, thyme and lavender.

Braïda was especially concerned with berries. This is interesting because the Cathars are regularly described as eating berries. After receiving information from such a source I wonder whether this practice was medicinal as well as dietetic. In her dreams and visions Miss Mills saw herself engaged in preparing potions with a wine base. This is a medical practice which has lasted until this century. She learnt that sloes in wine were an especially common and useful medicine, given as a tonic after debilitating illnesses. She was a little doubtful as to whether what she saw and heard described were really sloes because they seemed exceptionally big and were also darker coloured than our own.

I had had the same problem myself with the berries I had discovered in September in the Gorges de Frau near Montségur. They, too, were bigger than ours and with less blue-grey bloom on their surface. Nevertheless they were undoubtedly sloes.*

Miss Mills was very positive on the subject of rose hips. Her description of the latter was impressive. 'They are a differen shape from ours. They are longer and thinner and less swollen a the base.' I am not an authority on the different species of wilc rose but anyone can verify that what she said is true by looking at the bushes which grow in the Ariège. Rose hips are an especially concentrated source of vitamin C. The latter is useful in counteracting infections. To drink a strong potion of rose hip in the thirteenth century produced the same effect as the ingestion of a thousand milligrams of ascorbic acid in the twentieth. The latter is a common practice for staving off colds.

Miss Mills could not identify many of the berries she saw in her dreams and in Braïda's company. I myself have been exasperated by my inability to recognise so many of the low-growing, dry-leaved shrubs growing in the Ariège and the Corbières. Many of these shrubs produce berries. In producing their potions the Cathars had abundant local resources.

Miss Mills also mentioned a 'low-growing, stubbly sort of plant with large green leaves'. The latter were used in preparing a potion. She was unable to identify it. What was more exciting was the discovery not only that the Cathars used belladonna but that it was employed for exactly the same purpose as it is today. Miss Mills was unaware that belladonna is derived from deadly nightshade. It is interesting that the Cathars called the plant by the name we use in modern medicine. The lotion was prepared from the leaves and was used in the treatment of eye conditions. The active principle of belladonna is atropine. The latter is still used every day in eye hospitals and elsewhere in conditions where dilatation of the pupil is advisable or necessary.

The Cathars in Montségur to some degree specialised in the treatment of wounds. For this purpose they used the roots of plants which Miss Mills could describe with perfect clarity but

* I was fascinated to learn from Dr. L. R. Twentyman, of the Royal Homoeopathic Hospital, that he regards extract of sloes as the finest available tonic after debilitating illnesses.

97

which neither she nor I could identify. One plant used for this purpose had roots shaped like those of salsify. Another resembled in form a small beetroot but was pale pink rather than purple. These roots were cleaned and ground up in a kind of mortar before being made into a paste. The latter was applied directly to the wounds.

What was fascinating was the use of moulds in the treatment of wounds. This anticipated the use of penicillin by seven centuries. What I found thrilling was that a species of moss impregnated with a mould was especially valuable. When Miss Mills was telling me about this particular preparation I interrupted her to ask, 'Was it staghorn moss?' She confirmed that it was. I remembered how at one time in the First World War we were told that this moss was still very useful if applied to suppurating wounds. I remember how thrilled I was, as a small boy of nine or ten, when I found it on the Cumberland fells. While she was speaking to me the memory of those days was particularly poignant. Was it simply looking back, and, if so, how far?

Another form of therapy was the application to wounds of what seems an insanitary concoction of cobwebs and moulds. The former were to control haemorrhage and the latter to combat infection. Miss Mills particularly remembers collecting cobwebs. I feel this must have been a first year probationary occupation. It was obvious that she positively enjoyed her therapeutic sessions with Braïda. She spoke firmly and with intense interest of what she called the Thirteenth Century Health Service. This libellous description was not justified. All the evidence goes to show that the Parfaits were gentle, sensible, conscientious, of wide culture and devoted to their patients.

Some time previously Miss Mills had asked me if what the old lady had dictated in her messages referred to her own life or that of Miss Mills' precursor, Esclarmonde. I had not really been able to answer. I think the two motives were intertwined. Miss Mills had a slight bias in favour of the recollections being related chiefly to Braïda's own career. She was, after all, establishing her own identity and giving a convincing picture of the times she had lived in. But in the matter of medical treatment there was no doubt whatever that the two motives were inseparable from each other. They had worked together in the thirteenth century. After seven centuries they were recalling their common interests and occupations. There can be no doubt that this deduction is correct because of the switch of interest which occurred at this time. Braïda went over completely to the subject of healing.

One could say it was a happy chance that, with all this interest in plants, berries, moulds and mosses Miss Mills was so proficient at natural history. But to take such an attitude would be to mistake the whole nature of the operation. In these matters there is nothing fortuitous. Miss Mills was chosen as a vehicle for the expression of Catharism and primitive Christianity because she had certain qualifications. When a spiritual hierarchy is operating on earth it cannot do so unless it uses common sense. Braïda spoke to Miss Mills about berries and plants because she knew she was experienced in these matters. She was carrying on where one had left off in a previous incarnation. There were other ways in which she was continuing directly her previous vocation. Ever since the summer of 1970 she had continued to be inundated by people wanting help from her. For some months now the nature of the help she gave them had become more specific. She had at first compulsively stretched out her hands to people. Was she now developing her capacity to heal? I made no comment and waited for further evidence. Some of those she touched commented on the heat in her fingers and the 'power' that came from her. They said how peaceable and relaxed they felt after she had touched them. Now she went a step further. With patients suffering from migraine she asked if they would mind if she stroked their foreheads. She made the same request of people with common minor ailments like fibrositic shoulders. As far as I could ascertain what she did was some kind of stroking movement approximating to what is called effleurage by the physiotherapists. It was obvious that she had a diagnostic gift in her fingers and that she could pick out areas of maximum tension in fibrositic muscles. In a few cases it was clear that she prodded or rubbed harder at more resistant areas. There was reasonable evidence that she had some capacity to heal. I was not to know that the woman and the hour had met and that, at the moment when she was ripe to benefit from it, she was to receive instruction which would enhance enormously and immeasurably her healing gift.

The frank and unmistakable shift towards healing took place at the end of December 1971. In the middle of that month I had two strange dreams. On the night of the 13th I dreamt that I was back at Oxford. I was to sit for a degree in a few days time. I had done no work for it. I was afflicted with a profound sense of waste. I felt that I should never have embarked on this particular degree. At the same time I kept remembering, but only fitfully, that I had already a living and a medical qualification. Nevertheless I went to one of the lectures. It was delivered by a sharp-featured and handsome woman and the subject was philosophy.

I have no idea what was said at the lecture. During its course I was taking a belladonna mixture, in half doses. Was this, in part, a flash back to the Cathars use of belladonna for eyes? Was the purpose of the lecture to make me see better? However, the main significance of this dream was that years ago I was given tincture of belladonna for the rapidly emptying stomach which has been the curse of my existence. This medicine had been my sheet anchor. For the last few years before 1968 I had taken $7\frac{1}{2}$ minim doses perhaps two or three times a year for periods of two or three days. I had used this modest dosage because I did not wish to take more medicine than was necessary and also because if I took it for longer than two or three days I became nauseated. The medicine had not had this effect on me when it was first prescribed. I had become nauseated because at different periods of life the body rejects medicines it has previously tolerated. When one moves on to a psychic plane this tolerance for drugs and alcohol is often reduced. There was another and more powerful reason. At this time I was returning to my Cathar roots. I was accepting how I was made and reacting less to the inevitable flaws in my constitution. Since my illness in 1968 I have not taken a single dose of belladonna. The doctors did not wish me to do so because they feared it might quicken my pulse rate.

I interpret this dream as meaning that my approach to life and people must now be more total and philosophical. That I was taking half doses of belladonna during the lecture, I translate as meaning that, while I must move out of the limits of what is called science, I should not abandon what I have learnt from it and that I should still continue to utilise it where it is useful. I should, in fact, use it in half doses. It was significant that the lecturer should be a woman. One can put this down to my pre-occupation with the Mother Goddess or the eternal feminine principle. As the dream came at this particular time I wonder whether one should turn a little more positively in the direction of Braïda. Certainly, within a fortnight of this dream, I was presented with another concept of medicine.

Before Miss Mills received her more specific instruction in healing there occurred what to me was a fascinating phenomenon. She picked up a word or two of Braïda's language. She could not be sure that her spelling was correct. It was a hard and throaty language and difficult to interpret. One word she obtained at this time was potentia. I wrote to André Maynard, the Occitan and French poet who is a laureate of the Académie Française. He identified the word as meaning power. From the context in which it was uttered it is clear that Braïda was re-ferring to the power of healing. Among other words which came through were estancon and pel. When I visited André Maynard in July 1972 he had on his table what is called in Occitan an estancon. This is a vessel so designed as to make it difficult for liquid to escape through the aperture. It is significant that Miss Mills should have picked up this word in a conversation on heal-ing. Was the estancon used to contain one of Braïda's potions?

Pel has different meanings. It can mean either the hide of an animal or parchment. The significance of this latter word was clear. Over a period of some weeks Miss Mills was seeing parch-ment covered with script. While a knowledge of Occitan was unnecessary to Miss Mills, who was in direct psychic contact with Braïda, one can see clearly why eight years ago I was led to Ash Hanson who, devoted to the very different culture of mathematics, had nevertheless taught himself Provençal many years previously. It was necessary for me to have, through others, a flirting acquaintance with this language, in order to satisfy my own critical nature and in order to transmit knowledge to those of rationalistic inclination.

What was clear beyond all doubt was that healing, for Braïda, was essentially a matter of using the hands. She divided the process into two categories, the high- and low-powered. The former was characterised by heat and vibration in the fingers of the healer and the flesh of the recipient. In her first discussions she limited herself to the question of heat.

Healing was achieved by laying both hands on the patient's body. This was the bedrock of the ministration. Always two hands, and always still. I thought immediately of the early Christian ceremony of the laying on of hands. I could not fail to do so because this was the basis of the Consolamentum. But if I ever thought that this rite was merely putting the hands on the heads of the recipients and wishing them peace and relaxing them a little, I was soon disabused. I discovered soon that the laying on of hands was not only an art but an anatomically based science. It was infinitely more than a religious symbol. It could be applied to many parts of the body and for many purposes.

It is impossible to give Braïda's instructions in the order of their appearance. This is for the simple reason that so much of Miss Mills' knowledge was derived from answers to her own questions. She slipped quite early into the habit of questioning her nocturnal visitor. When I discovered that this was going on I felt sure that it would not be efficacious. It was so contrary to my own rule, 'Don't ask and you might be given.' In actual fact there were certain kinds of question Braïda never answered but on her own subject of healing she was completely accessible.

The physiological principles behind the Cathar laying on of hands were radically different from anything I had encountered previously in any system of massage or relaxation. To my surprise I learnt it was based on certain bony points in the body. I would have thought that the great nerve and circulatory centres would have been more likely landmarks. Certainly the head and the solar plexus loomed prominently in the system but for the most part the points at which the hands were placed were established in relation to bony structures. In treating a pathological lesion, the hands were placed on the two points between which the afflicted area was situated. For example, to treat a lesion of the shoulder one hand would be placed at the appropriate point at the nape of the neck and the other at the prescribed area in the vicinity of the elbow. The whole system was based on putting the hands on two of the most convenient fixed parts in such a way that the afflicted area was enclosed between them.

An alternative method was to put one hand on the inflamed or otherwise afflicted area, and the other on the nearest fixed point. It was emphasised, however, that this was no more likely to be efficacious than placing both hands on the prescribed areas with the pathological lesion between them.

Braïda's technique was radically different from that commonly employed in present day massage. She was hostile to the idea of kneading or exerting pressure on any muscle. If one was dealing with a patch of fibrositis the aim was to relax the whole muscle or group of muscles in the vicinity. This relieved or cured the condition without a direct and brutal frontal attack on the afflicted part.

In the main there were two kinds of healing. In one, cure was by the easing of tension and in the other the patient was also recharged. It was the difference between, on the one hand, soothing people and relieving their pains and, on the other, restoring their strength. It follows that, generally speaking, the former techniques were used for local and also less serious lesions, and the latter for more serious, long-standing and generalised conditions. Where the batteries needed charging the area of the solar plexus and different regions on the skull were utilised.

It must be made clear that this was not a system of physiotherapy as we understand it. In the Languedoc of the thirteenth century one did not put one's name down at the equivalent of the Chartered Society of Physiotherapists, produce evidence of good education and ask to be trained. Certainly there was training, and from what I know of both systems, the earlier would be at least as intensive as the present system which produces so many confident turners on of heat and electricity. One thing is irrefutable. In the Languedoc the selection of candidates was most rigorous. People were chosen because they had revealed a positive and innate capacity to heal. Contrary to recent and rather desperate opinion, the latter is only given to a minority. The idea that we are all latent healers is one of the sad, feebly comforting illusions of a dying democracy. In the Languedoc, instruction in healing was given by those with strong healing capacity whose gifts had been enhanced by self-abnegnation, meditation and asceticism. I know no such equivalents in the association of the Chartered Society of Physiotherapists.

What are the signs that this mysterious process of healing is taking place? Perhaps the best known are the sensations of heat and tingling in the hands of the healer and in the skin of the recipient adjacent to the hands. Braïda said that the heat was not inevitably felt at the point of contact of the hands. It could be experienced in other parts of the body. I knew this to be true. I myself had felt heat on the outer surface of the legs between the knee and ankle when in the presence of a healer.

I was surprised to learn that the heat and tingling were not the most important signs of healing. When the latter was operating at its maximum both healer and healed felt vibrations in the hands and forearms of the former. This was not limited to a sensation of vibration. Sometimes controlled and rhythmic tremors occurred. These could be felt and seen by the patient. What interested me above all was that the maximum in healing was being achieved when healer and patient were aware of the feeling of pulsation. This occurred in the hands of the healer and in the tissues they were touching.

It was only human nature that Miss Mills should require me as a guinea pig. A person of my age and medical history can always oblige with a few lesions. I suffered from a frozen shoulder. The honest and gifted doctor I had consulted had told me the diagnosis and treatment, or absence, of it. He said that a bit of heat might make it more comfortable if I was made that way but that he himself had no confidence in physiotherapy for this condition. Incidentally, the night before Miss Mills asked me to sacrifice myself in the cause of, was it science, I had been more disturbed than for a long time by the pain in my shoulder. The result was incredible. The pain had gone next morning. The difference in the mobility of my shoulder was astonishing.

On another occasion I was very tired and was suffering from sinusitis. Miss Mills put her hands on the appropriate points on my head. I felt, within seconds, an intense heat and tingling in both her hands and on my head and neck. After perhaps a minute I felt a fine vibration in the fingers on her left hand which was touching my forehead. This intensified to an obvious and visible tremor which spread from her fingers as far as her elbow. This tremor was quite uncontrollable and equally un-hysterical. Miss Mills was not in the least perturbed by it. She was changed radically since she had begun to converse freely with Braïda. This is not surprising. It is not given to everyone to receive practical advice from someone with the additional experience of speaking from another world.

At one stage I told her to move her left hand an inch to the left side of the prescribed area. It was as though the heat had been turned off like a light. When she restored her hand to the original place the heat returned in two or three seconds.

Feeling that she was accomplishing something Miss Mills kept her hands for a long time on my head. I felt I was being flooded by an intense power which I could hardly support. It was as though I felt the pulsations of electricity from a battery too powerful for me. I hung on because I did not wish to hurt her feelings. Finally I terminated the session. There was no sign of my sinusitis or the headache that went with it. There was certainly no question of my feeling tired. I was bristling and over-strung with energy. I felt like a caged tiger. It was dramatic, illuminating, and a little uncomfortable. Next morning I felt I could fight for a kingdom.

I was anxious to clarify this question of dosage. I diffidently mentioned this to Miss Mills. I had no idea she would raise the question with Braïda at the latter's next visit. I myself was chary about addressing questions directly to the oracles. I felt one should wait for them to speak first. Certainly in ancient Greece one frequently consulted the oracles, but these latter were living beings. Surely it was different to address oneself directly to dis-carnate entities. I was still clinging to my old axiom that when-ever you knock, the door stays closed. But Braïda gave her opinion with great precision and clarity. Dosage could not be estimated in terms of time. You could only go by results. This is a sad commentary on a civilisation which measures one's dosage of infra-red with a watch.

The feeling of vibration only occurred if there was some-thing very positive to treat. It could not be evoked by the malingerer. So far as the long-term aspect of treatment was con-cerned, the healer went on until he could no longer feel the evidence of his own healing capacity. The vibrations and pulsations diminished as the patient improved. When they disappeared there was no point in continuing. It was generally time to stop if the healer felt himself to be drained and if, at any time, he noticed that there was no sign of healing activity in his hands and fingers.

The feeling on the part of the patient that the treatment was too powerful was not felt in localised physical conditions like a carbuncle or a touch of fibrositis. It did not arise unless one had at least one hand on the two great receiving centres, the head and solar plexus. Where it did occur it was better, if possible, if the patient 'got beyond the feeling'. If he hung on long enough he would find that he would benefit especially from what he received when he had thought he could endure it no longer.

I thought that the feeling of a great battery being directed at me was what Braïda meant by pulsation. This was not the case. What I felt when Miss Mills' hands were placed on my head was a sensation of a strong and rhythmic vibratory energy. This was Braïda's particular kind of pulsation. I developed fibrositis in the neck from driving in a car on a cold day with an open window. Miss Mills put her hands at the sites described. I felt very soon the beating of the blood vessels in her own hands and in my neck. When she had finished I saw in the mirror that my own carotid arteries were pulsating visibly and forcibly. They settled down to their normal amplitude in a couple of minutes. There could be no doubt that the pulsation described was circulatory.

Another item of instruction was that the healer should use the palm of the hand as much as possible. This strong emphasis on the palm surprised me. So did the fact that Miss Mills added, 'She told me the same as you had done.'

'But did I ?' I said.

'You certainly did.'

I could not for the life of me think why I had made such a statement. It is obvious to me that this use of hands in healing had been erupting from my subconscious for a long time. For two years previous to my retirement I had been obsessively preoccupied in finding instruction in massage for a former patient. I was concerned that her recurrent depression was attributable to the inhibition of her gift of healing. I was satisfied that she had an immense power to heal in her fingers. I saw that patient during the time Braïda was instructing Miss Mills in the laying on of hands.

There was a striking change in Miss Mills since she started her conversations with Braïda. She said she felt wonderfully better and had never known such peace for years. She had ceased altogether to ask why this should happen to her. She had a clear sense of destiny and purpose. This could hardly be otherwise, for she had learnt from Braïda how she had been occupied in her other incarnation. It was clear from their conversations that she had been Esclarmonde de Perella and that she had been trained as a healer. She had also received a course in meditation. When she discussed this subject with Braïda the latter said that, in this life, she had no need to do anything except empty her mind when she felt tired. In her previous life she had acquired a heightened awareness from her practice of meditation. She had done this as a necessary preparation for healing. Her relaxation in this life should be to get into the country and look at the flowers. This was something which Miss Mills had already realised. The awareness she had learnt from meditation in her previous life had given her an incredibly sharp eye for the details of nature.

Braïda was fascinating on the subject of meditation. She never spoke of it except in relation to healing. It was clear that the latter was her major concern. She said that meditation was essentially a passive process of letting go and allow the batteries to recharge. When the individual was sufficiently relaxed and restored he was more receptive to what could give him strength. So far as she was concerned that was all there was to it. She did not advise any reaching out for higher selves. She did not encourage the obsessional desire to perfect oneself which is a characteristic of so many modern systems of meditation.

Miss Mills had already received instruction from the chubby-faced bishop on the higher flights of meditation, but Braïda was down to earth and practical. She was the ideal mentor for Miss Mills. They had been made for each other in both the thirteenth and the twentieth centuries. When, later, Braïda returned to the question of the mental as distinct from the manual aspects of healing, she dealt with one of the least abstract and most easily visible manifestations. When discussing the case of the severely wounded she said that, in bad cases, before surgery was undertaken, the patients were relaxed by the laying on of hands, following which they were hypnotised.

It was now quite clear to me that Miss Mills had more than one guide. Braïda, for all her gentleness, was so eminently practical and clinical that one simply could not visualise her dealing in discussions on the nature of time. I felt that Miss Mills' philosophical messages had come from another source.

One begins to see now why the early Christians laid such emphasis on the laying on of hands. One of the two primary injunctions demanded of them was that they should heal the sick. It was obvious that the laying on of hands was one of their principal techniques, and perhaps the most important of all. We can see why, when uncontaminated Christianity returned to the Languedoc in the thirteenth century, this rite regained its importance. It is obvious that it was, from the beginning, an art and a science. Among the early Christians the priest and the doctor were one.

The reader may be disappointed that I do not give full details of the points of contact used by the Cathars in healing. The curriculum of Miss Mills' previous education should supply the answer. She was shown because she had healing capacity. She was arduously trained. She was instructed in the necessary meditations, the prescribed medicines and, as we shall see later, dressed wounds. Even then, after years, she was only ready to embark on the use of her hands in healing. Her career was interrupted by her death at the stake. She had to wait seven centuries to take up where she had left off. In this life she could only begin in her forties. She is practising something which requires an innate capacity and an apprenticeship of more than one incarnation. If this is thought fanciful, my own case will, in due course, illustrate that in these matters there are no crash courses. My own period of qualification exceeded one incarnation. This protracted apprenticeship was not chiefly concerned with the acquiring of knowledge. Its main aim was to develop the capacity to heal in people specifically gifted. It is quite useless for people without healing capacity to practise this scientific version of the laying on of hands. What I say is not prompted by any love of mystery or of being occult for the sake of being occult. It is at the least profitless, disappointing and sometimes dangerous for these techniques to be practised by the enthusiastic and impatient. It is simply no use people running around laying their hands on people and hoping that their skin feels hot. It is equally no good for an orthodox therapist, without healing power, to adopt these techniques.

17

While Miss Mills was seeing and conversing with Braïda she continued her dreams and visions of people in blue robes. She heard them preaching in and outside a castle, but particularly in forests. By the end of 1971 five of these people were recognisable. The first was Braïda* and the second the chubby-faced man who always stood out because he looked so good-natured and was so constantly smiling. It was fitting that he made a great impression on her because he is one of the better-known Cathars. The third person was a young girl in her early twenties with fair hair and blue eyes and of less than medium height. Miss Mills saw this girl several times and concluded that this was herself. We have no evidence that she was right except her accuracy in other matters. The fourth face to register and recur was that of a Parfait whom she saw several times and whom she remembers particularly as giving a talk in a room to people seated at a table. The theme of the talk was that a table was an important symbol. It was a centre round which a family collected. It was a place where friends could discuss things peaceably together. Christ had eaten round a table with his disciples. It was important to remember the simple significance of such a meeting. It was fitting that bread and wine should be shared at a table by those who loved each other. It was obvious that the

* She never saw Braïda in or about the castle. She died before the siege of Montségur.

speaker had chosen his subject deliberately. The remains of pieces of bread were still on the table. In those days it was the habit of the simple *croyants* to collect morsels of bread left by the Parfaits. The preacher spoke simply but well. He was a tall, thin man, not strikingly good-looking but with pleasant features and an agreeable expression. His most memorable feature was a prominent Roman nose. When Miss Mills described him as tall, it was in relation to the people about him. He was not tall by present day standards.

After this man had appeared two or three times in her dreams and visions she knew it was me. She said that he wore a belt and buckle resembling those worn by bishops and the higher grades of the Cathar clergy.

At first I found this confusing. In *The Cathars and Reincarnation* I had never really defined my status as a Cathar. I had given the impression that I was some kind of intending priest. It seemed presumptuous to regard myself as having been a Parfait. I believe also my innate anti-clericalism made me reluctant to believe I had ever belonged to the cloth. Most of all, how could I have been a fully fledged Parfait and had an association with Puerilia? It was odd that at the time I wrote *The Cathars and Reincarnation* the obvious answer never occurred to me. I had lived intimately with Puerilia before I took the Consolamentum. This was permissible. People who had had such liaisons stayed with their womenfolk in the same way as husbands and wives intending to be Parfaits remained with each other until they were actually received. I made little comment when Miss Mills mentioned this for the first time. I needed more proof than this.

Mrs. Smith had always insisted that I wore a buckle. She referred to this many times verbally and in letters. It was obviously very important for her. Mrs. Smith's and Miss Mills' version of

the buckle differ but the ⊨(sign, so important to the former

is common to both. My explanation is simply that Mrs. Smith remembered part of the buckle and Miss Mills the whole structure.

So far as Roger's rank is concerned, there was never any

question of his being a bishop. It appears that he was something more than an ordinary Parfait.

I did not question Miss Mills much on the subject of Roger-Isarn. I did not wish to influence her to the slightest degree. But it came out clearly in her conversations with Braïda that I was Roger-Isarn de Fanjeaux. Miss Mills told me that I had been more important than I thought. She spoke quietly, with compassion, as though she came from a real world in which the errors of my own speculations were corrected. I had been something above the rank of an ordinary Parfait. I was constantly with the bishop. I have always thought that, as Roger, I was not a great deal in the public eye. It seemed that in this I was right, except for my preaching. I was mainly a scholar and addicted to philosophy. My main preoccupation was the nature of time.

This really made me halt in my tracks. In the last two or three years I have given lectures up and down the country. These have been on such diverse subjects as the nature of healing, reincarnation, a cosmic view of medicine and the vibrational aspects of disease. Those who have heard me will bear me out that in these varied subjects the nature of time has always appeared as a common denominator. This applies also to the books I have written in these years on obsession and on my concept of man as a transmitter. It must have been noted to what extent my concern with the timeless experience recurs in this book. Also there was the extraordinary episode of the note in Miss Mills' diary the day I made my speech in Paris. She had wondered, for no tangible reason, whether I would branch out from my set theme into the nature of time. Sure enough I did, and with good effect. It was extraordinary to know that I had carried over so much from one incarnation to another.

Braïda said that I had always been fascinated by the question of healing but that I had never received any training in it. This bears out what Mrs. Smith had previously said about me. I loved collecting herbs and brewing my own medicines. I was constantly pondering whether I should go more into the world or withdraw from it. Was I tossing up between healing and more philosophy? I cannot answer these questions. All I know is that a Cumbrian in his early teens with a great love of the country, an aptitude for literature and history and an incapacity to cope with maths and scientific subjects suddenly decided to be a doctor and condemned himself to study subjects at which he was mediocre and inept.

I knew that Braïda took a great interest in me. It was obvious that she knew me well in this life and the last. I am sure that it was she who indicated from the very beginning that I was to be trusted. She knew what I was thinking and feeling. Something happened which illustrated this to a striking degree. This event also provided a vivid example of the Cathar doctrine of the two basic energies of good and evil. Miss Mills developed what she called a cold. This was followed by sinusitis. This in itself does not appear of much moment except that Miss Mills rarely ever catches cold. Though she did not stop work she described herself as feeling absolutely ghastly. This was far from her usual form. After some hesitation she told me she believed the whole thing was attributable to a man she had met in the course of business. She had met him several times previously. On each occasion she had suffered from an attack of vomiting. She was sure that her present condition had been caused by contact with this man. She had only met him formally, in the course of business, but she attributed these effects to his presence. She dragged round for three or four days saying she felt abominable.

She asked if I believed that disease could be induced by evil and what could be done about it. I told her I believed it to be possible and that awareness that this process could occur was the best protection. Unsatisfied by this she put her case before Braïda who appeared that night. The latter said she had nothing to add to what I had said. She took a firm line with Miss Mills and said she had been stupid not to consult me more quickly. She told her to get me to treat her sinusitis by the technique she had taught Miss Mills. She said, 'It will do him good. He won't believe he can do it till he tries.' She was certainly familiar with my innate scepticism and caution. Her instructions were specific. She prescribed four treatments.

The next night Braïda did not appear. In the middle of that night Miss Mills had a strange sensation. She felt enormously strong. 'It was as though I had been given an immensely powerful injection.' Braïda was sending some immense force as a substitute for her presence.

Next day I started the treatment prescribed. I gave the required number of sessions. I did not think the last was necessary. Miss Mills recovered quickly. It could hardly be otherwise. Some time previously Braïda had said that, where there was psychic contact extending from another incarnation, the two individuals concerned could cure each other of physical maladies.

Miss Mills asked me more than once if I had seen Braïda. She said that she felt sure that one day I would. She asked Braïda if she had visited me. She replied, 'I am often there but I don't think he is aware of me.' I have never seen her. Occasionally I can feel something in the vicinity and for a few instants I have a kind of tingling, inner awareness but nothing eventuates. What is fascinating, and more important to me as a doctor, is that on several occasions when Miss Mills has practised on me the laying on of hands, I have felt again the sharp, subtle tingling on the left side of the tongue that I experienced when I suffered from sensory migraine. In those days I was satisfied that this sensation was a sign that I was picking up the vibrations of discarnate entities. I had not suffered this symptom for years. It returned again when I was receiving from Miss Mills the laying on of hands. This can only mean that Braïda herself is present at these times and that Miss Mills' hands are literally guided.

Though I do not see her I have felt at times that she is near me. It is difficult to describe my sensations at such moments. There is a feeling of going out of time and that the atmosphere is vibrating. What I am certain of is that my ideas on different subjects have been influenced by her. In what concerns conceptions like group souls and reincarnating for a common purpose I have come a long way in a short time. I know that Braïda had firm views on this subject. She did not regard it as a metaphysical nicety but as a basic feature of Cathar doctrine which ought to be widely known. I learned a great deal simply by talking to Miss Mills. It is profitless to ask how long she or I have been subjected to such influences. When we talk of time we can do so only in so far as it is registered by our personalities. From the point where they speak they are out of time and our converse with them is also essentially a timeless experience. Much of the philosophical material Miss Mills received was concerned with the nature of time. I cannot think that this originated with

Braïda. She was not the type. If these ideas came from one of the guides it was from the bishop. Nevertheless Braïda was the most immediately accessible vehicle. Perhaps the teachings of the bishop and others were transmitted through her. She was, like Miss Mills, another vehicle in the chain reaching towards me.

One of the most extraordinary phenomena in all this history occurred early in February 1972, the day I had spoken to Miss Mills about my literary intentions. I had said that I was at a loss what to write next after I had finished this record. I said that I would like to let myself go on something a little more lyrical. I quoted the theme of a poetical allegory I had in mind. I wondered if I should base it on Montségur. I did not mention to Miss Mills my intention of writing on the influence of Dualism in the practice of medicine. None of this was of pressing importance but for some reason Miss Mills seems to have taken it seriously. Before she went to bed that night she addressed herself to Braïda. The latter appeared immediately in the lighted room. This was the first time she had appeared by request. Miss Mills said, 'I must have looked completely shocked. I swear that she laughed to find me so surprised.'

Braïda coped with the problem with her usual this-worldliness. She said that very obviously I should do what pleased me most, but that, even if I made a poetical allegory, I should introduce somehow a Dualist theme. This was not propaganda. She recognised that Dualism was playing such a part in my life that I should not evade its influence. She warned, very emphatically, against my writing too lyrically. This was sheer horse sense. The contemporary importance of Catharism has sometimes been obscured by debilitated romanticism. She followed up with a suggestion for a book on the influence of Dualism on medicine. This coincided so closely with my own previous ideas on the subject that I could not but think the latter had originated with her.

Miss Mills said that Braïda did not emanate any atmosphere of great piety. She loved seeing her because she was so charming and good-natured and because of the peace which radiated from her. She had the same feeling about the male Parfaits she met. None of them were sanctimonious or even demonstrably pious.

She described them as 'rugged kind of people'. She said that for the most part they had classical features but that their faces were more heavily boned than those in Greek statuary. This is a good enough description of many of the present-day inhabitants of the Languedoc. The stocky, round faced bishop was less rugged than the others.

Miss Mills continued to help her protégés by a modification of what Braïda had taught her. Three times in the months of January and February 1972 different people made the same comment. Each asked her, in different ways, and with different manifestations of diffidence, why her hands had become those of an old woman. Why were the joints of her fingers so knobbly?

'Well, are they?' I asked.

'That is how I saw them. It was also as they were. Look, they've gone down now.'

She stretched out her hands. There could be no doubt whatever that the joints were still swollen. She insisted that they were less so than formerly. What was more important was that there was no sign of any recent or present inflammation. The condition had the appearance of being degenerative and due to age. It was not a manifestation of rheumatoid arthritis such as generally afflicts those of menopausal age or earlier. It was essentially the osteoarthritis of an old person. I felt her fingers with my own. Miss Mills is in her middle forties. She is twenty-three years younger than me. I cannot be said to be conspicuously well preserved but my finger joints were less swollen and deformed than hers. She had not noticed these signs before they were pointed out to her. They were unaccompanied by pain.

What this means is that she took the form of the old lady's (Braïda's) senile arthritis but without the symptoms. In this life, when one takes the symptoms of patients, it is usually for a brief period. One has the whole disease picture in miniature in a matter of a day, following which the condition clears up. This transfer of symptoms from one world to another is a different matter. I cannot enlarge on this because I have only encountered it with Miss Mills. After seven centuries she has the silent and eloquent testimony of the marks of the burning torch on her back. The latter phenomenon is just as remarkable as her acquisition of symptoms from someone dead seven centuries but returning as a discarnate entity. What I am describing is not the same phenomenon as that which enables people to see how the hands of healers change when they are working. It had been said that sometimes, when they are at work, their hands are changed, but this kind of transformation occurs only while they are working. I saw and felt in Miss Mills' fingers a recognisable and pathological change which lasted two or three weeks. From every orthodox point of view the change back from osteoarthritic joints to the normal is impossible.

The story of Braïda's advent into the life of Miss Mills is very interesting for those for whom the basis of life is vibrational. This latter view seems to me incontrovertibly true. All life is energy and all energy is vibratory. Miss Mills first became aware of the voice of Braïda through the tinnitus which was a symptom of her Menières syndrome. Braïda did not cause this symptom. Miss Mills was herself responsible for it because she at first resisted the message. Then the voice broke through by day. That was what Miss Mills at first described as an inner voice and which gradually became more audible. Then to ensure that her meaning was properly comprehended and her own credentials established, the voice dictated messages at night. Then the nature of the vibrations changed so that Braïda materialised through vision rather than sound. She first came out of darkness and then appeared, by request, in a lighted room.

I do not pray. I am incapable of formal supplication to a deity. It directs too much attention to myself and the God I have addressed has seemed too distant. Nevertheless in the last two years I have made a simple request to I know not who or what. This is the only intercession that has ever helped me and after I have uttered it I feel peaceful. The unspoken words are, 'You who are near me, help me.' In the past I have wondered to what I was speaking and how it was related to my psyche. Was there a presence near me and was it Braïda?

18

While Miss Mills was being showered in August 1971 with the names of sergeants-at-arms and other obscure individuals concerned with the siege of Montségur she was also having dreams and visions centred around the chubby-faced man. Apart from Braïda, of all the faces his was the most constantly recognisable. It was clear that his prestige was immense. At the meetings in forests and in setting out on journeys he had invariably a considerable and respectful escort.

To me everything pointed to him being Guilhabert de Castres. The latter was the most renowned of all the Cathar bishops. He was the living symbol of Catharism in the Languedoc. The name is imperishably associated with Montségur where he lived the last years of his life. To guess that the chubby-faced man was Guilhabert de Castres was not difficult. In the last years of Montségur there was only a maximum of three bishops. I dismissed him from my mind and made no attempt to read up the details of his life.

Miss Mills remembered the chubby-faced man giving her private instruction in a room and also in a cave. The latter was divided into two parts. There was a small compartment which led through a narrow opening to a larger chamber. I wonder whether this was the cave at Ornolac described to me by a learned friend who regarded it as of symbolic shape and ideally adapted to those undergoing spiritual initiation. An old French sailor had, years ago, pointed across the valley towards the same cave. This old man made a great impression on me. I saw him only once but he is one of those who remain printed on my mind with an intensity more real than memory.

Miss Mills remembered a good deal of the subject matter of the instruction she had received. In late August and September 1971 she was constantly reminded of the nature of time. There was a repetition of the written references she had received in May. At this time I was away in France but even there I felt the presence of the bishop's contact with Miss Mills. On September 30th I was due to give a lecture to the Societé Métapsychique de

France. On the 29th Miss Mills wrote in her diary, 'I wonder whether he will speak on the nature of time.' There was absolutely no reason why I should do so. I had been asked to lecture on my book, *The Cathars and Reincarnation*. I had every intention of sticking as closely as possible to the text. It was quite an ordeal for me to lecture and answer questions in French before an audience containing several members of the Institut Français and under the chairmanship of Gabriel Marcel, the foremost philosopher of France. This audience was of the toughest calibre I had ever encountered. When I saw them seated at the table with paper and pencils to make notes for questions my heart quailed at the prospect. It was all the more important for me to stick to the main theme of my book. I cannot remember the exact question which lighted the train. I think I was asked why I was sure that the phenomena I had described must inevitably be attributed to reincarnation. Suddenly I wondered, could I do it? I paused for one of those fractions of a second which, in the depths of one's being, are measured in terms of eternity. Could an audience as distinguished and exacting as this endure my ideas on the nature of time expressed in my three-tense French with constant repetitions? I was mortally afraid of being a martyr to the sharp and incisive cerebration of the French intellectual. I will not reproduce my argument in detail. It was to the effect that reincarnation is an indubitable fact seen from the standpoint of human personality. The latter is tethered in time and space. It cannot escape from past, present and future. People who recall previous incarnations are indubitably psychic. This means that in their far memory they are living under the direction of the psyche which is to a large extent emancipated from time. On the plane at which reincarnation becomes a reality, when we meet those whom we have met in previous lives, our confronted psyches make a kind of continuum which is a microcosmic version of the Holy Spirit or the universal consciousness. The latter is totally emancipated from time. My argument was that at the level at which reincarnation justifies itself it disappears. I cannot speak for individual members of this society but I felt an atmosphere of complete agreement and sympathy from this hard-bitten audience. I feel that to be accepted by them was a cardinal point in my existence. Miss Mills could not have known that I would touch on the nature of time because I myself had no intention of doing so. I made my split-second decision not because I felt that I would gain by so doing but because, in some mysterious way, this was expected of me.

Miss Mills was at times still hesitant in enlarging on the details of her philosophical instruction. Anything to do with the historical or healing aspects of Catharism she produced without inhibition. One would have thought she would be glad to dispose of what she understood imperfectly. I had believed that she hesitated because she was quoting esoteric instruction which was inevitably confidential. Braïda had foreseen this when she first got in touch with her and told her that I was to be trusted. It soon became clear that this was only part of the story. I had still to consider Miss Mills' reaction to another mentor from the past who has not yet appeared and who is of vital importance in the transmission of Braïda de Montserver's messages.

Miss Mills' recollections of the instruction she had received after the Consolamentum now went beyond the nature of time. She recalled that she had been required to contemplate and complete intricate designs shown to her. She had never heard the word Mandala and did not understand what it implied. She had a vision, accompanied by a voice, in which she was required to fill in the gaps in a design which consisted of three concentric circles with a rose at the centre. This was in some way glowing. Was it coloured with pigment as in an illuminated script? It will be recalled that the rose at the centre of my visionary Rose-cross was also glowing. She completed the Mandala by filling up the spaces between the circles. (See diagram on page 120).

Miss Mills said that all her professional life she had been addicted to "doodling' in the gaps between appointments. The designs she produces are always the same and are identical with the leaf patterns she saw in her vision of the Mandala.

The whole aim of completing the Mandala was to decide what kind of person one was dealing with. It was, in fact, a kind of typological testing. It is interesting to reflect that Jung in the twentieth century was fascinated by Mandalas and completed

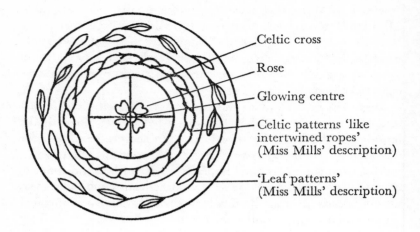

Celtic cross

Rose

Glowing centre

Celtic patterns 'like intertwined ropes' (Miss Mills' description)

'Leaf patterns' (Miss Mills' description)

one of his own. The Mandala technique is of oriental origin. Miss Mills' recordings on the nature of time have an Eastern flavour. The use of Mandalas reveals to what degree Catharism of the thirteenth century was scientifically valid and how so much of its thinking was strangely contemporary.

It was clear that the chubby-faced man had given Esclarmonde de Perella much deeper instruction in meditation than Braïda's simple advice to let go, let the batteries recharge themselves and let the power flow in. She remembers she was taught to concentrate on certain images and on some of the passages she wrote down on paper. The aim of these meditative practices was to purify the Parfait to a degree beyond that achieved when he received the Consolamentum. Essentially, the latter was evidence of his capacity to be trained for higher vocations. Miss Mills' studies in meditation were designed also for the purpose of enabling her so to divest herself of the sensations of the flesh that she could withstand persecution. It was then recognised by her mentor that she was a suitable person to become a healer. At this stage she was handed over to Braïda. The latter, when talking to Miss Mills, had a simpler attitude to meditation than the bishop. Her view was simply that, in this incarnation, she did not need profound meditation because she had done it already and developed the necessary awareness. What she had to do was to continue her healing. It was significant that during this period when Miss Mills was reliving intensively her sessions with the chubby-faced man, she was not visited by Braïda. It was as though, even in the twentieth century, they had agreed not to trespass on each other's territory.

In November, when she was receiving the last outpourings as to the nature of time, the chubby-faced man materialised. He appeared at the foot of the bed in Braïda's company. He was as smiling and affable as ever. He wore his dark blue robe and his bishop's belt and buckle. It was as if Braïda were producing him for identification and to lend greater authority to what he had said and still had to say. He only came with Braïda on one occasion. He returned alone on two subsequent visits. Miss Mills' dog made no audible disturbance when he came accompanied but growled when he came alone.

At this time there was a surprising return to lists of Cathar names. I myself had thought we were finished with this aspect of the matter. I had considered that, from now on, we would only be concerned with material related to philosophy and healing. Braïda had adequately identified herself and the time in which she had lived and instructed Miss Mills. I was slow to see that another was not only presenting his credentials but pinpointing the period in which he had lived and worked.

For four nights from November 26th Miss Mills poured out in writing a new batch of names. For the most part they were unfamiliar to me. I did not recognise Benoit de Termes. Certainly I knew Olivier de Termes. He was the stubborn defender of the castle of that name which capitulated only after the water supply was contaminated. I did not know that he had a brother called Benoit. Simorre, Hot and Roaix were unknown to me. Mothe rang a distant bell. I could not identify Razes. I felt it was a place rather than a person.

I did not bestir myself greatly to verify these names. I was not stimulated to further activity when, on another night, the names of Raymond Agulher and Raymond de Saint Martin came through on paper. As I saw it, Miss Mills was now tuned in so completely to Montségur that, given time, I saw no reason why she should not produce the names of the majority of the Parfaits and the garrison. I could not see that there could be any specific system in this latest crop of names. I did not realise that once again the guides were pointing in a certain direction. On the morning after this particularly prolific night Miss Mills asked me if the chubby-faced man had ever been connected with Toulouse. This was rather like asking if a business man had ever been to London. She was then more specific. Had he been a filius major there? I could not answer. Had he had anything to do with Fanjeaux? I responded as I had to her question about Toulouse. All the Cathar world in the Lauragais seem to have converged at one time or other on Fanjeaux. I gave her one specific item of information, that her namesake Esclarmonde de Foix had received the Consolamentum there. Miss Mills then asked if he had anything to do with Castelnaudary? I could only offer the feeble suggestion that he must have preached there at some time or other. He was, after all, incessantly active and a great traveller. At this stage I did not pursue my researches with any vigour. I went on the principle that if these names meant anything they would repeat themselves in due course and that their repetition would provide me with clues which would save me further effort.

It was more than two months later that I found Simorre. The discovery of this man enlightened me as to the whole problem. He was a learned and disquisitory Cathar bishop who was very active at the beginning of the thirteenth century. He was a friend and collaborator of Guilhabert de Castres. The latter was regarded as the most erudite of the Cathar hierarchy. Among the other especially learned Parfaits with whom he fraternised were Arnold Hot and Benoit de Termes. Guilhabert and these two were such formidable controversialists that they were chosen to represent Catharism in the famous discussion at Montréal in which they were opposing Pierre de Castelnau, the Papal legate and his confrères. One of Arnold Hot's stirring condemnations of Catholicism has been preserved for us. Raymond Agulher was also a formidable debater. On the night of November 24th Miss Mills had taken down the names of the most cultured, articulate and like-minded of Guilhabert's entourage.

The references to Razes was clear. Bernoit de Termes was a deacon at the time of the debate at Montréal in 1207. In 1225 he became Bishop of the new diocese at Razes, established to meet the needs of those residing between Toulouse and Carcassonne.

I learnt for the first time that there were at that time five Cathar Bishoprics. I had always been satisfied with four.

Miss Mills had asked me if the chubby-faced man had anything to do with Fanjeaux. The answer is simple. The first facts recorded of Guilhabert de Castres' career are related to this town. This was in 1195. There is another connection with Fanjeaux which, to me, is almost startling. He was filius major to the Bishop of Toulouse. (This answered another of Miss Mills' questions.) In that year he ministered at Fanjeaux. He gave the Consolamentum to Pierre-Roger the Elder, of Mirepoix. This was the father of the defender of Montségur. In the same year he bestowed this sacrament on Aude de Tonnens. The latter was the mother of Roger-Isarn de Fanjeaux, my antecedent in the thirteenth century. At an earlier date in my contact with Miss Mills I had asked myself to what extent the main characters in her history and that of Mrs. Smith were known to each other. I was now convinced that it was inevitable that they were known to one another. But to know that Miss Mills' bishop had received one's own mother was peculiarly convincing.

I found an answer to Miss Mills' question about Guilhabert's connection with Castelnaudary. Never recoiling from danger he was present there when the town was besieged by the Royal army in 1224. When Miss Mills drove through the town in 1954 it gave her the horrors. At that time she had never heard the words Cathar or Albigensian.

During the four nights and days from November 24th to the 28th she was constantly seeing meetings in woods. These were peaceful encounters when Parfaits were present. She also recalled again, on November 28th, the meeting which was violently interrupted and ended in a skirmish. She said that there were twenty people present at this meeting. Only one escaped. On the same night the name Pagan was written on a piece of paper by her bed.

Pagan was traceable as Pagan de Labecede. The name of the latter place had come to her previously, in dreams and visions, for over a year. It was clear that she was remembering some episode in a nearby wood.

There are certain interesting questions we can ask. Why did this event recur in her memory? Was she the single individual who escaped? But there is something here more positive for us and which asks nothing of our capacity for conjecture. This dream, and the name Pagan, occur in the middle of the references to Guilhabert de Castres. Is this especially significant? I find that Guilhabert, round about 1225, stayed in Pagan's house at Labacede. The latter had obviously a great respect for him. He also gave him shelter on a later occasion during the French invasion.

I found later in the records that a meeting of Cathars in a wood near Labacede was raided by the authorities. Of those taking part in this meeting only one escaped. There are other events in Guilhabert's life which tie up with our narrative. Some time between 1211 and 1215 he took refuge with Bernard D'Allion whom we have met previously in the story of the treasure. We have alluded already to my making a note of the extract from Roché in which he describes how Guilhabert was escorted by Isarn Bernard de Fanjeaux, Ramon Sanche and Pierre de Mazerolles. This was in 1232. It was at this time that it was decided to make Montségur the centre of the Cathar faith, so many bastions having already fallen in the course of the wave of persecution. Miss Mills always maintained that in her day it was a place not only for constant pilgrimages but where those qualified were regularly initiated into the mysteries. On the occasion described by Roché, which had seemed so excessively important to me, Guilhabert was in fact settling down to use Montségur as his last base and end his life there.

All the dates fit in with what was seen and heard by Miss Mills by her varied and mysterious methods of communication. She described Guilhabert as a well-preserved man who must have been well over seventy. He looked years younger than his age because of his boyish expression. It was only when she saw him close up that she realised that the skin of his face was deeply wrinkled. He must surely have been at least well into his thirties by the first years of the thirteenth century. It is hardly likely that a younger or less experienced man would have been trusted with the administration of the Consolamentum to a person as important as Pierre-Roger de Mirepoix the Elder. One must remember that Guilhabert moved in aristocratic circles and was personally concerned with the spiritual welfare of the chief families. At the time he was instructing Esclarmonde he was an old man.

On one occasion Braïda de Montserver appeared to Miss Mills as a young woman of thirty. At that time she had fair hair which, with her dark eyes, gave her a striking appearance. She had a dark, rather sallow complexion. Why should she have appeared at this age? She did so at the time the visions by day and dreams by night were pointing to Guilhabert de Castres. I think she was illustrating how she looked at the time Guilhabert began his mission. She died in 1242. Miss Mills describes her as about seventy. She must have been about thirty at the turn of the century when Guilhabert was establishing his reputation as filius major to the Bishop of Toulouse.

Braïda told Miss Mills that in my previous incarnation I was a favourite pupil of Guilhabert's. This is not to be surprised at. He had, after all, given the Consolamentum to my mother. The house in Fanjeaux was as much a shelter for the Parfaits as it had been a resort for the troubadours. Miss Mills is convinced that the messages about the nature of time were intended for me. 'Surely this only makes sense,' she said. 'I could understand some of them but not all. It was no good sending them to me.' Like Miss Mills I was to some extent taking on where I had left off, but in my case there was a difference. Miss Mills had put behind her all the metaphysical stuff she had learnt in the thirteenth-century course of meditation. She had dropped it so completely that she had difficulty in understanding some of the messages. I had certainly not forgotten the instruction I had had from Guilhabert. For several years I had been fascinated by the nature of time. In the last three years all I have written has been impregnated with the idea that time is an illusion. Before I knew that, as Roger-Isarn, I had been instructed as to the nature of time, I had in this life taken a bold turn back to philosophical matters. This was clearly evident in articles I wrote at that time for 'Light'. What it amounted to was this. In the Languedoc I had studied and been trained for philosophy but had had the impulse to heal. In this incarnation I gave vent to the latter but in my late years turned round to my old love. Nevertheless I think that with me, in this life, the impulse to heal is the stronger motive. Or perhaps there are other reasons why I feel drawn more strongly to Braïda than to Guilhabert. In any case I am now satisfied that to be a doctor and a psychiatrist was the ideal compromise for me. It enabled me to combine the healing and philosophical trends in my nature. Miss Mills, of a metaphysical intention in neither the last incarnation nor this, had decided finally on healing in her former life and in this had continued resolutely where she left off.

One evening Miss Mills' dog growled a little but quickly subsided. Guilhabert was standing at the foot of the bed. He had come alone. They did not talk much. He repeated some of the philosophical messages she had received. He was as friendly and agreeable as he had always been. He paid her a second visit early in January 1972. Looking back on this two months later, Miss Mills said she felt sure that he had only appeared to identify himself and that he had been introduced by Braïda for that purpose. She said his intention was to feed me with ideas, for writing and speaking. It is beyond dispute that in the last year I have broken through the shackles which inhibited me from talking and writing freely. My attitude to medicine is now completely cosmic. To me to consider healing in relation to the nature of time is more essential and practical than to differentiate between the actions of the different kinds of antibiotics.

I believe that Guilhabert de Castres only re-entered Miss Mills' life in a secondary capacity. In the thirteenth century she had passed through his hands. This was a foregone conclusion. He was the most scholarly exponent of Catharism; he lived at Montségur and she was the daughter of its owner. It was inevitable that he should undertake her spiritual education. When this was completed he passed her over to others. She went to Braïda for her practical instruction in healing. Possibly she still needed a general spiritual director.

Miss Mills asked me when and how Guilhabert died. I was able to answer this efficiently. Duvernoy has written that, while in his early years he was an inveterate traveller, he settled down to end his life at Montségur. He is not noted in the records after 1241. Duvernoy says, 'In the absence of all indications to the contrary, everything leads one to believe that he died a natural death at Montségur.'

Braïda confirmed Duvernoy's statement. On her next visit

she told Miss Mills that he had died at Montségur. He had left it on one of his missionary journeys. While away he had been taken ill. At his own wish he was brought home to die.

In rounding up the story of Guilhabert de Castres we encounter again the mysterious figure 609 which recurred so insistently in Miss Mills' story. There are many references to the Cathar bishop in Folio 609.

When Miss Mills' dog growled again later in January, Guilhabert was standing with another man beside her bed. The newcomer was dressed in the same dark blue robes and wore the same belt and buckle. He was taller and thinner than Guilhabert. He was darker and with sharper features. Though he was many years younger he seemed more serious. He had a pleasant face but smiled seldom. God knows he had little to smile about.

On the night when the two men appeared together Miss Mills did not know that Guilhabert de Castres was handing her over to the care of someone who had looked after her spiritual welfare seven centuries previously. She did not realise that he was repeating what had already happened in 1241. A number of patients have said to me, 'In some odd way I seem to be doing what I have done in a previous existence.' Miss Mills was experiencing a sharp, visual play-back of this phenomenon.

The second man came again alone. The spaniel growled. It was interesting that he learned to remain quiet with Braïda but never became accustomed to the male Parfaits. On this occasion the newcomer had little to say. Weeks afterwards Miss Mills said, 'He was only making himself known. He had come through the old lady.' He was introducing himself as he had been in the thirteenth century. She realised soon that he had another, more contemporary, identity.

Guilhabert died in or about 1241. When he passed Miss Mills over to the other man in January 1972 he was merely repeating what had happened in 1241. The second man was able to look after Esclarmonde-Mills for another three years.

19

In November 1971 Miss Mills was receiving a mass of information about potions, lotions and pastes for curing wounds. She was also being instructed by Braïda in the scientific application of the laying on of hands. Why should she at this stage revert to the horrors of the siege? Why should the latter be associated in her mind with the tall, thin man introduced to her by Guilhabert and who had visited her again in his gentle, sad uncommunicative way? I had strong suspicions as to this man's identity.

For a long time I had believed that, in the last three or four years of its existence, only two Bishops had lived at Montségur. This is not to be surprised at. For most of the history of Catharism there were no more than four Bishops in the whole of the Languedoc. It was only in 1225 that Miss Mills' Benoit de Termes raised the number to five. History tells us beyond doubt that Guilhabert de Castres handed over to Bertrand Marty. Miss Mills insisted rightly that there were three bishops at Montségur in the last few years.

It will be remembered that on November 26th she supplied a list of names and that I was able to prove that the majority of these were connected with Guilhabert de Castres. The names Roaix and Mothe remained unidentified. It was some weeks before I succeeded in tracing them. The verification of the identity of the tall, thin unsmiling man took longer than that of Guilhabert de Castres. This was quite logical. After all he appeared later in Miss Mills' previous life.

I discovered that the Cathar bishop Bertrand Marty, who presided over the spiritual destinies of Montségur after the death of Guilhabert and at the time of the siege, was born, probably of humble parents, on the estate of the Roaix family. Mothe was probably Bernard de la Mothe who was an active Cathar but, as far as I could see, not especially associated with Bertrand Marty. Then I had something of a windfall. The name Raymond Agulher was recorded by Miss Mills a few nights before the interrupted bulletins commencing November 24th. This formidable polemist became Bishop of Razes after Benoit de Termes.

Emile Bayard's representation of the burning of the Cathars at Montségur. The victims included those who reincarnated in England in the twentieth century and whose memories are recorded in this book.

Aerial view of Montségur, never designed to be a fortress. During the siege between four and five hundred people were accommodated in this restricted area.

He took refuge later at Montségur and died there on the fatal March 16th, 1244. He was, in fact, with Bertrand Marty at the end. We will hear more of Raymond later.

After that everything fell into place and it was obvious that Miss Mills' second male visitor was Bertrand Marty. The name Guillaume de L'Isle appeared several times in Miss Mills' writing. It figured prominently in the early days and reappeared later when Miss Mills was concerned with the siege. This was adequately accounted for by the fact that he had been mortally wounded at Montségur and had received the Consolamentum. There was more to it than that. Among all the nobility of the area he is described as the most devoted supporter of Bertrand Marty to whom he often gave refuge. There was still more to come. Duvernoy tells us that he was at Montségur while Guilhabert de Castres was still living. Then I stumbled on a piece of vital information. We have heard already that one of our central figures, Isarn de Montserver, received the Consolamentum on his death bed. I now discovered that it was from Bertrand Marty that he received the sacrament. This provides another striking link with Braïda's family.

Bertrand Marty is intimately concerned with others who appear in our story. In 1235 he preached at Montségur, in front of the donjon, to Raymond de Perella, his wife Corba, and his son Jordan. More important, in 1234 he administered the Consolamentum to Raymond's mother-in-law Marquesia de Lantar who, as we have seen, died with Corba and Esclarmonde herself at the stake at Montségur. Above all, there was the fact that he consoled Isarn de Montserver on his death bed at Queille. Miss Mills' story really began with Isarn de Monserver His name appeared with that of Queille in her first writings.

There was another very detailed item which was still more convincing. Miss Mills asked me if Cremone meant anything. I said that it was possibly significant because it was a town in Northern Italy and because Catharism was strong in that part of the world. Beyond this I could say nothing. She said she was sure that a message had been received from Cremone in the course of the siege. This was all too deep for me. I discovered later that Bertrand Marty had received letters from the Bishop of Cremone just before All Saints Day 1243. The siege was well under way at this stage. The Bishop of Cremone suggested that the time might be ripe for a few Parfaits from Montségur to take refuge in Italy.

In a book of this nature I will not bore the reader with too much confirmatory evidence. All that I know, as well as what I have quoted, proves that Miss Mills' second man was Bertrand Marty. Certainly there was another bishop present during the siege of Montségur. This was Raimond Agulher. I had only recently recognised, through Miss Mills, his status as a Bishop. But I know for certain that Raymond was not the second bishop who visited Miss Mills. As we shall see later, Raymond had assignments elsewhere.

What was fascinating was that Bertrand Marty was also concerned with the chief figures in *The Cathars and Reincarnation*. I had said previously how Miss Mills' revelations bridged the gap between the major characters in her own and Mrs. Smith's stories. Certainly his association with the Mazerolles is frequently recorded. In 1232 he is reported with Pierre de Mazerolles, the figure in Mrs. Smith's nightmare, in the region of La Selve. Another time he lends Pierre a sum of money against the cost of his escorting members of the Cathar hierarchy. Later he preached in a field at Gaja, for the benefit of Pierre and his mother Hélis. The latter was one of the most sympathetic characters in *The Cathars and Reincarnation*. We shall see further on why she meant so much to me. It is also interesting that at different times Bertrand Marty was concerned with the minor characters in that book, such as my thirteenth-century friends Mir de Camplong and Roger de la Tour de Laurac.

Miss Mills' contact with Bertrand Marty occurred against a background of tragedy. He was the acknowledged head of the Cathar Church at the time of the massacre at Avignonet. He continued this office till the surrender of Montségur. In the thirteenth century Esclarmonde de Perella saw him constantly under tragic circumstances. As Miss Mills in the twentieth century, she repeated the circumstances and the atmosphere. He came to her at the time she was reliving the terror of the siege.

One of the most dreadful aspects of the siege was the treatment of the wounded. The wounds were what she called 'mushy'. They were not only open but the tissues around them were horribly crushed. I asked what sort of weapon could have caused such wounds. She replied 'stones' without a moment's hesitation. On November 17th the words trebuchet and manganelle were written on a piece of paper. She had not the slightest idea of their significance. These are identifiable as huge stone-throwing engines used in siege warfare in the Middle Ages. They were especially important at Montségur. One of them was the favourite brainchild of a bishop with warlike instincts and a talent for engineering.

She asked me what the sergeants-at-arms wore in battle. I assumed that they had coats of mail and told her accordingly. She bowed to what she thought my superior knowledge but it was obvious that she did not think my statement was correct. I asked her what the sergeants-at-arms wore. She replied without hesitation, 'An ordinary kind of tunic strengthened with vertical strips of leather.' Some weeks later I came across a description of the death of a sergeant-at-arms. It says quite clearly that he might well have survived his wounds had he borne the armour carried by the knights. We have met previously Alzeu de Massabrac, the son of Raymond de Perella's sister Alpaïs. Alzeu was wounded at the same time as this sergeant but was properly armed and, in consequence, survived. The description bore out my contention that he wore mail armour. Whatever may have been Alzeu de Massabrac's personal habits, Miss Mills insists that breast-plates were worn by the knights at Montségur. I did not know at this time that another witness was to appear with a similar testimony.

This was not my only error. Miss Mills asked what time elapsed between the Crusaders seizing part of Montségur and the capitulation. I told her several weeks. This was nonsense. How could they have fought for weeks in its narrow courtyard? What happened was that a detachment of the invaders made a daring climb on the east side of the château. As a result of this they established themselves on a relatively flat platform of rock. I was muddled in confusing this platform of rock with a foothold in the castle. Some weeks later they captured the barbican, a fortified outpost just outside the walls. This was what Miss Mills meant when she referred to the Crusaders seizing part of the fortress. The besiegers poured out in an immediate counter-attack. She remembers that the casualties from this were appalling. The records indicate that the counter-attack failed grievously and that further resistance was impossible. This counter-attack occurred on March 1st, which was the date on which Miss Mills, in 1971, began her period of acute depression. The garrison surrendered. The terms of the capitulation were arranged the following day. Miss Mills was right when she maintained steadfastly that the first encroachment on the fortress was followed in a day or two by the capitulation. In this, and in the matter of the armour, she was not only right according to the records but persisted in her opinion after positive misdirection on my part. I suppose this was a literal example of the truth that seeing is believing.

But at this date, November 17th, 1971 or March 1st, 1244— the dates are interchangeable—there occurred a simple and more dramatic echo of what Miss Mills had suffered. There was a direct and unbroken link between the child who, in an English town, had been terrified by the trumpets of the Boys' Brigade, and the young woman who had tended the wounded on a mountain near Andorra in spring 1244. This tenuous but continuing link had been manifested in the first string of quotations she had received in the spring of 1971. In one of the biblical verses quoted there had been a reference to the sound of trumpets. The full memory returned on a day in November in Somerset. The trumpets sounded when the counter-attack on the barbican had failed. It was, in fact, a sign of capitulation. I have since read that the defenders launched this attack to the sound of trumpets. I can only repeat Miss Mills' version. I advise its acceptance because she was there.

During the siege she cared for the wounded. She applied to their wounds the pastes and potions she had prepared previously. It strikes her as curious that while so engaged she was not aware of her infirmity. 'How did I manage it? I can't remember any difficulty in getting about. Of course the whole thing was horrible. But I can't remember being handicapped by my limp.' I don't think these questions are difficult to answer. There are moments of supreme crisis when people forget their own infirmities.

She remembers how Bertrand Marty went about talking gently

to the wounded. He was grave and unsmiling and indeed she had never known him otherwise. In the history of Catharism he appears as a man of modest origin who rose to a position of great influence. He was a privileged administrator and an arbiter in disputes between the noblemen. She asked me if he had anything to do with the finance of the Cathar Church. She said she was sure he was interested in the handling of money. This comes out clearly in the depositions in which he is quoted as collecting legacies, paying for escorts and other such transactions. But though what we know of him suggests a commanding figure, this aspect of his character does not appear in Miss Mills' memories. He was rugged looking, not constantly smiling like his predecessor, but gentle enough in all conscience.

Miss Mills owes it to Marty to remember him a little. According to Duvernoy he was responsible for the disposal of the Cathar treasure and for the distribution of money and goods to the soldiers. He was especially generous to Imbert de Salas to whom he gave money, clothes, a linen hat, condiments and oil. Perhaps this was why Imbert's name was among those recorded by Miss Mills. But above all she should remember him because of the last celebrations of the Consolamentum at Montségur. He administered this rite to Brasillac de Calavelle, Raimond de Tournabois and Pons Narbona, all of whom were sergeants-at-arms whom we have met previously. Finally he gave the Consolamentum to Esclarmonde's mother, Corba, on March 15th, 1244. Esclarmonde was present. Her sister Arpaïs in her disposition described the agony of this last parting.

Once again Miss Mills was justified in her preoccupation with folio 609 in the Archives at Toulouse. In this folio, which I have not seen, there are, according to Duvernoy, over thirty references to Bertrand.

These numerous references to Bertrand Marty were justifiable for still more important reasons. When he first came into the picture, Miss Mills spoke little about him and quoted little of what he said. It was paradoxical that she was much more open about the philosophical communications of Guilhabert de Castres which were not what I would have considered of absorbing interest to her and which she confessed she did not understand fully. She was guarded about Marty and at first was reluctant to indicate which of the written messages she believed emanated from him. At the same time she was intensely interested in him as a person. She asked me if he had anything to do with the management of money. I was able to answer this readily enough. Wherever there is any mention in the records of Cathar finance and administration during the period with which we are concerned the name of Bertrand Marty invariably appears. This aspect of his nature and functions stuck in my mind because he was at one time concerned in a transaction with my first Cathar acquaintance, Pierre de Mazerolles. Miss Mills was more concerned to find details of Bertrand Marty than of any other of the characters I have mentioned.

I knew her well enough by this time to know that she had discovered something new but was reluctant to discuss it. She said, with an unimpressive show of nonchalance, that Bertrand reminded her of her father. She said it was odd that the latter, a wise, loving and generous man, had always been intensely interested in the management of money. I recalled how the messages she had received had intensified at the anniversary of her father's death. These details were something less than presumptive and I could not regard them as evidence. It was possible that Mr. Mills himself had intervened from the other side and tangled the wires a little. At the same time I had enough experience of her to know that her intuitions were almost always uncannily accurate. I had an open mind about there being any connection between Bertrand Marty and her father.

Later she produced more positive evidence. The philosophical reflections came in three waves. The first two batches were metaphysical in nature and often poetically expressed. There was then a final barrage of messages which involved enlightened but common-sense advice about living expressed in practical and everyday terms and, above all, in the modern idiom. The change of tone of these messages was quite unmistakable. More than this she recognised her father's favourite modes of expression. There was even a sentence which expressed word for word what he had said to comfort her on one occasion when she had been upset and he had told her that there is nothing living or dead worth worrying about except the universality of human suffering.

But, however much we respect Miss Mills' immense talents as a human receptor and transmitter, one cannot on this evidence identify her father with Bertrand Marty. We must wait for the testimony of two characters who have not yet appeared on the scene. In the meantime I must admit that at this stage I never considered seriously the vital question of two people from a previous life reincarnating in the same family. I was still not greatly concerned with the question of group reincarnation. I recognised that I had been led through more than one messenger to Mrs. Smith and from the latter to Miss Mills. I was convinced of the reality of the chain connection but not yet thinking in terms of reincarnation in groups.

20

When I returned from France at the beginning of October 1971, Miss Mills' psychic life was particularly active. She was being visited by Braïda, she was recalling her former instruction in healing and her sessions with Guilhabert de Castres. Above all she was remembering the horrors of the seige of Montségur. With her secret life, her career and her intensive social activity, she had enough to occupy two or three people. She remained, as always, very ready to lend a helping hand or to give advice to everyone who consulted her. She had the opportunity to exercise this in full measure when her friend Betty rang her from the Midlands to say that her fifty-year-old husband had died suddenly, without premonitory symptoms, from a heart attack.

Betty was inconsolable. She appeared to be disintegrating as a result of this appalling catastrophe. It was strange that she rang Miss Mills because, though they had been school friends, they lived in different parts of the country and in recent years had seen little of each other. Nevertheless, it was to Miss Mills that she turned in this crisis in her life. Sometimes she rang three or four times in a single evening. Miss Mills was distressed by her friend's loss but at one stage found these lengthy telephone calls almost unbearable. Her capacity to share other people's troubles was something beyond sympathy and identification with them. With her energy consumed by her other activities, there were times when she found it hard to share so utterly her friend's agony. She asked me what she should do. I said she could only continue to listen patiently and that she was the only person in the world who could console Betty. I did not know how right I was nor, above all, why I was right.

In a couple of weeks the telephone calls were less frequent. It was obvious that Miss Mills had helped Betty, but equally clear that the latter had not yet recovered. One day there was better news. A woman friend of Betty's was prepared to take her abroad for a change of scene. It was up to Betty to plan her itinerary. Without hesitation, she chose the Pyrenees. She said she had always wished to visit St. Girons. This surprised me because I had begun my last Pyrenean holiday at that place. From some points of view it is a good centre. There is beautiful country in the vicinity but, as far as I was concerned, it was not the perfect site. It is some distance from the great centres of Catharism. The town itself is not particularly attractive. Miss Mills was happy that Betty was prepared to accept the diversion offered.

When Betty next rang she appeared a little better. She said that she was visiting her parents who lived in the South West in a few days' time. She asked if she could see Miss Mills. The latter agreed willingly. She rang me and asked me if I could scribble a few names of places worth visiting in the Pyrenees. She said that she was sorry to trouble me but that she wanted to do what she could for her friend. I was very happy to do so. I love imparting information and sharing experiences with other people, and would have been happy as a Cook's guide. Betty wished to start her holiday at St. Girons and to move on in the direction of Carcassonne. I gave her a list of places I thought she should see. In making this list I was simply concerned to steer her in the direction of the most beautiful country and buildings. My choice was not based on whether or not these places had Cathar affiliations. My itinerary was sent on to Betty, who was very grateful. Miss Mills invited my wife and me to meet her for dinner during her impending visit. The day before the meeting

Betty cancelled the arrangements. She was staying with her parents who had contracted 'flu. She was apparently a conscientious soul and did not wish to spread infection to others. She sent me, through Miss Mills, a box of chocolates as a recompense for my trifling services. This was the closest contact between us, at any rate in this life. It was ordained that in this world we should never meet. She passed completely from my mind.

Occupied by her nocturnal discussions on healing and her recollection of her instructions from Guilhabert de Castres, Miss Mills had little opportunity to think of Betty. She received a postcard from her. It seemed that she was feeling much better. Miss Mills was relieved and happy to receive her postcard but the latter did not make a great impression on her.

On November 17th Miss Mills had a particularly harrowing day. The words Trebuchet and Mangonelle had been recorded in writing the night previously and all that day she was reliving the horror of the siege of Montségur and its bombardment by stones. She was really excited and relieved when Betty rang from the Midlands, not merely to announce her return, but to share an experience with her. She said that she was wonderfully better. The whole holiday had been remarkable, but what had affected her most was her visit to Montségur. It had been an unforgettable experience. She said, 'I was made whole by it. I was completely transformed.' Miss Mills was relieved that her friend was so much better and delighted that Montségur had been the chief factor in her recovery. I was myself pleased and interested but not unduly excited. To me it was merely that the mountain was exerting its usual beneficent influence.

Three weeks later Miss Mills had another telephone call from Betty. The latter had been out to dinner with friends in her home in the North Midlands. The hosts had themselves visited Montségur and knew a great deal about the Cathars. I still maintain that the number of people in Britain familiar with the Cathars are a small minority but that sooner or later I established a kind of contact with most of them. But something else had happened at the dinner party. Her host had lent her a copy of Saintsbury's French Mediaeval Lyrics. She had been fascinated by the poem which begins, 'Je vous ameroie Roger (I will love you Roger).' Miss Mills said that she was remarkably peaceful and happy and that the object of her phone call was very obviously to draw her attention to the beauty of the poem. I was certainly intrigued by this information. The poem in question is quoted in my book *The Cathars and Reincarnation*. In the thirteenth century I, as Roger-Isarn, used to sing this to the peasant girl I loved. Betty had certainly never read my book. I also found it hard to think that French Mediaeval Lyrics were excessively popular in the Midlands.

Miss Mills said that she felt sure Betty had some kind of far memory for Catharism in the thirteenth century. I indicated that one needed a world more evidence than had been provided. My attitude was more than justified except that I was allowing more for my natural caution than for the extraordinary accuracy of Miss Mills' hunches. She said that she thought sooner or later Betty would return to the subject. This disquieted her a little because she wished above all to preserve her anonymity and was not prepared to reveal to all the world how she was made and what she had experienced. My recording her secret life without disclosing her identity was one thing, to give herself away to her friends and her acquaintances and the public in general was quite another. At the same time we agreed it was not fair to Betty to inhibit her new and, it seemed, curative interests. During a later phone call, Miss Mills said to Betty that she might be interested in a book called *The Cathars and Reincarnation*, because it dealt with some of the areas she had visited in her recent holiday. On December 20th Betty rang again to say that she had read this book. She must have simply leaped at Miss Mills' suggestion to have obtained and read it so quickly. She said that she was absolutely fascinated by it. She said that an incident described in the book reproduced what had happened in her own life. When she was seven years old she had been very ill with scarlet fever. She possessed at that time a stuffed toy rabbit called 'Roger'. She remembered that she attributed her recovery to 'Roger'.

The story she told follows exactly the same outlines as the episode told me by Mrs. Smith which I had recorded in *The Cathars and Reincarnation*. Mrs. Smith was desperately ill at the age of eleven. She had a stuffed animal from which she would not be separated. During the night when her life was despaired of, she kept calling for Roger. In using the name of her toy animal she was calling across the centuries to another Roger.

Was there a good deal of suggestion in Betty's statements? It is easy for me to say that I dismissed them out of hand. It would not be true. I knew that another trail was being blazed through the jungle of unconscious communication. I had always found that, at the times of maximum psychic communication, the side roads were as open as the main arteries. But at this stage I would have sympathised completely with anybody who chose to regard Betty's contribution as irrelevant.

A few days later Miss Mills had another phone call from her. She was obviously serene and happy. What she said in the course of her phone calls reveals a little the peace of mind she had attained so rapidly. She said she had come across a quotation from Plato which had greatly impressed her. She read it aloud to Miss Mills. 'Every soul is immortal. For that which is ever moving is immortal; but that which moves something else or is moved by something else, when it ceases to move, ceases to live. Only that which moves itself, since it does not leave itself, never ceases to move, and this is also the source and beginning of motion for all other things which have motion.'

Her quiet enthusiasm for this passage communicated itself to Miss Mills. She wrote it down and rang me up and read it to me. I did not know how many professional women transmit passages from Plato in the course of their day's work. In actual fact she need not have done so. This passage had caught my eye the day previously. It had stuck out like a particle of gold in an enormous volume I had been obliged to peruse.

Betty died of a stroke a few days later. Such a calamity had not been anticipated. It was a consolation to her parents and her friends that her last weeks had been so happy. Her restored and enhanced serenity dated from her visit to Montségur.

Miss Mills was deeply stricken by the death of her friend. Braïda appeared to console her. She said that Betty was still asleep and being watched over by a 'Prudhomme'. This was one of the few words Miss Mills had been able to distinguish and retain from a conversation with Braïda. According to Larousse, this word, which is now archaic, means a person of probity and integrity. The fact that Betty was being watched is fascinating because it is recorded that often Parfaits stayed with the dead for three days to facilitate the passing of the spirit. In certain schools of Tibetan Buddhism this practice was also followed. It is interesting that when her father died, Miss Mills did not wish him to be cremated until three days had passed.

Miss Mills asked Braïda how long Betty would stay in her present condition. She was told the question was pointless because time does not exist.

Five weeks after Betty's death, her mother Jane was sorting her papers. She discovered that she had kept a brief record of her visit to the Languedoc. This had been written while she was in that region. I was not surprised that she had visited Montségur and Fanjeaux because these places were included in the itinerary I had written for her. In the latter I had made no mention of the history attached to these places. Montségur had certainly been emphasised as a must from the scenic point of view. Fanjeaux had only been mentioned *en passant*. As I have said, I had not been surprised that she had been impressed by Montségur, because this is a common enough reaction. What was more significant was that she had been made whole by it. But what was really astonishing was the reaction to Fanjeaux. She had put down in writing that she had felt that she belonged there, and that she had returned to what was her real home. Beneath this entry about Fanjeaux, she had written the words, Cecilia, Isarn, Braïda and Pelegrina. This could only apply to the Montserver family. The group included Braïda's two children, Cecilia and Isarn and her daughter-in-law Pelegrina.

This was astonishing enough in all conscience. She had in some way alighted on the names of the family with which, apart from her own Perella clan, Miss Mills had been most associated in the thirteenth century. Had she picked this up by telepathy from Miss Mills? The next entry took the phenomenon beyond the sphere of telepathy. Betty had visited St. Papoul. I cannot be sure that I even mentioned it in my itinerary. If I did it was unemphatically and merely to draw attention to a dilapidated abbey not regarded as of considerable interest to tourists but which I found attractive. Under the entry relating to St. Papoul were the words, 'Oh Roger, Roger, Roger, Roger.' We were back in the period and subject matter of *The Cathars and Reincarnation.* My thirteenth-century precursor, Roger-Isarn was, with a friend also called Roger, seized by the authorities at St. Papoul. He never escaped from their clutches and died later in prison of a chest infection.

Was Betty's Roger myself in the thirteenth century or his friend whom I had identified in my book as Roger de la Tour de Laurac? I could not be sure. Though I was fascinated, I felt no great impulse to investigate the matter further. All I wished to do was to provide evidence that men can communicate outside the limits of their own personalities and beyond the frontiers of time and space. I had ceased to be very interested in the exact mechanisms of communication. I also felt that sooner or later, the new links would be revealed in the chain of psychic contact. I did not have to wait for long.

Betty's mother Jane asked Miss Mills if she had any idea as to the identity of Roger. Her answer was evasive. She wished to keep the conversation at an everyday level. She did not wish to reveal her own psychic gifts or even her interest in such matters. One thing was clear. Betty had had some kind of revelation when she visited the Pyrenees. Her mother was emphatic that she had been transformed by it. Betty's peace and serenity in her last weeks were unmistakable.

Three days later, Miss Mills had another phone call from Jane. She had found an isolated piece of paper in Betty's effects. The names written on it were Tour, Camplong, and Pons. Was Tour an abbreviation of Roger de la Tour de Laurac? The latter, as we have seen, had been a friend of my antecedent, Roger-Isarn. So was Mir de Camplong. The tie up with the characters in *The Cathars and Reincarnation* seemed complete. I was strangely unexcited by this event. Perhaps I was becoming habituated to half existing in the thirteenth century. Betty had picked up these names by some form of psychic communication, but I had almost a surfeit of references from Miss Mills. I had become almost *blasé* about thirteenth-century personages.

Jane returned to the attack a few days later. She rang up Miss Mills and conducted for a few minutes a havering and desultory conversation which was so unlike her that Miss Mills knew that sooner or later she would ask some important and delicate questions. Suddenly she came to the point and asked bluntly, 'Do you believe in reincarnation?'

'Yes' Miss Mills said.

'Good. This is all I want to know. It explains everything.'

A week later, Jane rang to ask Miss Mills if she had heard of Blanche de Laurac. This was another name she had discovered later in Betty's papers. My immediate thought was that Betty might have made a note after reading my book but Miss Mills said her mother Jane was positive that the note had been made before Betty's return to England. She could not question Jane too closely because she needed all her energies to evade her questions. In the last two calls Jane had said that she was sure Miss Mills knew far more about these names than she admitted. Miss Mills put on what she hoped was a convincing front, indicated she was interested in the thirteenth-century Midi and admitted to believing there were people with the capacity to recall previous lives and to tune in to earlier centuries. She was adamant in refusing to share her psychical experiences with anyone but me. She considered that to admit to far memory would be an insupportable embarrassment to her professional life in a small town.

In the next few days things came rapidly to a head. Jane said she felt absolutely impelled to go to Montségur and the Corbières. I did not know why she mentioned the latter. These are little known and little visited arid mountains at the eastern extremities of the Pyrenees. I could understand that she had heard of Montségur but why should she mention it in the same breath as the Corbières? How was she to know that these two names were associated with Catharism? She herself had never mentioned the latter word. Betty's books had been disposed of *en masse* and Jane was unaware that she had read my book. Miss Mills did her best to dissuade her from the idea of a visit to the Languedoc. She pointed out it was too far and that we never find what we are looking for. She said that Jane gave the impression of being on the point of saying something and refrained from committing herself at the last minute.

Next morning, the story took a huge leap forward. Jane telephoned again and came to the point immediately. She admitted that the names she had mentioned had been written nearly forty years previously when Betty was a child. For the most part, they had not been written on paper but underneath drawings she had made at the age of seven when she had been very ill with scarlet fever. I worked out later that Betty must have been drawing and writing within a month or two of Miss Mills having her first recurrent dreams at the age of five when ill with diphtheria. Over the phone, Jane mentioned other names recorded by Betty. These included Massabrac, Congost and Pierre-Roger de Mirepoix. These three names were among those remembered by Miss Mills herself. Once again, we moved into the dark shadow of Avignonet. Betty's three names pointed clearly to the massacre. Those mentioned had all participated in it. This sinister affair had awakened memories in Mrs. Smith, Miss Mills and myself. But why should it affect a child in the North Midlands, stricken by scarlet fever in the mid-1930s? It was clear that in this age of outrageous materialism, Catharism had still a tremendous emanatory power.

Next day Jane arrived unheralded at Miss Mills' house. She had obviously made up her mind to share a secret she had kept since Betty's childhood. She brought with her five children's drawing books. She had bought them forty years previously to distract Betty during her tedious convalescence. Betty had obliged by furnishing historical details of an incident which occurred seven centuries previously in another country. The incident described was certainly important but not sufficient to merit mention in more than a sentence in a French child's history book. The importance of the Albigensian Wars are greatly minimised in many histories of France. Certainly at that time no French or English history book for children or others would give the names of the actual conspirators at Avignonet. Betty was drawing and describing in her annotations something known only to a tiny minority in her own country. But did this small, academic minority reveal the same attention to detail as Betty in her drawings?

Jane brought five notebooks with her. With the greatest difficulty Miss Mills persuaded her to leave one behind for my inspection. She described me to Jane as intensely interested in this period of history and as knowing a little about it. Jane consented reluctantly. She said she had treasured these books for forty years and that, until that morning, she had not told anyone of their existence. She could not bear them to be out of her sight. She finally agreed to leave one for me on condition it was returned immediately and that nothing in it should be utilised by me verbally or in writing. I quite understood her attitude. Investigators of psychic matters who suspect the integrity of those unwilling to part with information can be deplorably lacking in insight.

21

The morning I spent in Miss Mills' house poring over Betty's notebooks was in some respects the most revealing of my life. It is not given to everybody to see the evidence that a sick child in an industrial city saw across seven hundred years, to an incident which was the prelude to the destruction of the Mediaeval resurgence of primitive Christianity.

The drawings occupy nineteen pages. The figures depicted are childish and stylised. Men's arms and legs are represented by straight lines and their heads by circles. Trees receive the same treatment but in different colours. Men are always coloured in blue. In spite of the childish nature of these drawings, there is evidence in them of some kind of pattern. The latter is sometimes symbolic and contains signs of Cathar significance. At other times it is so woven that names are expressed in strange loops and convulsions. Whether the names are written straight or in a mysterious and embroidered form they are primitively executed by the same childish hand.

Betty's drawings, and their explanations, are given on the ensuing pages.

Diagram I

The left hand top corner of diagram I contains four Tau crosses. As we have seen, the latter are symbols of healing. At the base of the drawing the word FAN is clearly discernible. This is obviously an abbreviation of Fanjeaux, where there was a centre for training Parfaits in the art of healing. If this seems an over-dogmatic statement the reader should pause before passing judgment until he has seen the other drawings. If Betty was so unerringly accurate in other details, she can be allowed the abbreviation of Fanjeaux.

The Greek cross to the right of FAN is of no special significance except that, where they used the cross as a symbol, the Cathars affected the Greek variety. I do not know if the straight E above the Greek cross means anything in particular.

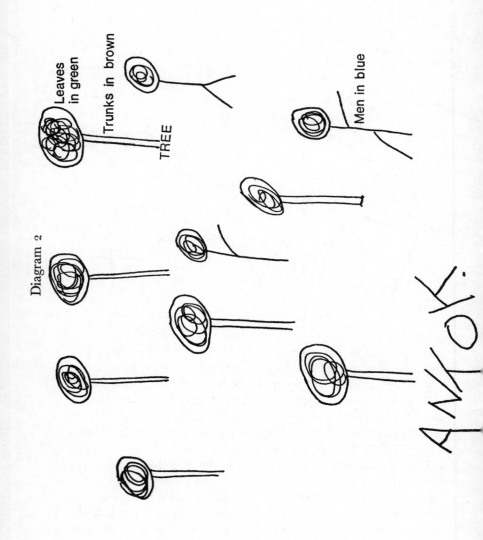

Diagram 2

Leaves in green

Trunks in brown

TREE

Men in blue

ANKOK.

146

The analysis of this drawing is impossible unless one knows the key word. All one has to go on are men and trees, or, if you like, men in a wood. But the whole show is given away by the word Antok. Before the massacre of the Inquisitors at Avignonet, the conspirators from Montségur and those led by Pierre de Mazerolles met in a wood near Gaja-la-selve. This wood was called Antioch. The name had always stuck in my memory for the simple reason that I could not imagine why a wood in the Languedoc should have a near-Eastern name. The whole matter was revived for me by the fact that, the night before she received the visit of Betty's mother, Miss Mills asked me if the assassins of the Inquisitors had met in a wood. Antok is Betty's attempt to spell Antioch.

Diagram 3

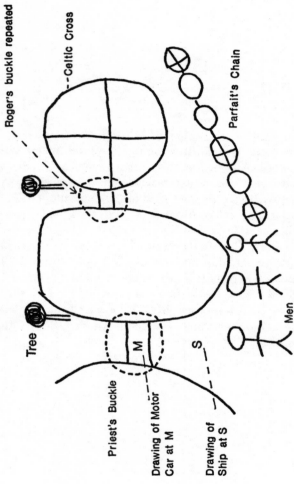

Roger's buckle repeated

--Celtic Cross

Parfait's Chain

Tree

Men

Priest's Buckle

Drawing of Motor Car at M

Drawing of Ship at S

In diagram 3 there are here three points worth noting. Scrawled across the child's schematic representations of a motor car and a ship is the clear outline of the buckle which was worn by Roger Isarn and which so obsessed Mrs. Smith. The latter spoke of Roger's buckle and the dark blue of the Parfaites' robes as though these were the two yard sticks by which her story should be measured. Secondly, in the bottom right hand corner, there is a Parfait's chain in which circles and Celtic crosses alternate and which resembles exactly that described by Miss Mills. What enabled Betty to draw thirteenth-century symbols which were recalled about ten years later by Mrs. Smith and nearly forty years later by Miss Mills?

There is another Celtic cross at the top right hand corner of the picture.

Diagram 4

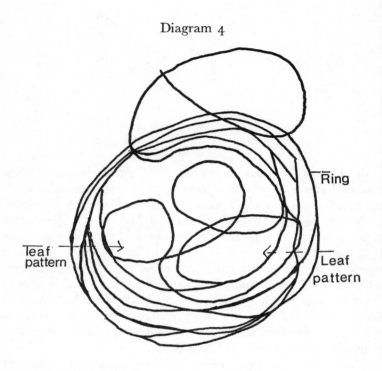

This diagram is only one corner of a childish scrawl. This particular design is the end of a series of indefinable loops.

We see here a circular design and a pattern of leaves. Braïda de Montserver says that the former is Betty's childish attempt to draw the ring she wore as a girl and young woman before she became a Parfaite. The pattern of leaves is Betty's effort to recall the design engraved on the ring. This leaf motif resembles, but not closely, that on Miss Mills' Mandala. Braïda states that this ring was commonly worn by Cathar sympathisers who had not been received into the priesthood.

Diagram 5

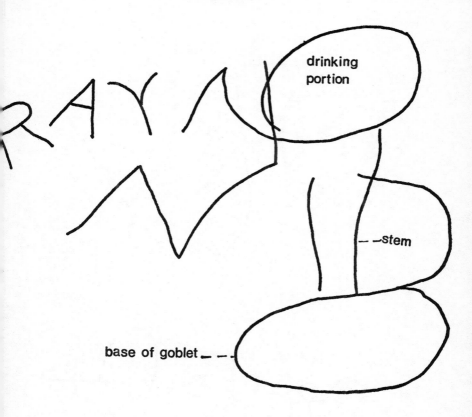

drinking portion

stem

base of goblet

The word 'Raymond' is obvious, except that the 'D' has a florid ending. The 'D' is joined to the 'O' in such a way as to resemble a goblet with a stem. Taken alone, this design should be regarded as having no special significance. It is, however, repeated on a later page.

Who was this Raymond? This name was so common in the mediaeval Languedoc that one can make no comment on this one example but in diagram 6 we are surely enlightened as to his identity.

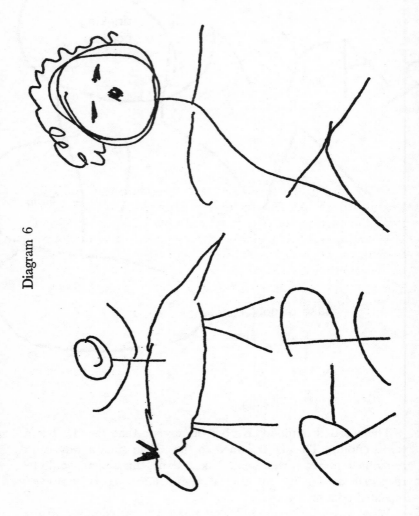

Diagram 6

152

In the bottom left hand corner of diagram 6 the letters R P are distinguishable. Against the background of the whole subject I think we can take these as indicating Raymond de Perella. I do not know what significance one ascribes to the man on the horse or the other figure. Presumably the first is a knight, which fits the description of Raymond de Perella.

Pages 7 and 8 of Betty's book were drawn with the book full open and make a single picture, as shown in diagram 7.

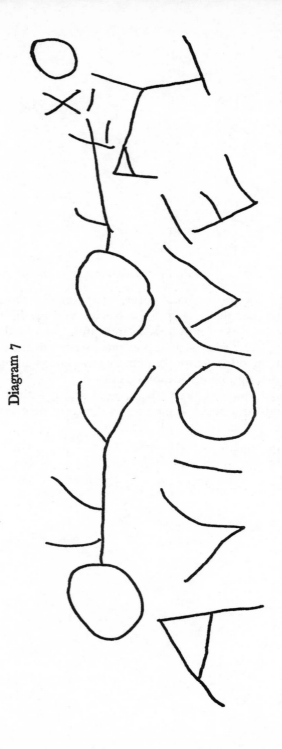

Diagram 7

There can be absolutely no doubt as to the significance of Diagram 7. Here are two recumbent human figures. In all Betty's drawings, these are the only men represented in that position. They are the two murdered Inquisitors. Underneath something is written in her peculiarly spidery and geometric capitals. This is the key word to the picture, and, to a large extent to her own story, to mine, Mrs. Smith's, and Miss Mills'. The letters AVIONEY are an exceptionally good attempt on the part of an English child of seven to render the pronunciation of Avignonet, in her own language. Perhaps the very active figure formed of the last two letters of the word Avioney represents somebody killing the Inquisitors.

This diagram was a two page affair with the book wide open.

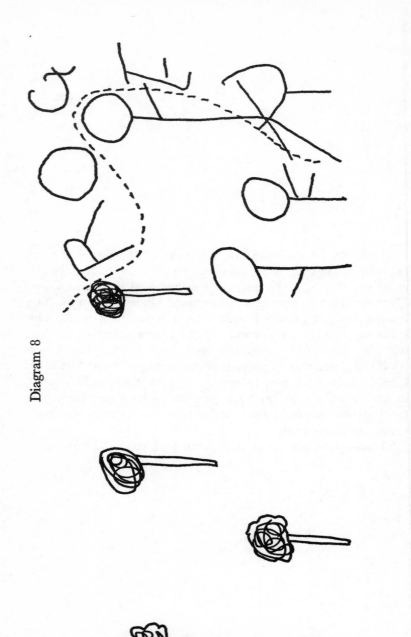

Diagram 8

Here, in diagram 8, there is again an emphasis on men and trees. The leaves are in green and the trunks in brown. The men in the bottom right-hand corner are in blue. To the right the word Roger is sketched in clearly. We are still in the woods. Are we still concerned with the Avignonet conspirators? But why the word Roger? We know from *The Cathars and Reincarnation* that Roger-Isarn was horrified by the massacre and unaware of the plot until it had been accomplished. But the next diagram points clearly in the direction of my predecessor Roger Isarn de Fanjeaux.

Diagram 9

bowl

stem

base
of goblet

Parfait's Girdle

← ‑ ‑ Signs on Roger's belt ‑ ‑ →

The name Roger is written clearly in the right-hand top corner. In Betty's original it was written in pencil. Note the repetition of R's which precede it. The rest of the drawing was in red/brown crayon. Secondly, the sign Roger wore on his buckle is reproduced twice towards the bottom left-hand corner of the picture. Thirdly, there is a further reproduction of the Parfaits' girdle composed of Celtic crosses. It will be seen that the links between the crosses, together with the adjacent part of the circumference of the circles, are actually reproductions of the signs which preoccupy Puerilia, and which she saw on Roger's buckle. Is it possible that in her recollections Mrs. Smith was concentrating, at times at any rate, on the junctions between the circles in the Parfaits' girdle?

The goblet appears again at the right extremity of the picture. There are those who would translate it as the Holy Grail. I am not among this number.

Two large R's are distinguishable to the left of the picture.

Diagram 10

The first line is obviously an abbreviation of Camplong. The G is at the right extremity of the second line. We are back in the world of Roger-Isarn. Mir de Camplong was one of his closest friends.

The word Camplong is a good example of the way in which Betty disguised her names in a design of curlicue. It is clear that even at seven, Cathar symbols had invaded her unconscious. This is shown clearly in her drawing of belts and buckles. There are also signs of a pattern in some of her less translatable scrawls. Are similar designs concealed in the way she writes proper names?

Once again a single tableaux occupies the whole canvas.

Diagram 11

Diagram 11 also occupies a double page. The name on the bottom line is easy to identify. This is indubitably Congost. Gaillard de Congost appears little in the records except as a participant in the Avignonet affair. The left half of the middle line is taken up by the word Pons. Pons Narbona, a sergeant at-arms, was also implicated in the massacre. We have two other names to account for, Pierre, above and to the left of Pons, and Rog directly to the right. These are the Christian name and surname of a single person, Pierre-Roger de Mirepoix, commander of the Montségur garrison and leader of the troop which left for Avignonet on the night of the massacre. Betty attempted to spell Pierre-Roger in either Medieval French or Occitan. She used only one 'r' but put the vowels in the wrong order.

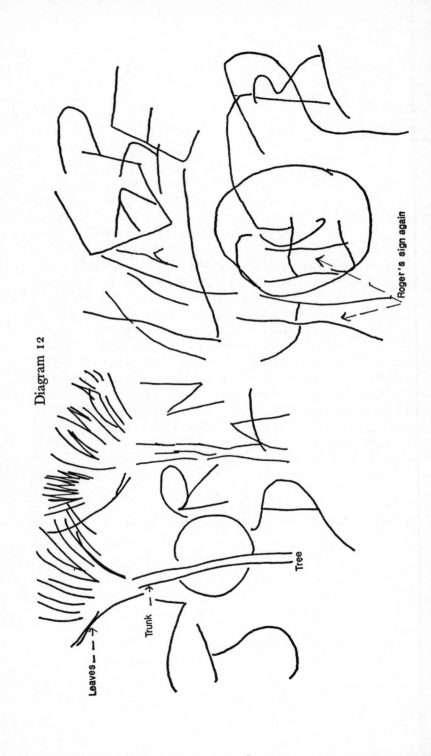

Diagram 12

Beyond any doubt diagram 12 is a reference back to the massacre at Avignonet. In some ways this drawing is the most significant of all because it is concerned with the most minute details. On the left of the picture is a wood. The word Jordan is scrawled across it. This refers to Jordan de Mas who rode out from Montségur with the band led by Pierre-Roger de Mirepoix.

Now the right side of the picture contains the word Leper. What in the world can this have to do with the massacre at Avignonet? A week or two later, Miss Mills asked if there was a leper house in the vicinity of Avignonet. I answered very positively, 'no' and added, which is true, that such an institution existed at St. Papoul. I went casually to consult a book which included a description of the conspiracy. I had no hope of finding anything new. I did my by now habitual trick of opening at the right page. I discovered that the two separate troops of conspirators, the one from Montségur, the other from La Selve, were met at the leper house at the outskirts of Avignonet by someone who guided them to the Inquisitor's lodgings. All this was recorded by Betty nearly forty years ago. At that time, was there any professor in England going into the matter in such detail?

Betty used two pages for this drawing.

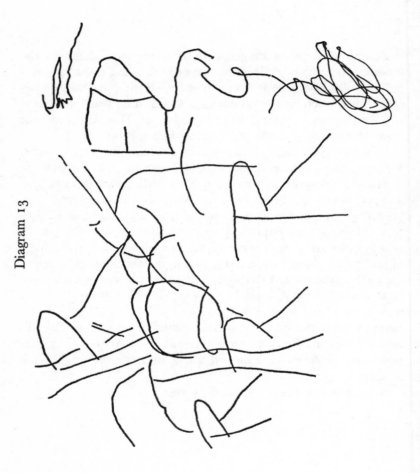

Diagram 13

In the final diagram of her notebook Betty returns, at the age of seven, to what she was to recall forty years later at St. Papoul and which she recorded in writing, 'Oh Roger, Roger, Roger, Roger.' The memory of her thirteenth-century brother seems to have remained always at, or very near, the conscious level.

Here we see a line of 5 R's at the periphery and Roger scrawled across the middle. For this single page drawing Betty used the back cover of her drawing book.

What does all this mean? It is clear that at the age of seven, Betty was remembering, or picking up the vibrations, of the massacre of the Inquisitors at Avignonet. This is not only proved by her drawings and the names appended to them. The names in the odd pieces of paper found by her mother were also concerned with this affair. Othon and Alzeu de Massabrac were clearly implicated and their names are unmistakable. Betty had also written Raymond on a scrap of paper. This could have been either Raimon Guiraud or Raimon de Ravat. These two rode with Pierre-Roger from Montségur.

But there is a second theme in Betty's childhood recollections. Why the concentration on Roger? Why the heart cry in her diary after the visit to St. Papoul? It was here that Roger-Isarn had been captured by the hunters of heretics. Was there some tie-up in the thirteenth century between Betty and Roger? Had there been, even in this life, some communication between Betty and myself? The exchange of thoughts over the Plato quotation was certainly interesting.

Betty's drawing book was duly returned to Jane. Two days later she rang Miss Mills and asked her if she had thought Betty had had a previous incarnation in the Languedoc and if these writings were signs of it. Miss Mills said, 'Yes.' Jane then asked if she thought it possible that someone had been trying to get in touch with Betty. Miss Mills replied that she thought it possible.

These questions were posers for Miss Mills. She had a two-fold aim in answering Jane's enquiries. She wished to console her as much as possible and, at the same time, to conceal her own psychic gifts. It was obvious to me that there was a good deal that Jane had guessed already. Her next question was, 'Has anybody ever tried to get in touch with you?'

Miss Mills answered with a shamefaced, 'No.' She had a bad conscience about these evasive answers. She was very fond of Jane and wished to help her as much as possible.

In this conversation, Jane made it clear to Miss Mills that my seeing Betty's drawings was a special favour and a complete confidence. She was afraid that the drawings and names might be utilised in a book. This natural fear was stranger than it looked. At this time Jane had no idea that I had written anything. I told Miss Mills to impress on her that I would not dream of writing a word about Betty without her permission.

But Braïda had something else to say. She appeared that night and told Miss Mills that Jane would change her mind and that she would give me permission to use this material. Miss Mills asked her who Betty was. This was a mistake. Braïda resisted over-direct questions. She was hostile to the idea of proof by definition. Miss Mills' identity as Esclarmonde de Perella and my own as Roger-Isarn had been established in the course of long conversations centred around these persons in such a way that their identity was unmistakable. The other people and incidents which entered into these discussions established beyond doubt our previous identity. Braïda occasionally pulled up Miss Mills sharply. When the latter asked her if the spring celebration of Montségur was a Manichean feast, she said, 'That you will have to think out for yourself. You have surely been given enough references to study.' By this she can only have meant that the Spring Rites were essentially the celebration of a Christian Easter.

By way of consolation Braïda said, 'You are going to meet another person who knows a great deal about Catharism.' I told Miss Mills that this was undoubtedly Betty's mother, Jane. She herself was far from sure that this was the case. She was in a low state that morning and not able to anticipate anything with her natural cheerfulness. The date was March 14th. This was the date on which the garrison marched out from Montségur.

The previous night had been an ordeal. Guilhabert de Castres had appeared. He had intoned a monotonous chant which Miss Mills found horribly depressing. She had heard these chants before, but previously they had been sung by a number of people and had not had a depressing effect on her. On this particular night the results were abysmal. Guilhabert de Castres then brought in Bertrand Marty and left him with her. This is as it should be. Guilhabert was dead before the siege while Bertrand was there till the last hours and died at the stake. Bertrand Marty repeated the Lord's Prayer to her. Miss Mills was conscious that she was not perceiving its full significance. This is understandable. She was looking back to a time when she could not be fully attentive. However much one has been spiritually strengthened, it must be difficult to concentrate the day before one is to be burned alive.

Jane rang on the evening of the 14th. It was almost a comfort to Miss Mills to find that Jane felt as low as she did. 'Why,' said Jane, 'do I feel so depressed?'

Miss Mills replied that this was the date on which the garrison had quit Montségur. In her previous conversation she had admitted to a certain knowledge of Cathar history because she did not wish Jane to think that Betty had been chasing a mirage. She told me that over the phone she could hear Jane's huge sigh of relief. The latter asked her how much she knew about it. When she admitted to some knowledge, Jane then described a dream she had had the night previously. She saw a castle on a hill. She saw men with jackets strengthened by strips of leather walking out from it. The description of the jackets is identical with that mentioned previously by Miss Mills. What stuck out most prominently in her dream was that a number of the men in leather jackets stayed behind with their wives. We are back again at the sergeants-at-arms. Jane did not know how many men stayed behind. She said there was something unbearably sad about this particular dream and that the whole dream was terrible.

What interested me specially was here was another with a taste for anniversaries. Like Miss Mills, Jane was always depressed during the first fortnight in March.

To Miss Mills' amazement Jane added firmly that she did not mind me using the material Betty had provided as long as her identity was concealed. Though I had never met Jane I had thought it possible, on the evidence of conversations reported to me by Miss Mills, that it would take a few months for her to change her mind. I was astonished by her sudden *volte face*. Braïda's forecast the previous night had been fulfilled well within twenty-four hours. It was obvious Jane was the next Cathar informant foretold by her.

22

In the small hours of March 16th, 1972, I woke up feeling literally like death. When I offer that description I mean what I say. I felt I could not get my breath and that to inhale at all required an effort of will. Had this been ordinary breathlessness I would have put it down to my heart condition. Even then, before or after my illness, breathlessness had never been my trouble. Nor was there any element of bronchial spasm about this sensation. It was as if there was no air left in the world. I lay awake for half an hour. When I discovered that my wife was also awake I switched on the light. It was four o'clock. I am not accustomed to waking up in the small hours. 'I hope the two others are all right,' I said. I do not know why I said the 'two others'. After all I had not met Betty's mother.

When I got up that morning I felt far from well. It was the anniversary of the burning of the Parfaits at Montségur.

I saw Miss Mills that evening. She had woken up suddenly in the night and had immediately vomited. I asked her what time this had occurred. She replied, 'Three-thirty.' This was the hour at which I myself had awakened. I was not in the least surprised by her symptoms. Braïda had appeared later that night. Her advice was simple. She merely counselled patience once more. Miss Mills heard Guilhabert de Castres chanting. Then Bertrand Marty appeared again. At one and the same time he encouraged and consoled. She was re-living their last meeting.

Jane hung on bravely until the next day, the 17th, before telephoning. It had been difficult to do so on the 16th because she had been visited by her doctor. She had woken in the small hours of that morning with excruciating pain in the feet. This spread in both legs, to above the knees. When she switched on the light, she found that both legs were fiery red and covered with huge blisters to the line above the knees to which the pain extended. She said that the pain was absolutely agonising.

It is interesting that the pain stopped above the knees. It has always been said that very often the victims of burning at the stake became unconscious and died early from asphyxia.

Because the pain was unendurable, she rang the doctor. When the latter examined her he said that the whole picture was exactly that of a burn, but that, if she insisted she had not been burned, he could only say that he had never seen anything like it in his life. He told her candidly that, if he called it an allergy, it was for want of a better description. He wrote her a prescription for an antihistamine. She told Miss Mills that she did not take the doctor's tablets. 'What was the good? I knew what had caused it.'

The lesion disappeared between two and three in the afternoon, but the pain persisted for some days afterwards. Jane could not say the exact time she woke up. I wonder what time the Parfaits were burned at the stake. Miss Mills says it was at dawn. A year ago, she had found by her bed, written in French, the words, 'dawn March 16th cold etc.' I do not know any authority which gives us the time of the auto da fé.

Medically speaking, Jane's burn is not as fascinating as the eruption on Miss Mills' back along the line of impact of the burning torch. I wonder if any other doctor knows of two skin lesions originating seven centuries previously.

Jane reported this to Miss Mills by phone on the 17th. Miss Mills was astonished enough by what she had heard but the end of the conversation was beyond anything that she had previously experienced. Jane asked if she had been visited by anybody recently. Visited by anybody is a vague enough phrase, but Miss Mills knew well enough what was intended. She answered, 'No'.

'Why are you lying to me?' said Jane.

'Why do you say that?'

'Come off it'. Jane spoke with unusual sharpness. 'I know for a fact that Braïda has been visiting you.'

At this stage, Miss Mills gave up the battle. She always had a horror of anyone other than myself knowing of her experiences. It was clear to her now that you cannot hide when eyes are watching you from other centuries. She made no attempt to deny what Jane had said.

Jane went on to say that she had been visited for years by a man in blue robes she had first taken to be a monk. She was careful to point out that he did not wear a hood. He only visited her when she was particularly worried about anything. So far as she could say, he appeared once every two months. He seems to have functioned as a kind of guardian angel.

Three days later, Jane appeared at Miss Mills' house. She spoke freely and directly about Montségur. Without hesitation or diffidence she described the siege. Like Miss Mills, she had helped with the care of the wounded. She described the pre-ponderating type of wounds and how they were dressed. Her description corresponded with that given me previously by Miss Mills. She mentioned especially the use of cobwebs for controlling haemorrhage. She described the plant resembling salsify which Miss Mills had seen pounded up in a mortar and used as a paste for dressing wounds. Jane said it was also boiled and eaten.

It was fascinating that Jane was able also to contribute to our knowledge of Cathar dress and decoration. All the Parfaits wore blue. Once again, Mrs. Smith was triumphantly vindicated. The Parfaits were never tonsured. Neither men nor women wore anything on their heads. Miss Mills has described how, to this day, Braïda de Montserver wears a Juliet cap. Braïda died before Montségur. The fashion could have changed by that time. It is also only reasonable to suppose that the rigours of the siege would simplify dressing habits. Mrs. Smith had a recollection of sometimes wearing a kind of net but recalls that for the most part, her hair was free. Mrs. Smith, Miss Mills and Jane are all emphatic that among the Cathars there was no elaborate head-dress like a wimple. They are all agreed that, in comparison with what obtained in other civilisations of that epoch, the hair styles were remarkably free and uninhibited. To me the minor differences they recall increase the reality of the picture.

Jane insists that the chains with the designs such as the Celtic cross described by Miss Mills, were not worn immediately after the individual became a Parfait. After receiving the Conso-lamentum, a girdle was worn. The right to wear the chain followed further initiation. She verified that the bishops wore buckles. These had the same design as those described by Miss Mills, but Jane insisted that there was also a cross in the middle of the buckle. In this matter of dress and decoration, once again the likenesses and experience of Mrs. Smith, Miss Mills and Jane far outweigh the differences.

For centuries the historians have agreed unanimously that the Parfaits never ate meat. For their protein, they relied on fish, nuts, pulses, and bread. Jane says positively that they did take meat on occasion. They would eat the flesh of an animal already killed to obtain its hide in order to make parchment. Miss Mills had foreseen this in her vision and dreams at the end of 1971, when she saw parchments and hides and wrote down the word 'pel'. The latter is the Occitan for hide and parchment. In this they seemed to have adopted the attitude of certain Buddhist lamas. One of the latter ate meat at my table, and said that there was no reason why he should not do so as the animal was already dead but that he would not co-operate in any circumstances with the taking of animal life.

Who was Jane? This is not at all difficult. She knew that her husband was a soldier. He was not in a position of authority but was nevertheless in her own words, 'not exactly a private soldier'. He wore a tunic strengthened by strips of leather. He was, in fact, a sergeant-at-arms. She was burned with him. No wonder the elucidation of the mystery of Brunarsendis had meant so much to me. Brune and Arsendis were the two wives who were burned with their husbands, Arnaud Domerq and Pons Narbona. Jane must have been one of these women. On a later occasion, Miss Mills asked her if Brune rang a bell. She admitted this was so.

Jane said that in her previous life she and her husband had two boys and a girl. If one could confirm that the family of Brune and Arnaud Domerq were so constituted, that would clinch the matter.

She returned again to the question of the Parfait who visited her. It was from him that she had learned Miss Mills was visited by Braïda. I had first wondered if this gentleman were Guilhabert de Castres, for no better reason than that the latter was so active, eminent and ubiquitous. The newcomer was also well acquainted with Braïda Montserver. It was clear from Jane's description of him to Miss Mills he could neither be Guilhabert de Castres nor Bertrand Marty. Far from being chubby faced and short like the former or tallish and thin faced like the latter, he was a big burly fellow in all respects. He was tough looking and broad headed. She always thought of him as the rugger forward. It seemed he resembled in build those admirable French forwards who are recruited from the Cathar country and who do not in the least demonstrate the Cathar capacity for non-resistance. He was inextricably associated with her memories of Montségur. At the time of the siege, there were only two bishops left at the château. Emphatically he was not Bertrand Marty. He could only have been Raimon Agulher, a formidable speaker who, nearly forty years before the siege, had confronted the odious St. Dominique in the famous debate in the house at Fanjeaux, in which in my previous incarnation, I may well have been born. His appearance gave no clue to his capacity as a preacher.

Jane told Miss Mills that she was going to the Midlands to settle Betty's affairs. After that she proposed to go to the North of England for a holiday.

When Jane appeared at Miss Mills' house she was still suffering from the acute pain in the legs which had started on the morning of the 16th. Miss Mills gave her treatment according to Braïda's methods. The pain stopped in a couple of minutes, another example of cure by resumed contact after centuries.

Braïda appeared the following night. She said that Jane would be away for some time and that, when she returned, she should not be contacted or encouraged to meet me. She said that it was possible that Jane would pass through a stage when she did not wish to speak further. Essentially she should be left to do what she wanted in her own time.

Three days later I had to go over to the B.B.C. at Bristol to do a small item for 'Woman's Hour'. I was very tired and depressed and wished the assignment could have been at another time. That evening I was visited by Miss Mills. She had not intended to do so because she herself was very busy, but had been told by Braïda that I needed support. She had also another item of information to communicate to me. Miss Mills had suggested I mix together, in what she called an Anthology, some poems I had recently composed with short items of prose I had written in the last two years. At first I thought this a good idea. In the last twenty-four hours I had gone back on this decision. It seemed to me wiser to utilise the ideas expressed in the prose pieces and to translate them into poetry. The night previously Braïda had expressed the identical opinion. It seemed more than ever clear to me that what I thought my own ideas were injected by her into my subconscious.

After Miss Mills had reported Braïda's opinion, I had a sudden inspiration. Some months previously I had written at great speed a piece of rather lyrical prose poetry which was difficult to classify and which involved a Dualist theme concerned chiefly with the forces of good and evil. It began at the landing stage on Bassenthwaite Lake and ended in an underground room in Florence. There was no real story to it. It resembled two cinema flashes joined together by fragments of dreams and visions. The picture in my mind of the road from the landing stage at Bassenthwaite Lake to the Pheasant Inn was particularly intense. At the time I had raced through this piece I recalled how I felt the presence of my father beside me on the road from the Lake to the Pheasant Inn. My father had been dead fifteen years. To me there is something sacred and crucial about this stretch of road. I did not know that in a few days another would feel the same way about it.

It was curious that two days later I went to visit a sick nurse who worked for a hospital with which I had been connected for thirty-five years. My connection with the hospital was not so close as it had been and I had not seen this nurse more than six times in my life. Towards the end of the interview she told me that she had dreamed about me last night. She had been aware of my presence throughout the night but the only detail she could recall was the phrase, 'Il povero parfait' which kept repeating itself throughout the night. She asked me what it meant. Naturally my mind was concentrated on the Languedoc. I said that *povero* was obviously the French *pauvre* with the 'e' pronounced audibly as is often the case in the Midi. The nurse said that she had no knowledge of French but was insistent that the word was not *pauvre*. I admitted to her that what she had said did not make grammatical sense in French and suggested the phrase was translatable as, 'the poor Parfait.'

I may appear obtuse but I have to admit that it did not occur to me that this phrase was Italian. The *il* was of course the masculine definite article in that language. I did not know if this nurse at this time was picking up fag ends of my Bassenthwaite-Florence vibrations. A month later she said that once again I had disturbed her sleep and that my presence had been accompanied by the word 'Orvieto', repeated several times. This was one of the places written down by Miss Mills on her nocturnal excursions to Italy. This nurse had no knowledge of Italian.

The flashback to Italy is interesting. I never discovered why Miss Mills had, earlier in this history, wandered off in that direction.

Though Miss Mills had desired above all to preserve her anonymity, once she had recovered from the shock of knowing that Jane was aware of Braïda's visits, she was glad to share her secret with her. After all Jane, too, had no desire to impart her experiences to all and sundry. Miss Mills was relieved that she had no longer to be so guarded with her. Jane herself also became more communicative. The next time she rang up she revealed that, in her thirteenth-century incarnation, her husband had been Arnaud Domerq. She recalled also that before she was burned she was 'given something which gave her strength'. She attended a ceremony in which she made a 'kind of general confession'. The Lord's Prayer was repeated in an abbreviated form several times in the service. Like Miss Mills, but independent of her, she insisted that its form was different from our own. Towards the end of the ceremony a book was placed on her head and she was led round the room by someone who took her by the arm. The description of arm rather than hand is interesting. In actual fact women who received the Consolamentum were led by the elbow.

Jane is describing the same ceremony as seen by Miss Mills in her dream. More than that she is dealing with the identical occasion. She said that other people were present at the ceremony. We have said enough previously to know that Esclarmonde de Perella was one. It was obvious that Miss Mills and Jane were well known to each other in their previous incarnation.

At this time I was completely saturated with Catharism. I spent part of my time entering in my journal what was being revealed to me. Braïda told Miss Mills that if I felt any lyrical impulses I should express them directly in poetry as a relaxation from writing this book. I had two or three short bursts in which I produced several poems. I also planned a book on Dualism and medicine. Medicine would not be the fulcrum of this book but would be treated against a Dualist background. As I have said I felt that in these matters I was indebted to Miss Mills' guides.

It was odd that when Jane next rang Miss Mills she had light to throw on my recent intentions. She had been recently visited by the rugger forward. He had told her that very shortly she would read a book which would be of great interest to her. It was inevitable that within a couple of days a friend gave her a copy of my *The Cathars and Reincarnation.* She rang Miss Mills. She told her that I had poetic potentialities and asked why on earth didn't I express them and write a book on medicine with Dualism as its background. In a word she repeated what had come to me through Braïda and Guilhabert de Castres.

Then came what to me was the most important part of the message. Her Parfait told her that what was happening between her, Betty, Miss Mills and me was at the moment happening all over the world but that, if it were not recorded, evidence of it would be lost. This was sheer horse sense. Wherever people are joined together by psychic communication there is a tendency on the part of each group to think of themselves as islands of experience in an ocean of materialistic indifference. The statement that this was happening all over the world, that, in fact, there were many such groups, bore out my own clinical experience over the last ten years or more. This statement of the rugger forward was to me the most invigorating tonic. It confirmed me in my belief that I could not be better occupied than in telling the story of what I had experienced. Jane concluded her telephone call by telling Miss Mills that she was going to Cumberland for a holiday. She was staying at an hotel well known to me. In my home in Somerset I had switched on the television the evening previously and had recognised the view from the hotel window. The programme had nothing to do with the beauties of Cumberland. The appearance of the hotel in it was incidental. After Jane had been a day or two in Cumberland she telephoned Miss Mills. She was now staying at 'The Pheasant' at Bassenthwaite Lake. Of all the hotels in Britain this is my favourite. It has played a great part in my life and has always brought me happiness. The lake itself had returned vividly to memory in recent weeks and had provided a background for one poem, and one item of prose.

Jane told Miss Mills that on the road outside the Inn she had suddenly felt Betty's presence. This was the road I had in mind in my poem which alternated between Bassenthwaite Lake and Florence. It was here I had felt so intensely my father's presence. I said to Miss Mills, 'Did she say it was between the Hotel and the landing stage she felt Betty near her?'

'She certainly mentioned the landing stage.'

Jane told Miss Mills that she felt very much at peace but very tired. She knew that Miss Mills was feeling the same way and it was for this reason she had telephoned. She also knew that Miss Mills was suffering specifically from a pain in the chest. I will describe this in more detail in the next chapter but one. She said that she was convinced that she, Betty, Miss Mills and I had all been very closely connected in a previous incarnation. She and Betty had had a more than mother and daughter relationship. She was not speaking sentimentally or with presumption. She believed they had a very close psychic contact with each other.

23

Three days later Jane rang me for the first time. She was over seventy. She had the light and musical voice of a woman thirty years younger. At one time in the conversation I could hardly believe that I was not talking to Miss Mills. Jane told me later that her daughter Betty had always commented on this resemblance. When I raised the question with Miss Mills she said she had always thought that their voices were similar.

Jane rang because she was worried about Miss Mills. At a distance of three hundred miles she was completely aware of her condition and of the chest pains which I will describe later. For a first telephone conversation we exchanged a good deal of information. I asked her the name of the rugger forward. She said Raymond. I was able to add that his surname was Agulher. She was aware of his capacity as a preacher and debater. I spoke of Miss Mills' night visitor. She seemed surprised that I had not yet been visited by her. I said, 'I suppose she is Braïda de Montserver.'

'But surely,' she answered.

She returned to the question of Miss Mills. She said she was concerned about her because she did so much and seemed so deflated at the moment. She excused herself for ringing me because she felt sure that no one else knew Miss Mills as well as she did. I am sure that she was right, even though over the years they had seen each other no more than once every six months.

I was diffident about asking her where she had first felt Betty's presence so clearly. It was between 'The Pheasant' and the landing stage on Bassenthwaite Lake.

A few days later Miss Mills asked me who I thought Betty had been in her previous life. I told her that when *The Cathars and Reincarnation* was being published someone asked me if I thought reincarnation was the only explanation of the phenomena I had described and whether it could be someone from another century who had been trying to contact Mrs. Smith. I agreed that this was possible but not necessarily an alternative and that clairaudience and other such phenomena were among the mechanisms necessary for far memory. Often from that time I had wondered whether anyone from the thirteenth century had been trying to contact me. Till Braïda appeared on the scene I had from time to time a curious feeling that Hélis de Mazerolles was still close to me. Hélis had been my sister in my thirteenth-century incarnation. I felt that it was possible she had tried to speak to me through Mrs. Smith. I told this to Miss Mills. I said that when people talked of being associated with others in previous incarnations it was almost always a matter of wives and sweethearts. I said that there was no reason why brothers and sisters should not remain in phychic contact with each other over centuries. I pointed out that this was conjecture, complicated by hindsight. In my own mind I still felt that my idea might also include a modicum of intuition.

The night of April 15th/16th I was abominably restless. I started off with a nightmare in which I shrieked so loudly that my wife had to waken me. I cannot remember any details except that there were sounds and shadows below a staircase and that my reaction was to scream the house down. It was not a repetition of the old nightmares I had shared with Mrs. Smith, and in which Pierre de Mazerolles was returning from Avignonet. But if it was not specifically connected with the massacre, it could well be an echo of those agonising years revealed in all the testimonies pouring in on Miss Mills and through her to me. Anyway, I awoke feeling like the wrath of God. I thought I would call on Miss Mills because I owed her a visit, because I wanted to see if she was completely recovered from her recent indisposition and also because, when she is in good form, she is the most bracing company.

That night Miss Mills had fared a little, but not much, better than me. She was obviously putting a good face on things but was evidently tired and had not had a good night. She handed me two sheets of paper without any comment, other than, 'Does this mean anything to you?'

I recognised it immediately. It was the quotation about the immortality of the soul which Betty had found so beautiful that she had telephoned Miss Mills from the Midlands about it. She had done so the day after I had noted the beauty of this passage as a quotation in an enormous tome I was studying at the time. I told Miss Mills what it was. 'I thought so' she said rather listlessly. 'I don't want all this writing to start again'.

'Did you see Braïda too?'

'She's always a comfort. She always makes me peaceful. But the writing is far too tiring.'

'I wonder if Betty is trying to get in touch?'

'That's just what I thought. In any case I dreamed about her.'

'What did you dream?'

'You and she were together in a wood. She was dressed as a Parfaite in a dark blue robe.'

'How do you know it was Betty?'

'It wasn't difficult. It was obviously in another age but there was a good enough general likeness. You were in the wood with her. Your features have not changed much except that your face was thin and your hair was not grey.' It should be remembered that Mrs. Smith, too, recognised my appearance as that of Roger. 'Two things stood out. She was very agitated about something and you were comforting her. Also you were very much younger than she was.'

'And so you think I was comforting a sister much older than me?'

'I don't know enough about it.'

When Hélis made her depositions before the Inquisition in August 1243 she was recalling events as far back as the previous century. She mentioned her brother Roger-Isarn. It is clear that he was much younger than she was. Was I also wearing dark blue in the dream?'

'No, a black cloak. It was not a priest's robe at all.'

'If this was me, it must have been me before I became a Parfait.'

'Do you think it was?'

'It is only a day since I put forward the brother and sister idea to explain the tie-up with Betty. Anybody at all would be justified in saying this was suggestion acting in a dream.'

I returned home and took part in my grand-daughter's birthday celebrations. I was glad of a little ordinary, one-level human activity. I was thoroughly tired. Braïda told Miss Mills that there was nothing more exhausting than moving from one plane of consciousness to another. I had only done so at second hand but nevertheless found the experience fatiguing. However, we were not yet finished. In some ways April 16th was the most crucial day of my life. It was not wildly exciting for the simple reason that I had got beyond any emotional reaction to these experiences. But I did want other people to know the news and had to inhibit myself from talking about my experiences. I had the feeling that nobody had ever been provided with more dramatic evidence. I was past wondering why I had been chosen to take part in such an experience.

Miss Mills rang in the evening. She always rang me immediately anything exciting happened. It enabled her to share what at best was a great experience and at other times a painful burden. Jane who was still on holiday in the North, had phoned to ensure that Miss Mills was completely recovered. We shall see later that more than one person was intensely concerned at this time with Miss Mills' health. The latter was no longer on the defensive when she spoke to Jane. On this occasion she opened the attack. She asked Jane if she knew who Betty had been in her previous incarnation.

'Oh yes,' said Jane. 'She was the daughter of Bec de Tonnens.'

I could hardly believe my ears. We were back with Mrs. Smith with a vengeance. I knew that Hélis and Roger were the descendants of Bec de Tonnens. I could not recall for the moment if the latter was father or grandfather. This was stupid of me because I knew well enough that Guillaume de Durfort was Roger's grandfather. 'Go on,' I said.

'It seemed that Betty ran a house for Cathar women near Fanjeaux. There were several houses like this in the locality. Another was run by Blanche de Laurac. I remember having heard this name before.'

'Mrs. Smith wrote Blanche de Laurac several times on bits of paper and also mentioned her in letters to me.'

'Jane says there were also two women called Feranda and Biona. They were also the heads of these houses for women.'

'I don't know these two from Adam,' I said.

When she had rung off I went to a particularly jumbled and chaotic file. The genealogical tree prepared for me in 1969 by the meticulous Monsieur Duvernoy almost presented itself for my inspection. Bec was my father and Betty's in a previous incarnation. Betty could only be Hélis. I searched absolutely without hope for Feranda and Biona. These turned up with equal ease as Ferranda and Baiona. They were mentioned as heads of Cathar houses along with Blanche de Laurac and Guillelme de Tonnens. The latter was Hélis' grandmother. Hélis herself was not mentioned in this particular reference but I knew from Mrs. Smith's recollection and from other sources that she functioned in this capacity.

We were back once again where I had started. It appeared that I, as Roger-Isarn, bridged the gap between the Fanjeaux and Mazerolles families, celebrated in *The Cathars and Reincarnation*, and the Montserver and Perella clans in Miss Mills' memories. More important was the fact that we had all in this life reincarnated in the same circle and in some cases in the same area. Puerilia had returned as Mrs. Smith, Esclarmonde de Perella as Miss Mills, Hélis as Betty, Jane as Brune and Roger-Isarn as myself. Mrs. Smith, Miss Mills and Betty had been born in this area. Jane and I had lived here for years. It must have been an especially strange experience for Jane to talk over the telephone to the man who had been, in a previous life, the brother of her daughter in the latter's thirteenth-century incarnation. From our first conversation we spoke as though we had known each other for centuries. She told me that in her other life I had had a great influence on her daughter. She said it in level tones as though I had been a private tutor who, in this life, had conscientiously prepared her daughter for an examination.

There are considerable differences between the scenery, climate, flora and fauna of the Languedoc and Somerset but the latter seems to offer a favourable background for the group reincarnation of Cathars.

There was still more to come. Miss Mills had a second call the same evening. This was from Kathleen who had been recently in hospital in the east of England. She had been a schoolfriend of Miss Mills, but they had not seen each other for years. I have to abbreviate her history at this juncture. It is dealt with more fully later. Kathleen rang to say that she was not completely recovered from the anginal condition for which she had been admitted to hospital. She thanked Miss Mills for all she had done for her. What this amounted to, at the conscious level, was that she had rung Miss Mills two or three times and the latter had listened to her with her usual sympathy and attention. 'Anyway, thank you for everything. I don't know how I would have got through without you.'

'But all I did for you was to listen to you on the telephone.'

'Oh nonsense,' said Kathleen. 'You took my pains and well you know it.'

Miss Mills was too flabbergasted to reply. She had never indicated by the slightest nuance that she herself had been under the weather.

'By the way,' continued Kathleen. 'Do you ever hear anything of Betty these days?' They had all been at school together. The school had been in the west of England, in the zone which perhaps one can now describe as impregnated with the vibrations of Catharism.

Miss Mills told her that Betty had died.

'That's odd,' said Kathleen. 'I had an extraordinary dream about her last night. She was in a wood with a man much younger than herself. She was dressed in a funny dark blue robe. She wore a silver chain around her middle with an extraordinary dingle-dangle thing attached to the chain.' This must have been the loop described by Miss Mills as being worn over the left hip. 'It was Betty all right. I could recognise her features. She was obviously terribly upset about something. The man was trying to console her.'

'What was the man like?' said Miss Mills.

'Oh, he was tallish and thin. He had Roman features and he wore a black cloak.' Miss Mills had also described me as tallish but about the same height as in my present incarnation. This is no more than five feet eight inches, but she also made it clear that I was above the average for the thirteenth century. This is in accordance with historical fact. As for thinness, I suppose that, apart from any tendency that way, the chest condition from which I suffered at that time did not allow me to put on much weight.

Miss Mills was always a little disappointed that I had not yet seen Braïda. She often asked if I had felt her presence. I would have been very happy to see Braïda the night of the 16th. She did not come. I cannot believe that anything ever comes if you want it too badly. What I did feel was a strange and tender yearning for Betty. Our only contact was a box of chocolates left for me at Miss Mills' when she could not keep her dinner appointment. Miss Mills described her as one who always gave freely and had a completely open nature. Mrs Smith described Hélis as a sweet natured woman and that without her she would never have supported the death of Roger. It was Hélis who returned to her her will to live.

Miss Mills and Kathleen had identical dreams the same night. At this stage I am disinclined to discuss the processes involved. At the back of my mind there is the industrious gnome who finds it necessary to point out that when Betty was introduced to the Cathar world at seven there were no accessible works in English or French which could have given her the obscure names she wrote in her drawing books. People like Schmidt and Lea in the nineteenth and beginning of the twentieth century did not quote such names as Congost, Camplong, etc. These were still locked up in legalistic latin in the inquisitorial records. The whole experience has become so oceanic that I can now do little more than record it. To discuss its detailed mechanism is like refusing to look at Niagara until you have calculated the amount of energy embodied in a single jet of spray.

Five weeks later Jane rang Miss Mills to say that, in her final clearance of Betty's effects, she had discovered another sketch book with drawings and accompanying names. One drawing was headed Monréal 1204 and showed two of her stylised and insect-like men in blue. The two names Coldesi and Guirau were written beneath them. In a second drawing it was obviously women who were being depicted, because long skirts were appended to the stylised figures. Underneath were written the names Ermengarde and Berengaria. The third drawing repeated the heading Monréal. The list of names following was Pateria, Dulcia, Sornia, Guiraude and Pontia.

I felt certain that these names referred to the Cathar homes for women in the neighbourhood of Montréal. The individual names were so unfamiliar that I thought it impossible that I could verify them. I was as usual guided to the references. There are some slight differences in Betty's spelling, for example Coldesi is really Coldefi, and Pontia should read Poncia. These details are unimportant. What matters is that these names coincide with those made in the appropriate deposition in the Doat collection in the Bibliothêque Nationale in Paris. The deposition says that Bernard Coldefi and Arnaud Guiraud lived at Montréal and that the above named women came to their meetings. This was described as happening in 1204. Betty at seven, in bed with scarlet fever in her home in England, was unable to read the mediaeval Latin in the Bibliothêque Nationale in Paris.

It is interesting that three of the seven women named were widows. One of Mrs. Smith's most vivid recollections is of the number of widows in the house of heretics in which she lived after the death of Roger. Mrs. Smith, as Puerilia, regained her desire to live with the help of Hélis de Mazerolles. From the latter's deposition made in 1243 it is clear that her devotion to Catharism dated from the previous century. I have no doubt whatever that, when Betty as a child of seven, was drawing in her home in the Midlands in the early nineteen-thirties, she was recalling the days when, as Hélis de Mazerolles, she was in charge of the Cathar convent.

Jane had still another contribution to make to our story. Her belief in, and her affiliations with, Dualism had begun when she was in her twenties. She had never studied the history of Catharism nor had she been concerned with its philosophy. She could not support books of a metaphysical flavour. What she knew had been revealed to her and when she read she did so for entertainment. It was amusing that she shared Miss Mills' and my own drug addiction for John Buchan. She recalled by far memory several of the main characters in my story. She knew beyond doubt that her daughter Betty had been Hélis de Mazerolles. When she said that she and Betty had a deeper relationship than that usual between mother and daughter she was speaking the literal truth and without sentimentality. She was a forthright and direct woman with great common sense and no special capacity to suffer fools gladly. Her special link with Betty was due to the fact that she had been Bruna and Betty Hélis and that they had known each other at Montségur and elsewhere. She was also certain that Miss Mills had been Esclarmonde de Perella.

In my conversations with Jane I never fed her with suppositions as to the identity of my characters. I waited for her to produce her evidence. In everything that concerned the main personages in my story it was always identical with my own.

She spoke often of Miss Mills' father. She was greatly attached to him and described him as a wonderful man. She had seen little of him for many years preceding his death and her assessment of him, as far as this world was concerned, was based on their meetings when Betty and Miss Mills were at school together. When I asked her, with a calculated absence of pressure, whether she thought he had been anybody in particular in a previous incarnation, she said in her cool and detached way that there was not the slightest doubt that he had been Bertrand Marty and it was clear that she had recognised him as such. As she knew Hélis, Esclarmonde, Arnaud Domerq and others connected with Montségur we should accept her testimony that she knew one who was its presiding bishop in its ultimate agony. We should treat her statements with respect all the more so because there is another witness, as yet uncalled, who is able to support her evidence.

24

During the period in which Miss Mills was resuming, after centuries, direct contact with Jane, her psyche was stirred in another direction. At this time she was remarkably fit. She had been both relaxed and fortified by contact with Braïda. These shifts of consciousness from world to world can be excessively exhausting. Despite the fact she was working hard, extending her knowledge of healing in the small hours, and opening her soul to Jane, she was remarkably well and relaxed. She was then suddenly inundated by calls made on her by people in distress. Some of the latter were also living partly out of time. They were almost more than she could manage.

It began with Penelope. She was Miss Mills' own age, about the middle forties. Years ago, they had been business associates. Miss Mills had not seen her for about ten years. She knew that she had been ill for a year with cancer. After the middle of March she received a letter from Penelope saying how much she would love a visit. Miss Mills said she wished she could take time off to see Penelope. This was impracticable. Penelope lived about a hundred miles away. Miss Mills made some commonplace remark to the effect that it was a pity we had not time to see everybody who would like a visit from us, but that was life and there wasn't very much we could do about it.

Towards the end of March Miss Mills looked in to see me early one evening. We were talking about nothing in particular, when all of a sudden she 'went away'. I can think of no better description. One moment she was talking to me with animation and eyes sparkling. In an instant the light was extinguished in her eyes as if by a switch. Her face was frozen immobile. The whole thing happened with the suddenness of a *petit mal* but there was no interruption of consciousness and no movement of the eyes, and she conversed with me, tersely, reluctantly but very much to the point. 'What's the matter with you?' I said. 'You have gone off somewhere.'

'No,' she said, 'it's just nothing at all.'

'It very obviously is.'

'Something is happening to somebody.' She spoke in a low voice but her face had come to life and wore an expression of abject misery.

'Some kind of premonition?'

'Yes, but something is happening. I hope it's not too bad.'

'Everybody gets premonitions. You cannot tell me that every one you have had has come true.'

'No' she said. 'But I wish I knew what was happening.'

She left shortly afterwards. Her smile was as wide as ever but obviously determined and her breeziness was equally fabricated.

She rang a couple of hours later. She was restrained and apologetic. 'I am sorry to bother you with a phone call and I hope you don't think I am doing it just to justify myself. I must have been awfully offhand when I left. Penelope's husband has just phoned to say Penelope died this evening.'

'About what time?'

'Six-thirty.'

'So that was it.'

'Yes.'

'There are other things which he said which would interest you. Just before she died she uttered the word Brasiac. This was the last thing she said. Does it mean anything to you?' Her voice was flat and listless. It was obvious that she had no emotion except grief for her friend. In giving me this information, she was doing what she thought a necessary chore.

Even at this juncture in the story of my contact with the Cathars I was completely astounded. Brasiac was the phonetic pronunciation of Brasillac. The latter was another sergeant-at-arms. He had fought at the siege of Montségur and had opted to go to the stake with the Parfaits. He had also been implicated in the affair at Avignonent. 'This beats anything I've heard,' I said.

'Jack (Penelope's husband) told me that before she died she was almost transfigured. He said she was utterly serene and he could not really describe what it was like. He was sure she suffered no pain. He said something extraordinary, he said it was as if she were returning to someone she had greatly loved, as if she knew for certain where she was going. He said that what happened to her in the last days before death was so extraordinary that it removed from him all fears of dying. She had seemed so radiantly happy that he could no longer feel that it had been a tragedy for her. They were a completely devoted couple, but he said that after the peace and joy she had obtained in the last weeks, the only person he could be sorry for was himself.'

'Why did he get in touch with you?' I asked.

'Well, we were friends.'

'How many years was it since you had seen her?'

'Oh, about ten.'

'Did you write or phone often?'

'No. It was the kind of friendship where you meet after years and take on where you left off. And there was another thing. It seems that in the last two weeks of her life she was always talking about me.'

'I expect that's why her husband rang you so soon, even though you hadn't seen her for years.'

'I expect so,' she said.

But it wasn't the sole reason. Just before the Easter holidays she received a letter from Penelope's husband, repeating what he had said over the phone and saying that he felt he must see her because he was sure there were things she could tell him. She hesitated a day or two before replying. She was again harassed by the question 'How much do I want people to know about me? I can't have a past life interfering with my present career.'

Finally, when she settled down to write the letter, she found she had mislaid his. As Braïda said later, there is a pattern in these things. Had Miss Mills answered the letter immediately, in her usual conscientious way, Jack would not have appeared in person.

Miss Mills told him there were things she herself remembered about the thirteenth century. She did not admit to Braïda's visit but said enough to indicate that she had far memory. She did this because it was consoling to him to know that she was on the same wave-length as Penelope. He told her that he had found among his wife's effects some pieces of paper with a few words written on them. First there were the names Pons Narbona, Arnaud Domerq and Brasillac. We are back among the sergeant-at-arms who opted to die with the Cathars. On another piece of paper she had written, 'For all the sins we have committed, or said, or thought, or aided we ask forgiveness of God, of the Church and of you all.' This was the last statement made by the croyant before he received the Consolamentum. After this his head was touched by a copy of the Gospels and the company repeated the Latin passage beginning, *Pater Sancti suscipe servum tuum in tua justitia,* an item recorded several months previously in one of Miss Mills' messages from Braïda or her colleagues.

There cannot be any doubt that once again we are listening to the celebration of the Consolamentum in the last days of Montségur. It was transmitted by Braïda to Miss Mills in 1971. It recurs in the life of another in the early spring of 1972. These memories were recalled in the last three months of Penelope's life.

Jack said that for years Penelope had dreamt of a castle on a hill and of men in blue robes who lived there. All her life she had been afraid of fire. Was it that she too was burnt? It is reasonable to suppose that she was the wife or sweetheart of Brasillac. There is no record, as in the case of Pons Narbona and Arnaud Domerq, of his wife having died with him. What was more significant was Penelope's irrational dread of stones being thrown at her. Her husband indicated that at times this bordered on absurdity. If she went down the road she was often afraid, without the ghost of a reason, that some child might throw a stone in her direction. This, in itself, would have been no great calamity, but the possibility of it was enough to touch off at some level of consciousness the horror of the great stones hurled at Montségur by the trebuchet and the mangonneau so vividly described by Miss Mills.

Her husband said that Penelope had always believed in reincarnation. He himself had had an open mind but was now as convinced as she had been.

Before he left, Miss Mills suggested that he should visit me. She said that I knew a certain amount about the thirteenth-century Languedoc. He refused the offer and indicated that what he had said was for her ears alone. By the time he had driven home he had changed his mind. He expressed no wish to see me but said that if anything he had told Miss Mills would help to enlighten others I was at liberty to use the evidence he had given, provided I did not reveal his or Penelope's identity.

With Penelope we are once again with the sergeants-at-arms. We are with them in their last moments when they are receiving the Consolamentum. I noted that in Penelope's recollections there was no direct reference to Avignonet. She mentioned Pons Narbona, Arnaud Domerq and Brasillac. The former was certainly at Avignonet. Arnaud Domerq is mentioned by one authority and not another. Brasillac is also described as one of the conspirators. It would seem that Penelope only remembered her old acquaintances in their more inspired moments.

After ten days Jack paid another visit. Miss Mills was not sure whether he had business in the locality or whether he wished to unburden himself further. He produced three sheets of paper on which Penelope had written in the last three weeks of her life. The names written on the first sheet were as follows:

Antiock—Trees
Avigney—Blood
Alfari—?? Magistrate

At this stage these names are easy to translate. Antiock and Avigney are phonetic renderings of the wood called Antioch, and Avignonet. So, after, all, we return once more to the massacre of the Inquisitors. Antioch was the name of the wood where the bands of conspirators converged. Avigney—Blood, refers clearly to the massacre. Alfari should be d'Alfaro. The latter was the *viguier* of the Count of Toulouse. Magistrate is a good enough description of this office. The Inquisitors were lodged in d'Alfaro's house and it was with his connivance that they were massacred.

On the next sheet the names Marciano and Lille were bracketed together, with the word Breastplates written opposite. Lille is an elided phonetic description of our old friend Guillaume de l'Isle, who appeared several times in Miss Mills' writings. Once again this is how the name would be taken down in a state of clairaudience. Marciano was a new name to me. I discovered that it referred to Raymond de Marciliano. Is there any significance in the appearance of a new character at this stage in the proceedings?

Raymond de Marciliano and Guillaume de l'Isle are bracketed together as wearing breastplates. They are presumably in action. We are further enlightened by the names appearing on the third sheet of paper. This list is headed by Penelope's Brasillac. I find that Brasillac, together with Raymond de Marciliano and Guillaume de l'Isle, were among the defenders of the east tower of Montségur at the moment when the knight Jordan de Mas was mortally wounded. They clustered round him while the dying man received the Consolamentum. We have had descriptions of the siege from Miss Mills and Jane. The former recalled the horror of the casualties sustained in the attempts to retake the barbican. The east tower was the part of the main building nearest to it. It is fascinating that, in our memories of Montségur, we can recall after seven centuries not only the names of its obscure defendants but the part of the fortress in which they fought.

As well as Brasillac the third sheet of paper contained the names of Bruna, Arnalde, Pons, Rege, and Belvise. Bruna is the occitan version of Brune, the wife of Arnaud Domerq in the thirteenth century and the mother of Betty in this. Arnalde is another rendering of the name Arnaud, which would be Arnold in English. Pons is obviously Pons de Narbona, the sergeant-at-arms we have met on other occasions.

Who are Rege and Belvise? I found both names in the list of those who were burnt at Montségur. The latter was a cross-bowman from the Château d'Usson.

Finally, like Miss Mills, like my hostess at Montségur, Penelope had been given a list of Biblical references. As in the case of the other two participants in the chain of communication, there was a marked preponderance of citations from John and Corinthians I.

On April 29th Jack rang Miss Mills again to say that, on completing the sorting of Penelope's effects he had found a small notebook. It was filled with names of people, authors and book titles, and of poems or isolated verses. It was clear that Penelope had recorded items of literature which she loved and which seemed of great importance to her. But this may not be the sole explanation for the existence of this notebook.

Kipling's *Hymn to Mithras* was written out in full. Two or three days previously Jane had asked me, in the course of a telephone call, whether I knew this poem. I have always adored it. The significance of this reference is that the cult of Mithras was unmistakably Dualist. Mithras also occurs in one of Miss Mills' dictated messages. There were other Dualist references including Zarathrustra, an alternative name for Zoroaster, the founder of Persian Dualism, and the *Golden Verses* of Pythagoras. As with Miss Mills, Plato and Epictetus were included in her list of authors.

There was another Kipling poem in Penelope's list. *The Sack of the Gods* is a clear statement of belief in reincarnation.

The question arises as to how many of these references were dictated. We have seen that she had noted Biblical references similar to those recorded by Miss Mills. At the same time it is unlikely that she would be directed, by discarnate entities from the thirteenth century, to copy down a whole poem by a modern author. It is quite impossible to say how much in these writings was dictated by her own tastes and how much was specifically directed. One can say with certainty that some of it was a product of far memory, clairaudience or discarnate guidance. From what Miss Mills told me of Penelope she would not have been naturally inclined to the study of such writers as Pythagoras and Epictetus. What is absolutely certain is that some proportion of Penelope's notebook was of psychic origin. Among the names she recorded were Amiel Aicart, Clamens, St. Martin and Taparelle. The three first names we have already encountered in the disposal of the Montségur treasure. (The full name of the third individual is obviously Raymond de St. Martin.) I discovered that these four Cathars gave a present of money, in the form of deniers wrapped up in a blanket, to Pierre-Roger de Mirepoix, in gratitude for his efforts to defend them. Penelope had previously redirected us to the Avignonet affair. In her latest communication she points to two other of the main themes which traverse this book, the disposal of the Cathar treasure and the siege of Montségur.

The story was not yet complete. I had wondered if Jack himself had far memory but had thought it safer to assume that what he knew he had acquired from Penelope by telepathy. Two months later he rang Miss Mills early on a Sunday morning. He told her that he was suffering from an intestinal cancer and was going into hospital that day for an operation. He said that it was absolutely necessary for him to tell her of two dreams he had had repeatedly during the last two months. In one he saw a peculiar kissing ceremony at which men and women in dark blue robes were present. The people in dark blue wore the distinctive girdles and belts described previously by Miss Mills. All the men present at the ceremony kissed each other. The women did likewise but there was no kissing between the sexes. He remembered also fragments of prayers, particularly the beautiful passage Miss Mills found written on her appointment pad and which runs, 'We are not of this world and this world is not of us'. Here was another who remembered the last Consolamentum.

He went on to say that in his second dream he saw the fighting in the castle on the hill. There were many wounded and he was among them. Lotions were applied to his wounds and he was also given medicines to drink. Among the women who looked after the wounded there was one he would always remember. It was for this reason that he had rung her this morning. As he was going into hospital it was necessary for him to put himself in her hands as he had done in the thirteenth century.

In the last few weeks he had heard repeatedly certain names. The one which struck him most was Tournabois. This was the name of another sergeant-at-arms. Raymond de Tournabois died at Montségur with his comrades Pons Narbona, Arnaud Domerq and Brasillac.

At this stage Miss Mills was talking freely of her memories of those days. She had forgotten her desire to conceal her gifts and was only concerned with a sick and bereaved man awaiting an operation. He told her simply and frankly that in the last few weeks he had felt himself helped enormously by some presence about him. Miss Mills said that for a man who had recently lost his wife and was now afflicted with cancer his fortitude was amazing. She asked him if he had any feeling that Penelope was still near him. He said, 'Quite frankly, no,' but that he certainly felt some presence and that its influence was enormously fortifying.

She then asked him if he had any recollection of having known Penelope in a previous life. He said that he remembered clearly a girl who was thin, dark and with aquiline features. She did not at all resemble Penelope who was fair, fresh-complexioned and buxom. He knew that he had lived with this girl but felt convinced that they had not been married. In the last few weeks her name had kept repeating itself in his mind. It sounded something like Silla.

I think this rounds off perfectly the story of Penelope and Jack, or, in another age, of Brasillac and his sweetheart. I do not think there is any doubt that in speaking of Jack we are dealing with Brasillac. Once again, in the former's telephone call before his admission to hospital, we are back at the last Consolamentum at Montségur. Was the mysterious Silla Penelope in a previous incarnation? I do not think there is much doubt of it. We have evidence of a group of people known to each other in the thirteenth century and who reincarnated in the twentieth. We know that Penelope belonged to that group. The last word she uttered was Brasillac. She mentioned this name only once. I have described the peace she achieved at the end of her life and how its radiation was transferred to Jack. It seems to me that, in the last moments together in this life, they recognised each other for what they had been in a former.

Can we do anything to identify Silla? So far my efforts to trace her have failed. Of course there was Cecilia de Montserver who was married to Arnaud Roger de Mirepoix but we have no evidence she was separated from her husband. It is recognised that a number of the garrison at Montségur had their girl friends with them, a fact which is disquieting for those to whom Catharism is a puritanical creed. From the records it would appear that Brasillac was unmarried. We cannot say whether or no Silla died at the stake but then, of the two hundred who perished there, history only records the names of twenty-nine. Of these eight belonged to our group, if we are allowed to include husbands and spiritual advisers. It is really not a bad proportion.

What is the meaning of these side channels of communications? Have the contributions of Betty, her mother Jane, Penelope and Jack anything special to offer? What stands out a mile is that a group of people who lived together seven hundred years ago and who shared a common cause have reincarnated in present-day England and have re-established contact with each other. What is crystal clear is that all, in their different ways, are tuning in to the same events. The first of these is the massacre of Avignonet. For years my slumbers were disturbed by it. If Miss Mills' recollections did not refer directly to Avignonet itself she wrote down the names of several who had taken part in it. Judging from her drawings the massacre was reverberating in Betty's mind as a child of seven. The memory of it returned to Penelope in the course of her mortal illness. But, however strong the chord struck by Avignonet, it does not echo in memory with such intensity as the last Consolamentum at Montségur. Miss Mills returns to it repeatedly, Jane remembers being given strength by it, and Penelope recalls it as clearly as Miss Mills. The two latter can repeat details of the service of the Consolamentum.

Is it surprising that Betty, who knew so much at seven and who later expanded her knowledge, should not also have recalled the celebration of the Consolamentum when Montségur was in its death agonies? After all, a number of the persons she mentioned were members of the garrison who took part in the massacre and returned to fight at Montségur. There is an obvious reason for this omission. Betty, as Hélis de Mazerolles, was not at Montségur during the siege. She was interrogated by the Inquisition in the August of the previous year. We do not know what judgment was passed on her. Certainly she was not burnt at Montségur or present in the last months of the siege. Had she been it is inconceivable that a person of such importance, the head of one of the Cathar houses for women, would not have been mentioned in the records.

In a way the sergeants-at-arms seem the heart and centre of this group which reincarnated seven centuries later in England. Miss Mills is constantly producing their names. Jane had married one and died with him seven centuries previously. In 1972 Penelope died with the name of still another on her lips. It is easy now to understand my emotion when I first read of these men preferring death with the Cathars to quitting the fortress as free men. There was no question that those among them who had taken part in the affair at Avignonet might as well die at the stake because the authorities would seize them later. The terms of the truce of Montségur involved a free pardon for all implicated in the massacre. Remarkably enough this article was observed.

At this stage in the proceedings one ceases to ask oneself how all this came about. I cannot explain the mechanics of group reincarnation. All I know is that it occurs. What I also know, which is of still greater value, is that when one has been engulfed by revealed truth one has less interest in its mechanisms. One is more concerned that others like-minded should hear the story and should be confirmed in convictions they have often maintained in loneliness and isolation.

25

Miss Mills had been so fit and so calm and peaceful that it was a little disappointing to find her looking pale and tired. She confessed to being completely exhausted. This, in itself, was quite out of keeping with her 'press on regardless' attitude to life. On April 6th she complained of pain at the left border of the breast bone and extending to the region of the heart. The pain radiated towards the left shoulder. At first it appeared with undue exertion. It was particularly noticeable when she climbed upstairs or carried a heavy basket. There could be no doubt whatever that this was a coronary pain. Certainly it did not amount to a thrombosis but it clearly involved a spasm of the coronary arteries. The condition is commonly called angina pectoris.

At first I was not unduly worried. Though she looked tired at the moment she was normally the picture of health. Of course these days one hears so often of coronary disturbance in people in their forties but really she was not this type, and in any case women are less prone than men to these conditions. Also the term pseudo-angina has been used for years for vague pains of coronary distribution occurring against a background of tension and not to be regarded too seriously. I could only hope that Miss Mills' symptoms were of this nature. Certainly she was going through an exhausting experience. Two days previously she had seen Penelope's husband. She was also in regular communication with Betty's mother. As Braïda had said, shuttling between worlds is a wearying experience. Taking into account that in the last two years she had been used as every kind of instrument of communication between this world and the next, it is not surprising that she should produce a few symptoms.

Miss Mills' pain in the chest became constant for two days. It was intensified and accompanied by breathlessness when she climbed the stairs. I began to feel less happy about her. I said that she should go to her doctor who would surely arrange for an electro-cardiogram. She turned down my suggestions with a bang. She said she had more faith in Braïda and me than anyone. I knew her own doctor and one could not find a kinder or more competent fellow anywhere. I found her condition a little disturbing. I did not like the persistence of the pain. These days there were so many cardiovascular catastrophies which came out of a clear sky to so many unlikely people. I consoled myself with the thought that she was possibly picking up someone's symptoms. She had registered Penelope's death immediately across a distance of a hundred miles. Nevertheless it was a little disquieting.

I gave her some treatment according to the methods described by Braïda. She said she felt less tired and that the pain was less, but it had not disappeared and was still accentuated when she went upstairs. Then she told me that Braïda had sent a message through her for me. She was to ask me whether I now understood the fusion of psyches. I affected to understand but in actual fact I did not translate the message correctly. I was flooded with all sorts of disquieting ideas. Was she going to follow my example and have a coronary? Would she emulate Betty in having a cardiovascular catastrophe at an early age? I was not at all happy and wondered if Braïda was preparing me for something. The mystery was solved the same evening. Miss Mills had a telephone call from Kathleen, a friend in the east of England who had been at school with her thirty years previously. They had not seen each other for ten years. Kathleen was in hospital suffering from coronary spasm. She had felt that she simply had to telephone Miss Mills. From that moment I felt relieved. Miss Mills still had to endure a few more days of pain but I knew she was past the worst.

Three days later, on April 12th, Miss Mills received another call from Kathleen. The latter was much better and had returned home from hospital. She had been given some green tablets to dissolve under her tongue if she had a pain. She had not needed any since the previous Saturday. It was on that day, April 8th, that Miss Mills' pain, which had grumbled below the surface for a couple of days, had first intensified. Miss Mills was not wildly surprised. She accepted that she could take other people's symptoms. What she found fantastic was that Kathleen began suddenly to talk about forces of good and evil. These had been in the world from the beginning and life was a varying balance between them. In the past, for the most part, evil had triumphed. It was possible that in the future the situation could be reversed.

In this matter of Dualism Miss Mills had recently become less passive. She took care not to mention the word Catharism but asked Kathleen if she had ever read any French mediaeval history. She said vaguely that a lot of people at that time were interested in the struggle between the forces of good and evil. Kathleen's reply was seemingly irrelevant but very significant. She said that she had read no French mediaeval history but that she had been to Foix ten years ago. She had been fascinated by it. She felt that it was completely familiar and that she had lived there before. 'That was why I was so thrilled to get your card from Foix two years ago.'

'But doesn't this mean that you believe in reincarnation?'

'Good heavens, yes,' said Kathleen.

This was the night on which Jane, Betty's mother, rang me for the first time because she was worried about Miss Mills. She herself admitted to a frightful cold. I think she was suffering from being on the same wavelength as Miss Mills. I told her the present situation and that Miss Mills seemed better.

That evening Miss Mills had catarrh of the nose and throat and felt she had a cold coming. As I have said before this was a rare condition with her.

Next day Jane rang me again. She was very apologetic. She said that it was merely that she had been so worried about Miss Mills but was now completely satisfied that she was better. Her cold had entirely cleared up. She excused herself for ringing by repeating that she felt sure than no one in the world knew Miss Mills as well as she did. I am sure she was right.

Miss Mills' cold had disappeared overnight.

Next day Kathleen rang Miss Mills about Betty. In the last twenty-four hours she had been thinking a great deal about her. She said that even as a schoolgirl she felt that Betty was unique. She was sure that even then she emanated peace. Kathleen said to Miss Mills, 'You could take my headaches away but she radiated peace.' She said also that she had only met Betty's mother twice but that she felt that she had known her all her life. She reacted to Jane the same way as I did.

Nearly three weeks later I told Miss Mills that I felt intuitively that Kathleen had more to tell us. I added that for some reason I felt that she was an approachable person and that one could ask her questions. I had never met her, spoken with her by phone, or received a letter from her. Nevertheless I added that I saw no reason to abandon the passivity I had hitherto practised. I had gone on the principle that if people had anything to tell me they would do so in due course and I had no intention of changing my habits.

Next day Kathleen appeared completely unheralded and visited Miss Mills. In the course of their conversation she referred again to her dream of seeing Betty in her dark blue robes. She also mentioned that for some time she had had dreams of people similarly attired. Miss Mills told Kathleen that she should contact me because I knew more than she did of the period involved.

The day after I was told that I was wanted on the phone. The name of the caller meant nothing to me. I did not know Kathleen's surname. When I picked up the receiver her voice was identical with that of Jane. It was light toned but deep and had exactly the same musical quality. My wife, who answered the phone, was also under the impression that it was Jane. It was Kathleen speaking. She was gentle, unassertive and very calm. She spoke of her recent illness and asked if it were possible to be cured by other people taking one's symptoms. I said I believed this to be true. She then disclosed that she had read most of my books. What was more significant was that she had discovered that I was the author of *Silent Union*. I had published this book under a pseudonym.

I asked if there was anything she wished particularly to discuss. She asked me if the name Laureta meant anything to me. I told her simply that she was a person whose name appeared in a deposition made before the Inquisition. I said that if I remembered rightly she was in some way associated with Guillaume de l'Isle. Without my notes I could not be more specific than this. She commented immediately, 'She was his mother.' It is almost superfluous to say that she was correct.

It appeared that these two names kept repeating themselves in her mind. The name Fanjeaux also forced itself continually on her attention. She had never been there and knew nothing of its history. The name Fanjeaux was accompanied by visions of what she called medallions decorated by crosses like little t's. These were the Tau crosses described by Miss Mills and worn by Braïda and those Parfaites who specialised in healing. Kathleen had no book knowledge of Catharism. She asked me if the Cathars had anything to do with healing.

She dreamt repeatedly of men in blue robes. All her life she had had a recurrent dream of being shut up in a small, dark space. Of itself a dream like this is of no special significance, but in view of what we already know of our other characters I wonder if she was recalling being imprisoned. She had always been afraid of fire.

Her most astonishing statement was her suddenly expressed conviction that Miss Mills had had 'a lot to do with Bertrand Marty'.

Kathleen was surely another link in our chain of Cathars. I thought this not necessarily because of her specific memories but because she fitted so neatly into the general pattern. In addition her symptoms had been removed by Miss Mills. This was another example of Braïda's statement that those who had known each other in previous incarnations and who have remained in psychic contact are able to cure each other's physical illnesses.

But who was she? I felt we would hear more from her but I did not hope that here was another we would be able to identify. She felt very close to Miss Mills, Betty and Jane, in spite of the fact that she had seen little of any of them for years and had only met Jane twice in her life. She also felt she had known me for years. A couple of years back I would have regarded this remark as of no significance and possibly as an irritant. Now I assess such statements in relation to those who utter them. I felt that Kathleen was another member of a circle closely connected in the thirteenth century and resuming contact in this. It was too much to hope we could put a name to her.

At this time my sense of time was dislocated. So much was pouring through from my secondary sources as well as from Miss Mills and Braïda. When I received a telephone call from Kathleen on May 28th it seemed an epoch since I had heard from her. On this occasion her voice was weaker and more distant. It is a strange thing to feel the moods and to estimate the character of a person you have never met, in the sense in which the world understands meeting. I felt her to be open hearted, generous and candid, but that a certain diffidence was imposed on her by a secret life she could not share with others. I felt that she was low and depressed. This was revealed by her voice. She herself was uncomplaining and not preoccupied with herself. She never referred to her previous illness except to express her gratitude to Miss Mills for what she had done for her.

I could not be sure of her exact motive for this call. I had now enough experience, from Mrs. Smith, Miss Mills and Jane, to know that people of this type, however honest and conscientious, can only impart in a fragmentary fashion the items of a secret life which has been previously known to them alone. She began by asking about Jane who was ill at that time. She knew that Miss Mills had had news of her. She repeated emphatically and sadly how close she felt to Jane. Even at this stage in the proceedings I translated this in general terms. I thought she implied how much they were on the same wavelength in this life. I did not tumble to it that their closeness to each other was of longer duration.

Kathleen then asked me if anything particular had happened today. I asked her why she wished to know. She did not say she felt awful. In our conversations she referred remarkably little to herself or her feelings. She merely repeated that she felt that something of importance had happened on this day. It was obvious that the event had been of tragic significance to her. I told her that it was the anniversary of the massacre of the Inquisitors at Avignonet. She did not seem at all surprised. Because I thought she was depressed I changed the conversation. In these matters I was now less than formerly the silent recorder. I asked her if she had been bombarded by any names other than the two she had mentioned formerly. She answered slowly but without perceptible tension and I felt she was prepared to confide in me. She said, 'Yes. A funny name like Bruna. It always makes me think of a bear. Does this mean anything to you?'

'Yes. She was the wife of a sergeant-at-arms. She was burnt with her husband at Montségur.' I paused a little before my next question. I was still afraid of a too positive approach. 'Have you any idea what your own name was on your last appearance?'

'Yes. I can't be accurate. It was something like Sendis. There was something else at the beginning.'

I had always known that the night when Miss Mills wrote Brunasendis on a scrap of paper was one of the peaks of my experience. At that time I had been deeply moved and excited by it. Even now it was difficult to control my feelings. 'Your name was Arsendis. You were burnt with Bruna at Montségur.'

'How did you find out?'

'Your name was written together with Bruna's on a scrap of paper. It came out as Brunasendis.'

'Where did you get the piece of paper?' I had not imagined that Kathleen would be capable of such a direct question, but when you are reliving your own death it tends to sharpen your manner.

My tension was rising and I burbled inadequately, 'It was found by a woman by her bedside—'

'Clare?' she said sharply. (This is Miss Mill's Christian name.)

'No,' I spoke in firm tones but I cannot think I sounded convincing. For a moment I was feeble and vacillating. I felt completely inadequate. I was experiencing the same emotions as Miss Mills when Jane had said to her sharply, 'Come off it. I know for a fact that you have been visited by Braïda.' I hesitated and plunged. 'Look,' I said. 'It's just no good. You're right—it was Clare. But you mustn't say a word to a soul. She just can't stomach people in her job knowing how she's made and what happens to her.'

'I won't say a word.' She spoke very gently. I think she felt that my request was superfluous.

'And of course you know who Bruna was,' I said.

'Jane.' It was characteristic of Kathleen that she made no further comment on why she felt so close to Jane. She was not the type to say, 'We died together and that is why I feel close to her.' She said later in our conversations that words were not important in deep communication. 'Who was Betty?' she continued.

'Beyond doubt Hélis de Mazerolles, my sister in the thirteenth century. You dreamt about us both.'

'And Clare?' '

'Esclarmonde de Perella. Her father was the owner of Montségur. How long has this been coming back to you?'

'A bit more than six months,' she said.

I knew she had more to say and that she did not consider this was the moment to say it. When she had rung off I felt worried and self-accusing. I had broken my word to Miss Mills. I had told her previously that I was sure that Kathleen knew already a good deal about her. These reassurances addressed to myself did not comfort me in the slightest. When I give my word I am rigid, unimaginative and literal minded. I had broken a promise and had to meet Miss Mills later that day. When I told her she took it well enough but it was obvious she was far from happy about it. 'It's a bit of a shock, that's all.' She changed the conversation and commented on environmental details with enforced cheerfulness.

She rang me later that evening. She was breathlessly and unreservedly happy. She said, 'I can't thank you enough for telling Kathleen. She's just rung me up. It is such a relief to be able to talk freely without checking one's words. And she really let her hair down. I can't tell you how happy it made me.'

I suppose it is a unique joy when two people who have known each other in a previous incarnation admit for the first time their previous connection. I could not raise this question because Miss Mills was borne along by a positive tornado of explanation. She gave me a full account of her talk with Kathleen. She was happy to discover a third person who felt so depressed that she had to drag herself through the first half of March. Reassured by the fact that there were others who remembered their life in the thirteenth century Kathleen had gone into greater detail. She mentioned the majority of the sergeants-at-arms whose names have come down to us as dying with the Cathars at Montségur. Her own husband, Pons de Narbona, was among this number. She mentioned also Jane's husband Arnaud de Domerq and Brasillac whose name was the last word uttered by Penelope. She recalled also Raimon de Tournabois and Raimon de Marciliano. What was more striking was that, like Miss Mills, Jane and Penelope, she returned to the last celebration of the Consolamentum at Montségur. She bore out what I had thought previously, that in this narrative all roads lead to the massacre at Avignonet and to the last Consolamentum. Betty alone did not recall the latter ceremony because, as Hélis, she had already been apprehended before 1244. Kathleen described in full detail the ritual of the Consolamentum, the white cloth and the book on the table, the words uttered, the perambulation round the room guided by the Parfait, and the ritual kissing between members of her own sex. She stressed particularly the care with which the Parfait and the recipient washed their hands before the ceremony. She said that when she herself was in her teens she passed through a phase in which she could not stop washing her hands. Miss Mills told me that she herself had manifested a similar ritual at the same age. I need hardly say I was also similarly afflicted. The reader will be familiar with some of the Freudian explanations for the handwashing ritual. It is not easy to explain, on Freudian lines, why this should occur in two people with conscious memory of their lives in the thirteenth century and in a third, myself, who beyond doubt lived at the same time. Phenomena such as these not only prove that obsessional symptoms can have their origin in a previous life. They reveal also that in two persons the same ritual is traceable, after seven centuries, to the same strictly localised set of circumstances.

What was most fascinating of all was that Kathleen remembered that she was among the last to receive the Consolamentum. Perhaps the wives of the two sergeants-at-arms were considered as a separate group and received the sacrament close after each other. In any case, we have enough evidence already to see why Kathleen and Jane were so close to each other and why the former reacted so intensely when the latter was ill. It constituted some kind of bond when you spend your last hours together before being burned alive.

Kathleen remembered an older woman who received the Consolamentum. It may be remembered that Jane recalled that she and Kathleen were quite young when they died at the stake as Bruna and Arsendis. Kathleen said that the older woman had something to do with Lavelanet. She is identifiable as Guilhelma, wife of Berenger de Lavelanet.

Kathleen recalled also a young girl with fair hair and blue eyes who was very active at the siege of Montségur in caring for the wounded and comforting everybody. She recognised this girl as Miss Mills in a previous incarnation. She said that the colour of her hair and complexion were the same in this life as in the thirteenth century but that one could not say that the features were identical. Of one thing she was positive—the eyes had not changed. She described them as, 'farseeing' and as, 'eyes you could not get away from.' This is a good description of Miss Mills' pale blue and peculiarly luminous eyes. Kathleen had not remembered the thirteenth-century name of the young girl who was so active in the siege but she knew she was the same person who could take away her headaches when they were schoolgirls and to whom everyone went with their troubles.

She shared with Miss Mills another memory of the siege. When a building in her neighbourhood was being demolished she felt the noise to be intolerable. She was re-living, with Penelope and Miss Mills, the horror of the bombardment by the trebuchet and mangoneau. Miss Mills said that great stones had crashed against the walls of Montségur every ten minutes by day and night. Penelope had been terrified of the possibility that children might throw stones at her.

Kathleen's other great memory of the siege was Bertrand Marty who, like Esclarmonde-Mills, was so active in comforting the wounded. Speaking in the same brief, positive yet unassertive manner as Jane, with whom she shared the same voice in this incarnation and the same death in her previous life, she said that Bertrand Marty was Miss Mills' father.

Kathleen was naturally more open with Miss Mills than she had been with me. One cannot blame her. She had never set eyes on me. They had been great friends at school and had remained very close to each other despite their geographical separation. There was also the little matter of their previous acquaintance in a moment of destiny seven centuries previously.

Kathleen told me later that she had had Dualist ideas for as long as she could remember. She had always believed in positive forces of good and evil and that individual lives follow what seems an ordained pattern which is part of a universal order. The individual only realises his place in that order after many incarnations. It was only in recent years that she had been able to put the word Dualist to such convictions. She had not had specifically Cathar recollections until the latter end of 1971. No names had come to her before the date on which Braïda had appeared to Miss Mills.

I wonder to what extent the fact that Kathleen had angina is related to her far memory. I suffered from an allied condition. Certainly after my illness in 1968 I was to receive revelations beyond anything I thought possible. Any illness can facilitate psychic activity by separating to some degree that psyche from the human personality. Certainly it seems that after illness Kathleen's memories were more copious and intense.

It is odd to think of Miss Mills, Betty and Kathleen as teen-age girls at their boarding school. Even at that age Kathleen felt that there was something different about both her friends. But did they have at that time any fully conscious remembrance of their previous incarnations? As a schoolgirl Miss Mills' memory was unawakened. She had only her dreams and her fear of fire and trumpets. It is clear that Betty's memories were very near the conscious level as a child of seven. Was she clearly recalling as a schoolgirl? Kathleen told me that her specifically Cathar recollections have only occurred in the last three years. Was her far memory stimulated by the sudden increase in Miss Mills' psychic activity? The latter's indubitably Cathar recollections cover the same period. Or did Kathleen pick up some psychic trail from reading my books? Certainly her memory was not reawakened by reading *The Cathars and Reincarnation*. The latter was published after she had begun to remember. It does not contain the names Laureta or Guillaume de l'Isle.

It is fascinating to reflect as to which of the trio was the most effective in starting the process of ignition. I cannot conceive of anyone more liberally endowed in these matters than Miss Mills. But was she the first in the field? Is it possible that as a school-girl Betty was the most incandescent? The more one is saturated in these matters the more one realises that such questions are superfluous. Where one is confronted with what Braïda calls a fusion of psyches one is concerned with the indivisibility of consciousness. At the level of the spirit time, space and individual contributions are no longer measured. We keep the individuality of our separate spirits but all else is merged. Nevertheless it is fascinating to think of these children at a boarding school pre-paring, against a background of hockey, tennis and formal edu-cation, for their true function as disseminators of light. As for the question of reincarnation in groups these can be no more precise example than that three girls, so much on the same wave-length, should have attended the same boarding school. Even the most progressive cannot attribute this to Anglo-Saxon snobbery.

26

I thought it was clear now what Braïda meant when she asked if I now understood the meaning of psychic fusion. Surely she was referring to Miss Mills' assumption of Kathleen's symptoms. The degree of union between them was also revealed in their shared dream about Betty. There is another aspect of the matter worth considering. I was surprised, and even a little disappointed, when Braïda did not visit Miss Mills during the days when she was suffering most acutely from her pain. I knew there was some good reason for this, but my human fallibility could not really grasp it. She did not visit because at this time I was treating Miss Mills to the best of my ability and according to her own ideas. Braïda told her that this was so. I had previously noticed that if I gave Miss Mills any special support or advice Braïda absented herself over that period. It was clear that I was functioning as a locum on her behalf. The degree to which Braïda entered into me on these occasions was another example of the fusion of psyches.

Or perhaps she was merely referring to the whole chain of communication which abolishes time and space and which is accomplished beyond the limits of human individuality. Perhaps her reference included what happened on April 18th. For twelve hours, for reasons I cannot easily define, I had longed for Jane to ring me. The phone rang just before lunch. As I reached for the receiver I felt a presence behind my shoulder. I heard what I can only describe as a swishing sound. I was aware of a white line sloping diagonally from ceiling to floor somewhere to the right and behind me. The call was a dud. When I took off the receiver there was silence. A few minutes later it rang again and I heard Jane speaking in her musical, light voice. She said that she had rung because she knew I had wanted her to do so. She confirmed that she had phoned a few minutes previously and failed to get me. We discussed Betty's friends and family connections in the thirteenth century as though this was a commonplace of conversation. I do not know how we got on to the subject of Braïda. I said that the latter had told Miss Mills that sooner or later I would see her. Jane said, 'You will see Betty before you see Braïda.' Because I had felt something but seen nothing I did not mention my experience. But had Betty come to console me because the call had not come through? Whatever way I looked at it I thought I had enough examples of psychic fusion.

What happened next made me wonder if there was any need to think or analyse at all. I wondered whether, if our hearts and souls are open, everything will be revealed to us by waiting. I believe this to be true but I am prepared to accept that our patience must be extended over years, over centuries, over different lives. What was so fascinating at this time was that so little was asked of one's patience, and that one had to wait so little.

On Friday, April 21st, I woke feeling weak and ill. I got up, had breakfast and felt positively frightful. I sat in my room in a state of complete exhaustion. I was burning hot and sweating steadily. Although it was a cold day I opened the windows wide but it made no difference to my symptoms. All that day I felt weary and weak beyond measure. Miss Mills rang to tell me that Betty had appeared to her that night. She was now dressed in a blue robe. It was clear that she had reverted to her earlier role as Hélis de Mazerolles. Miss Mills told me also that Jane had telephoned. She, too, had seen Betty the previous night. She had been with Miss Mills. It appeared that she and Betty were resuming their previous relationship as Esclarmonde de Perella and Hélis de Mazerolles. In their previous life, as Parfaites belonging to eminent Cathar families living in the same locality, they had been well known to each other. I was not excited by this information. I had become habituated to these relationships falling into place both in the twentieth and the thirteenth centuries. Most of all I felt too dreadful to manifest a glowing interest in anything.

I crawled through April 22nd. It was like existing in a badly-lit aquarium. On the 23rd I awoke to the same shadowy existence. I was visited by Miss Mills who told me that Braïda had appeared the night before and that the writing had begun again. I was sorry for her. I knew she had found the writing exhausting. If she felt as tired as I did at the moment she merited sympathy. Nevertheless I stirred from my aching torpor when she told me what she had written. There was a repetition of the Biblical references headed, true to form, by the Gospel according to St. John and Corinthians I. There was the statement, 'He who created by means of His wisdom' which I could not trace. The third contribution was breathtaking. Scrawled on a separate piece of paper were the words, A Creed, Masefield.

I consulted the collected works of Masefield. The poem was an unmistakable acceptance of the fact of reincarnation. I had scarcely looked at Masefield since my undergraduate days half a century earlier. I had no idea that he had such pronounced ideas on this subject. But who had dictated this particular reference? The Biblical citations and the unidentified statement could best be ascribed to Guilhabert de Castres or, at a pinch, to Bertrand Marty. They were not Braïda's line. In any case she had appeared in person the previous night and had no need to communicate by writing. Was it reasonable to attribute the Masefield reference to any of these inhabitants of the thirteenth-century Languedoc? It could only be that Betty also was beginning to transmit messages. Braïda's verbal messages to Miss Mills had been simple. She was advised not to get attached to place or person. She was told that Betty was happy and also that she was preparing to look after someone else. This gave me a shiver down the spine because Braïda's predictions were so immediately realised. When she had said that Jane would change her mind about permitting me to write Betty's story her forecast was fulfilled within twelve hours. I wondered if anything tragic was in the offing. I felt this was enough for one morning. I went out to see a particularly perceptive friend of mine who commented on my profound exhaustion and healthy appearance. She attributed my fatigue to living in two worlds at once.

When I returned home for lunch my wife appeared immediately in a state of acute distress and told me that she had bad news for me. My best and oldest friend was dead. His daughter had phoned from Paris to say that he had died in hospital on the 21st. He had had a successful and not very serious operation, had appeared to be progressing favourably and had collapsed and died suddenly of an internal haemorrhage. After I had telephoned Paris I rested a bit. In spite of the loss of someone for whom I felt a deep affection I felt better towards evening but was still tense and tired when the phone rang. The call was from Miss Mills. She herself had just heard from Jane. The latter had seen Betty last night. Betty had a message for me and Jane was anxious that Miss Mills should transmit it as she herself was unable to ring me that day. Betty had said that 'he' was all right, that he was sleeping and that there was no need to worry about him. The simplicity of these messages may not be satisfying to some but they are significant as much for their timing as their context. What is important is that Betty, in the next world, and Jane, in this, knew of Simon's death before I did. In this life their paths had never crossed.

On April 24th I awoke completely different. I was still tired but no longer excessively weak. I was free from the sweating and the burning sensation. Later that morning I had a phone call from Jane. She confirmed Betty's previous message about Simon. She added that Betty had told her last night that she would see me soon.

It seems that the guides from other ages themselves recruit messengers. Betty was one of these. The quotation from Plato a few days previously and the reference to Masefield were surely sent by her. When Betty died Braïda told Miss Mills that she was being cared for by a Bonhomme of probity and experience. She was now giving to Simon the love and care which she herself had received. She was fulfilling the same rôle as she had done in her life as Hélis de Mazerolles.

But where does Simon come into the picture? Why was Betty deputed to take care of him? Is it because he was my friend and she and I were once brother and sister and that the link is still close between us? Or is it that Simon himself was a former and unrecognised Cathar?

When I returned from my first visit to the Cathar country I saw him in Paris. The next day I left for England. He handed me *The Massacre at Montségur* to read on the return journey. All I had ever said was that I was interested in the Cathars. We had never discussed Catharism at all. On a subsequent visit I arrived at his flat before he had returned from work. His wife gave me his deceased father's journal to read. There was in it a passage which testified clearly to the old man's belief in reincarnation. Those were the days when I was excited to meet anyone interested in the subject. When Simon returned I scarcely took time to say good evening. I said that it was clear that his father had believed in reincarnation. 'But of course,' he said. 'But one should never try to discover one's previous incarnations.' I do not know if he was giving me advice. Perhaps he was advising patience. It is impossible to say because we never discussed Dualism. Certainly if his words were intended as advice I accepted them. I have never tried any means to remember previous incarnations nor have I ever advised others to do so. I did not seek the Cathars. They came for me.

I do not know if this gentle and saintly creature was himself a reincarnated Cathar. He was a keen student of Steiner. Among the modern exponents of Catharism the circle responsible for *Cahiers d'Etudes Cathares* are eager to point out the affinities between Anthroposophy and Catharism. I do not think it profitable to speculate further on Simon's real nature. I have learnt enough from Braïda, Miss Mills and Jane to know that if he had Cathar affinities these will be revealed in due course.

27

It was obvious that Miss Mills, Jane, Penelope, Kathleen and I were on the same wavelength and that Betty had been similarly constituted in life and had remained so after death. It was clear that we tuned in not only to the same period in history but to specific events. In this life we were in the closest psychic contact with each other. Often, in April and May 1972, I said to Miss Mills that I wondered whether Jane and Kathleen had had such and such an experience. Within a day, or often less, the latter would be telephoning one or other of us with the answer. What was more striking were our common reactions both to places in this life and events in the Middle Ages.

There was first the business of Rievaulx. I have described how I visited it early in the nineteen-sixties and had an indefinable experience in which I felt the whole of history to be winding back on me like a tape recorder. This experience preceded my first visit to the Languedoc and was accounted for later when I learnt from Professor Nelli's book that Alfred, Abbot of Rievaulx had, in the thirteenth century, held Platonic ideas of love similar to those expressed by the Troubadours. Miss Mills had reacted more violently. Like me her visit had preceded her first trip to the Languedoc in 1954 which, it may be remembered, occurred on impulse. She got as far as the Loire and felt she simply must go to Carcassonne. What I did not know, till Jane told me in 1972, was that Miss Mills had been overcome by emotion and fainted when she visited Rievaulx. Jane described the place as having a wonderful atmosphere and said that Betty had loved it. Kathleen was more specific. She told Miss Mills on May 23rd how, when she had visited it, she had heard music like plain-song which she normally disliked but which, on this occasion, she found beautiful and not at all doleful. It is odd that of the six main characters in the Montserver epic five should have visited what cannot be called a popular place of pilgrimage and should have reacted in this way. I do not know if Penelope ever visited Rievaulx. It is still more fascinating that all five of us had known each other in the Languedoc of the thirteenth century. This may indicate a closer tie between Rievaulx and the Midi than that provided by the ideas of its one-time abbot. Professor Nelli has always been fascinated by the conjecture as to whether or no there were Cathars installed in England. Perhaps he should visit Rievaulx.

Then there is the matter of the lepers. When I spoke over the phone with Jane in May she mentioned that I had written a novel about the Cathars.* We talked a little of how it came to be written and I said that it was curious that I had painted myself as a troubadour and that my first love had been a leper. I said that there had in fact been a leper house at St. Papoul and that a certain Raymond Barthe, who lived there with his mistress, had organised a sortie in an attempt to set at liberty two Cathar Parfaits who had been seized by the authorities at St. Papoul. For Mrs. Smith this latter place was of bitter memory. It was

* _The Gibbet and the Cross_, Neville Spearman, 1971.

where Roger and his friend, from whom he was inseparable, had been seized by the authorities. Jane said in level tones that, of all the places Betty had visited on her trip to the Pyrenees, St. Papoul had moved her the most. She said that 'it hit her for six'. In the first papers she had found after Betty's death the name St. Papoul was written and was accompanied by an imploring 'Oh, Roger', repeated four times. The reader may remember that the word leper was written on one of Betty's sketches of the Avignonet affair. Was the fact that the two troops of conspirators met at the leper house the sole reason for her interest in this malady? Jane said that when Betty was a schoolgirl she and Miss Mills had wished to work among lepers. They remained steadfast in this idea and when each had finished her business training they expressed it with renewed insistence. I mentioned this to Miss Mills. She said that her intentions caused considerable anxiety to her parents and that it was only with difficulty that she was persuaded to abandon the idea.

It did not surprise me unduly that Miss Mills had failed to tell me of her interest in lepers or that she had fainted at Rievaulx. I knew that there are some women who can only tell everything to other women. This is all right by me. I, too, favour the Mother Goddess and distrust the aggressive male deities. But perhaps her continued diffidence in certain matters was the reason for the congested night of May 3rd. She was visited in turn by Braïda, Betty, Guilhabert de Castres and Bertrand Marty. All uttered the same refrain, that she should confide in me completely.

I could bring dozens of witnesses to prove my own outspoken interest in leprosy in the last year. This conscious interest coincides with the growing intensity of Miss Mills' revelations. A large number of people have been bored by my insistence that of all charities this is the most worthwhile. One of the results of this crescendo of Cathar recollections was that I arranged to send yearly a minute donation to the leprosy association. Until I spoke to Jane in May 1972 I had not considered that my interest in leprosy stemmed from the thirteenth century.

The degree to which my instructors were tuned in to each other was also shown by their reaction to anniversaries. Miss Mills, Jane and Kathleen were all depressed the first fortnight in March. They also had their reactions to individual dates. Kathleen felt the resonance of Avignonet as much as Miss Mills felt the fall of Carcassonne. What was especially interesting was that Jane, even though until 1972 she had been seeing Miss Mills only twice a year, could recognise this phenomenon as quickly as I could. On May 3rd she met Miss Mills. She found her depressed and noted that she spoke more than once of Lavaur. She asked me if anything disastrous had happened on that date. I found that Miss Mills had been celebrating the capture of Lavaur by the Crusaders.

At this time Miss Mills said she was afraid of May 13th. Braïda appeared and told her that, on this date, she would always feel depressed. I discovered that this was the date on which the siege of Montségur started in 1243.

On May 5th it was clear that her celebration of anniversaries was not confined to misery on the appropriate day. In the matter of Lavaur she was obviously remembering in detail. Lavaur was in many ways the worst slaughter perpetrated by de Montfort's crusaders. Over four hundred Cathars perished there. This was twice the number who died at Montségur. Miss Mills asked if something horrible happened to somebody called Guirauda and if 'anything went wrong at the executions'. Guirauda, the châtelaine of Lavaur, was thrown down a well and stones heaped upon her. What went wrong at the execution was that the mass gibbet on which Aimery de Montréal was suspended gave way under the weight of its victims. Aimery and Guiraude were brother and sister and the children of Blanche de Laurac. The latter was a name recalled by Jane from her previous incarnation.

I, myself, am not gifted, or plagued, with Miss Mills' conscious memory for anniversaries but every year in May I have suffered from a spastic colon. I had never previously considered that this could be an unconscious memory of Avignonet. In May 1972 I did not suffer in this way. Perhaps this was because so many others were reverberating to, or conscious of, this ghastly affair and raising my own state of awareness to something nearer the conscious level.

One of the most interesting phenomena I encountered was the voice common to Miss Mills, Jane and Kathleen. The former had two or three voices. The one I am referring to is the one she used when talking of Catharism. I cannot explain this phenomenon at all. Is it that the same entity is speaking through these persons? These people speak in their throats with a vibratory intonation, nevertheless the effect produced is clear and light and quite distinctive. Is it that Braïda is speaking through them? Miss Mills says that she speaks a language with loud consonants a little in the throat but with a light accent. The idea that an entity from the thirteenth century is responsible for these voices should not be rejected out of hand. This would be no more remarkable than that Jane should have blisters on the anniversary of the burning of Montségur and that Miss Mills should carry on her body the injuries she sustained on that occasion.

There was another way in which my last five witnesses remained faithful to their Cathar past. In their last incarnation Miss Mills, Betty, Jane and Kathleen had all received the Consolamentum and, in so doing, had died to the flesh. We do not know what happened to Penelope but if she died with Brasillac's name on her lips and felt she was returning to him it may well be that they, too, received the Consolamentum and died together at Montségur. The echoes of this last ceremony were sufficiently strong to restrict the reproductive activity of these women, of whom four married. The whole group could only produce one child between them. The three with whom I was able to talk said that the physical side of life was distasteful or impossible for them. It seemed that the undertaking they had given before receiving the Consolamentum was to some extent still operative.

We have seen enough to know that the reactions and memories common to seven people are due to the fact that a closely knit group seven centuries ago have established links with each other in the contemporary world. Braïda said that it was vital that the evidence of reincarnation in groups should be disseminated as quickly and as widely as possible. She told Miss Mills that the matter could be taken further and that evidence should also be produced that people joined in one incarnation in a common good cause can reincarnate in the same family. This has already been revealed in the case of a mother and daughter. Brune returned as Jane, and Hélis de Mazerolles as Betty. There is also strong evidence that Bertrand Marty and Esclarmonde de Perella reappeared in this century as father and daughter.

It should be noted that a reverse process can also occur. Hélis de Mazerolles and Roger-Isarn were sister and brother in a previous life. Betty and I were separated in this but established some kind of psychic contact with each other which continues and increases from beyond the grave. She is looking after Simon. She appeared to her mother on May 21st and said she was helping with this book. Because of her I recovered from a period of staleness and exhaustion and saw in what form I should express the last pages of this testimony.

28

I acquired a fair knowledge of Catharism in verifying Mrs. Smith's story. As that of Miss Mills began to unfold I wondered if some of what she told me was due to telepathy. This was more because of her own statements than from my convictions. At the time she was producing Italian names she kept asking, 'How much of this am I getting from you?' The clinician in me knew that this was not telepathy. Nevertheless, in view of the fact that I had a certain knowledge of Catharism by the time I met her, anyone of scientific or rationalist inclination would be justified in raising the question of telepathy to explain some of the details of the story. To apply such explanations to the whole story does not make sense. But all that changed with the appearance of the old lady and the Parfaits who followed her.

Before Braïda de Montserver stepped on the stage her approach was announced by a physical symptom. Miss Mills had a prolonged attack of tinnitus. The lines were being tested by a new system of vibrations. Then the amplitude of the vibrations changed. There was a voice, and voices. Later the voices dictated words and messages. Then the chief entity with whom she was in contact appeared visually so that Miss Mills was able to describe her appearance in detail. Later the lady in blue introduced the two male bishops. With their introduction and recognition what I had strongly suspected became absolutely certain. I had thought that there were two voices dictating different kinds of messages. The first was responsible for the historical detail and later the instruction in healing. The second dealt with the philosophy of Catharism. This supposition was clearly proved with the appearance of Braïda and Guilhabert de Castres.

The phenomena leading to the appearance of the old lady takes us out of the realm of telepathy. Certainly Miss Mills did not get her from me. It is not in my power to call up spirits from the next world. And also Braïda informed Miss Mills of details of treatment the application of which were remarkably successful. This story cannot be explained by telepathy. The latter threatens to become another umbrella word like suggestibility. It is a kind of reflex incantation enabling the sceptical to deny the reality of what they cannot explain.

How by telepathy does one account for Miss Mills' tie-up with certain other contemporaries? What was the nature of the contact established with my hostess at Montségur who received the same quotations from Corinthians but ten years previously? Is this telepathy? If so it is a special kind in that it manifests itself after a ten years' interval.

To dwell too much on telepathy or on any single psychic mechanism neglects the fact that Miss Mills' recurrent dreams ceased after she had met me. This occurred also in the case of Mrs. Smith. This effect of psychic reaction is, in my experience, a clinical fact. Braïda stated that such psychic contact enabled people to heal even their physical maladies.

During the whole campaign Miss Mills was wandering in and out of time and from one language to another. She knew the contents of depositions before I had seen, not the original documents, but their French translation. I sometimes did not know that the latter had been made. What more need one say of this except to quote St. Paul on the diversity of gifts? Miss Mills developed those of prophecy, the interpretation of tongues, and healing. It is no doubt useful to transcribe these into a modern idiom. What is important to remember is that according to St.

Paul all come from the Spirit. One can only add respectfully, 'and are conveyed by spirits'.

At the back of *The Cathars and Reincarnation* there is a considerable bibliography. This represents the books I consulted in order to verify what I could about the characters in Mrs. Smith's story and about what she remembered of Catharism. These books were consulted but not studied intensively. I was more concerned with identifying Pierre de Mazerolles than with the acquisition of a comprehensive historical knowledge. If the latter was acquired it was not with intention. It came as a by-product. I read the passages referring to my characters or to specific statements of Mrs. Smith. It should be remembered that at this time I was working for the most part a seven-day week as a doctor. Very emphatically I did not study the names of obscure sergeants-at-arms and their wives. The story of their receiving the Consolamentum remained in my mind. Their names never registered with me. The idea that I might have remembered so much detail is ludicrous. But suppose one argues that Miss Mills could have obtained from me by telepathy names which I had forgotten, how can one account for the astonishing selectivity of her memories? Ultimately she read my *The Cathars and Reincarnation*. This contains one reference to Raymond de Perella. None of the other members of the family are mentioned. The Perellas and the Montservers were her main consideration. The latter do not appear at all in its pages. How do we explain the innumerable references right outside not merely the contents but the scope of that book? How account by telepathy for the reference to the Nikolski gospel? When more than two years previously I went through Obolensky's book on the Bogomils I was only concerned with the specific reference to the Cathars. I am certain that I saw no reference to the gospel of the Slav heretics. Had I done so it is the kind of item which would have remained in my mind.

Could telepathy be as purposeful and selective as this? Why did the names converge so accurately on three special themes, the disposal of the Cathar treasure, the Avignonet affair and the last Consolamentum at Montségur? It must have been telepathy operating through a shutter and with a highly focussed lens. And why is the story concentrated at the same time and in the same region as the apotheosis of Mrs. Smith's story? Not from anything Miss Mills derived from me but because she, and Mrs. Smith, lived through the same tragic years.

Certainly Miss Mills did not obtain from me by telepathy the scriptural and classical quotations. I am neither a Bible student nor a classical scholar. I had never heard of Iamblichus or Chrysippas. Until Miss Mills drew my attention to him my knowledge of Plotinus was limited to the fact that Dean Inge was one of his admirers.

Of course Miss Mills must be to some degree telepathic. All Europeans with a memory of past lives are psychic. This is one point on which I am prepared to be dogmatic. Among psychic gifts telepathy is the most common. The rôle it plays in our story is minimal and of a different nature to what one might anticipate. In their conversations there was more exchange of thoughts and feelings between Braïda and Miss Mills than there was between the latter and me.

If we look at the whole picture we see a chain of circumstances far beyond the contact established between Miss Mills and myself. It is beyond the scope of this book to demonstrate that I was born a Dualist and that before I even encountered Mrs. Smith I met several patients whose function it was to awaken the Dualist in me. I have described these patients in other books and articles. I was led by neatly graded steps to Mrs. Smith and Miss Mills. All my life of feeling, all my career as a doctor, was directed towards this culminating experience. What was initiated years ago cannot be dependent on single processes like telepathy.

It was clear that this operation was not only beautifully organised but adapted to the needs and qualities of its human agents. It is comforting that the heavenly hierarchies are more efficient than the earthly bureaucracies. Without my interest in Catharism I would have made nothing of Mrs. Smith. Without my taste for history I would not have looked for the names she produced. Had I not been awakened by her I would not have 'met' Miss Mills, that is to say, I would not have been aware of my psychic contact with her. In everything that came from Braïda there was clearly a sense of purpose. Miss Mills and I were being used in this life for something for which we had been trained in a previous incarnation. She had to heal and had died at the stake. In this life she was called upon to apply what she had been previously taught. This was difficult for her in a world of decomposing rationalism. She was given the solace of her former instructor. I myself was in the same situation. In my previous incarnation I had been fascinated both by healing and the nature of time. It was ordained that in this my present life I achieved the fusion of my medical and philosophical tendencies in the practise of psychiatry. My personal evolution has been immensely accelerated in the last two years. There is no doubt whatever that this is attributable to the guidance of Braïda and Guilhabert de Castres.

What was the basic purpose of an operation so well devised and so perfectly executed? The answer is simple. To disseminate knowledge of Catharism, which is not only the resurgence of primitive Christianity but also one of the long line of those cults which see the universe in terms of emanation and for whom goodness is a primary energy and a solvent for the other primary force of evil.

The prolonged and beautifully designed purpose behind this revelation shows that it cannot be accounted for by any single psychic mechanism. What involves a number of living people and three discarnate entities needs other explanations. People talk of far-memory and reincarnation as one and the same thing. The former is the process which presents the evidence for the latter and which uses several mechanisms. Was Miss Mills clairaudient? She must have been to have heard the voices. The same applies to Mrs. Smith when she took down the poems and messages as a schoolgirl. Clairaudience must be a common mechanism of recall in those remembering their previous incarnations. Was automatic writing a feature of Miss Mills' and Mrs. Smith's reportage? Emphatically not. They did not take up a pencil and let themselves float. Was Miss Mills exhibiting a form of trance mediumship when she recorded her messages? Possibly, but she was exhibiting a curious variety of this phenomenon in moving into this state from sleep rather than from waking consciousness. One can certainly describe her in broad terms as a medium. It may be that this is one of the prerequisites for far-memory. But is she acting as a medium when she is talking to the old lady? If so it is a very 'conscious' form of mediumship. It is, indeed, something occurring in a state of heightened awareness.

So often one is asked whether a collection of phenomena implies reincarnation or whether it can be explained by clairaudience, mediumship or even possession. What is not sufficiently realised is that the latter processes are often essential mechanisms in the process of recall of previous incarnations. Miss Mills' case is a gold mine because it illustrates so many such mechanisms. First the memory of her past erupts in two recurring dreams. The latter began in the course of an illness in which her life was threatened. When a patient is on the point of death the psyche is more loosely attached to the personality. It uses its emancipation from time to look backward or, less commonly, forward. When the patient recovers, what remains of the visionary experience which occurred on the threshold of earth is reproduced in dreams. The same process occurs in the case of Mrs. Smith.

When Miss Mills met me the nightmares were abolished in the process of psychic recognition. After an interval she communicated again with the past by other systems of vibrations. She saw what she called visions by day. She heard what she described as an inner voice and which the specialists would classify as clairaudience. She had other dreams specifically related to her previous incarnation. She had compelling intuitions which dovetailed accurately with what the voices said and with her dreams and visions. After this she recorded the messages in writing. It was as though a discarnate entity were slowly materialising in the course of these different varieties of psychic communication. Then the old lady identified herself. Can she be called a vision? Dogs do not bark at visions neither does one talk with them on a question and answer basis. Still less does one take one's personal problems to them. Miss Mills did all these things. Her history is one of reincarnation with varied and fascinating mechanisms of recall.

There are certain inescapable conclusions to be derived from these experiences. The reality of reincarnation is established beyond doubt. So is the phenomenon of group reincarnation. I express myself a little less dogmatically on the subject of reincarnation in families but this is only because of the limited number of cases I quote. The inhibitions of scientific method die hard. I am also convinced beyond any doubt that human individuality is indestructible and that it is possible to have illuminating contact with the so-called dead.

When we speak of reincarnation we should always realise that we do so from the standpoint of a human personality based on a world where time, the fundamental illusion, is measured in terms of duration and as though it were a reality. But we must not forget that we experience the evidence pointing to reincarnation on the psychic plane. It is at this latter level that we have also our clairvoyant and telepathic experiences. We undergo the latter because the psyche is, compared to the personality, freely emancipated from time and space. So it comes about that, in those psychic activities which enable us to look back on past lives, we are operating in a sphere where past, present and future are of little moment. When we pass through the psyche to the plane of the spirit time has ceased altogether. A fly perched at the circumference of a wheel is aware of its rapid revolutions. There is a point at the centre of the hub which is motionless. The lives we have had are both those we will have and those we are living in what we call the present. Perhaps what we are intended to learn from the case of Miss Mills is simply the timelessness of truth. This was, after all, one of the main themes in her philosophical revelations. Cases such as that of Miss Mills teach us that, at the level of reality, eternity and the instant are identical.

29

What were the fundamentals of the message which Braïda and her confrères wished to be transmitted? Beyond doubt they wished it known that Catharism was primitive Christianity. How otherwise can one explain the abundance of scriptural references and those to the neoplatonists who had so much in common with

Christianity? At the same time it is inescapable that Braïda was disseminating Dualism. She was constantly concerned with its basic principles, such as the belief in Reincarnation and in the primary forces of good and evil. She said clearly that it was essential to inform people as fully and as rapidly as possible as to these fundamental tenets. We must inevitably conclude that Catharism was a Christian form of Dualism. I myself am convinced that primitive, non-theocratic Christianity was essentially Dualist, but I will not labour this point because I cannot here marshal all the evidence.

So far as special issues are concerned it is indisputable that Braïda was overwhelmingly preoccupied with the art of healing. In this she was returning to what made primitive Christianity unique among the world religions. No other major cult so emphasised the necessity of healing the sick. In the thirteenth century Braïda, Esclarmonde and Hélis were so engaged. Miss Mills remembers a house near Fanjeaux where she and others were taught to heal. She remembers a second house in the same vicinity where she never saw the cross of healing worn by Braïda and others. In *The Cathars and Reincarnation* I describe how Roger advised that if anything should happen to him Puerilia should go to Fabrissa. Fabrissa de Mazerolles was a Parfaite who ran a house for Cathar women near Montréal. The latter could well have been a home for general training. It is possible that Esclarmonde went there before she specialised and that, within its walls, she met Puerilia. This encounter may be the basis for the intense emotion Miss Mills felt the morning I received Mrs. Smith's letter.

In this life Miss Mills continued her healing vocation under Braida's direction. In a different way I can be regarded as similarly occupied.

To me, as a doctor, there is something of specific importance transmitted by Braïda's messages. Dualism is an important antidote to the materialisation of medicine. The next step in our evolution as doctors is to recognise more the influence of the psyche imprisoned in matter. Its recollections of experience in past lives are related to present symptoms. The recognition of two basic energies of good and evil is vital in any cosmic concept of medicine. Healing is a particular expression of the emanation

226

of goodness. On the other hand, it is indisputable that many disease symptoms and syndromes are attributable to the power of evil. Discussing such factors is beyond the scope of this book. All one can say here is that Braïda's messages enlarged enormously one's medical horizons.